# The Writing of America

# The Writing of America

## Literature and Cultural Identity from the Puritans to the Present

## Geoff Ward

Polity

First published in 2002 by Polity Press in association with Blackwell Publishers Ltd

*Editorial office*:
Polity Press
65 Bridge Street
Cambridge CB2 1UR, UK

*Marketing and production*:
Blackwell Publishers Ltd
108 Cowley Road
Oxford OX4 1JF, UK

*Published in the USA by*
Blackwell Publishers Inc.
350 Main Street
Malden, MA 02148, USA

A catalogue record for this book is available from the British Library.

**Library of Congress Cataloging-in-Publication Data**
Ward, Geoff, 1954–
    The writing of America : literature and cultural identity from the Puritans to the present / Geoff Ward.
        p. cm.
    Includes bibliographical references and index.
    ISBN 0–7456–2621–1—ISBN 0–7456–2622-X (pbk.)
    1.  American literature—History and criticism. 2.   National characteristics, American, in literature. 3.   Nationalism and literature—United States. 4.   Group identity in literature. I. Title.
    PS169.N35 W37 2002
    810.9'358—dc21                                                        2001005547

Typeset in 10½ on 12 pt Sabon
by Kolam Information Services Pvt Ltd, Pondicherry, India
Printed in Great Britain by TJ International, Padstow, Cornwall

This book is printed on acid-free paper.

# Contents

# Acknowledgements

First and foremost I would like to thank the Leverhulme Trust, whose award of a fellowship was of immense help in the creation of this book, and the University of Dundee, for sanctioning an extended period of leave. *The Writing of America* was researched and partly written in Washington DC, and I am grateful for the assistance of the staff of the Jefferson Building in the Library of Congress, particularly Bruce Martin, Research Facilities Officer. I would also like to thank Mark and Megan Turner for the use of their house in Silver Spring, and neighbours and friends both for their hospitality and for helping me understand more clearly the way America works: in particular, Will Smith, Coletta Youngers and their families. I also thank John Ashbery, Ian F. A. Bell, Charles Bernstein, Ted Danforth, David Herd, Marjorie Perloff and Neil Rennie.

It will become rapidly apparent that, for good or ill, independence of judgement is a marked feature of what follows. I do, however, have two specific local debts. The information on the history of capital punishment in America used in chapter 2 was drawn largely from a review of books on the subject by Thomas Laqueur, in the *London Review of Books*, volume 22, number 19 (October 2000); and it was a piece in the *Washington Post* of 17 July 2000 by Sarah Mark, summarizing previous literature on the subject, that set me on the trail of Congressman Daniel E. Sickles, whose activities on one and two legs are discussed in chapter 4. I owe a great deal to my editors at Polity. Lynn Dunlop offered every encouragement at the early stages. Sally-Ann Spencer guided the book thereafter, and was always ready with constructive, imaginative and detailed advice. I could not have wished for a better editor. As always, this book is for Marion, Richard and Robert Ward, who never wavered in their encouragement of the project, voicing concern only when pre-war music of the rural South took over the house, and I became a prisoner of the banjo. This book is also a doorstop for the Chelsea Hotel, a belated eightieth birthday present for Clifford Ward, a suggestion of Rod Mengham's, and a glass raised to Tony Tanner (1935–1998).

The author and publisher would like to thank the following for permission to use copyrighted materials: for 'A Poem for Vipers', copyright © 1986 by John Wieners, reprinted from *Selected Poems 1958–1984* with the permission of Black Sparrow Press; for 'Often I Am Permitted to Return to a Meadow' by Robert Duncan, from *The Opening of the Field*, copyright © 1960 by Robert Duncan, reprinted by permission of New Directions Publishing Corp.; for 'Coming into the Country' by Gish Jen, reproduced by permission of the author, c/o Rogers, Coleridge & White Ltd, 20 Powis Mews, London W11 in association with Maxine Groffsky Literary Agency, New York; Gerrit Lansing and the estate of Stephen Jonas, for permission to reprint poems by Stephen Jonas; the editors of *Critical Quarterly*, and The *Cambridge Quarterly*, where earlier versions of material in this book first appeared in essay form; Professor Orlando Patterson for permission to quote from his article 'Everything Changes Money', The *New York Times*, 7 May, 2000; Marsilio Publishers, NY for permission to quote from 'Symphony Sid' by Amiri Baraka.

# Introduction
## Paradise™

'In the four quarters of the globe, who reads an American book?' The assumptions behind Sydney Smith's notorious question of 1820 in The *Edinburgh Review* have long fallen away. Rather, it might be asked now, what writer could hope to succeed without an American readership. It is now the non-American literature, economy or nation that either clamours tinnily for attention, sits constrained in a posture of servility, or strives destructively for escape. Reality has become American, in the first instance. Everything happens in the shadow of the giant, yet the giant's own visibility sometimes makes him lumbering or vulnerable. Moreover, the giant's sense of his own identity is, and always was, in flux.

The terrain of American literature is vast, and its shapes and borders shift like a desert in the wind. Alongside the difficulties of cartography come more conceptual uncertainties about where, precisely, the bounds of literature itself lie. So many of the forms of American rhetoric, from Puritan sermons and the Declaration of Independence to hip-hop lyrics, can be analysed and valued from a literary perspective, but always with a rider that their first purpose or discursive context lay elsewhere. Even those American books that have enjoyed classic status display a more overt relationship to the dynamics of the society from which they emerge than do many European classics, particularly those belonging to traditions of aestheticism or other essentially monastic literary models. Whatever else American independence meant, it meant severance from residually feudal patterns of rule, commerce or the scene of writing. And so, for example, Herman Melville's *Moby-Dick* (1851) is indeed a cornucopia of cetology, a neo-Shakespearean drama and a series of poetic meditations; but it is also a book about whaling, a key commercial activity of the time, and one of which the author had first-hand knowledge. Melville's still underrated novel *Israel Potter* (1855; treated in chapter 3) incorporates copious amounts of non-fictional material about the wars with Great Britain, just as in the era of Modernism and in the form of poetry, Ezra Pound's *Cantos* would incorporate Chinese ideograms alongside diatribes on Social Credit or quotations from Jefferson's letters. One persistent implication of American tradition has been that literature is the form that can include all the rest.

Equally traditional has been the drive to include the hitherto excluded, to say the conventionally unsayable. Literature is what a writer says that the rest of America won't admit, be it in Toni Morrison's treatment of African-American history in *Beloved* (1987), the incorporation of graphic sexual material in the work of William Burroughs and others (see chapters 6 and 7), or indeed the whole vernacular tradition exemplified by Mark Twain. As Tom Sawyer observes to Huck Finn as they whisper of 'dark, deep-laid plans' to spring a man from captivity, 'we got to do the best we can with the materials we got.'[1] Anti-establishment improvisation runs back to the founding of the nation, which, despite the Puritan legacy and the periodic eruptions of redneck biblioclasm, continues to celebrate the border-blurring, rapscallion and morally unbuttoned proclivities of a democracy: 'Well then, says I, what's the use you learning to do right when it's troublesome to do right and ain't no trouble to do wrong, and the wages is just the same?' (128). Huckleberry Finn's archetypal quest-narrative in which dark themes of violence, captivity and impoverishment are negotiated by juvenile escapade would go forth and multiply not only in fiction but in the images of cinema, the music industry, televised ads for running shoes and all other cultural projections of America's obsession with youth. The act of dissidence that severed colonies from motherland (see chapter 2) and the gun culture that began to dominate in the aftermath of the Civil War (see chapters 4 and 5) combined to give the juvenile delinquent classic status.

It's a male thing. Leslie Fiedler in *Love and Death in the American Novel* (1960) worried that Americans did not want to grow up, one consequence being the novel's shying away from the themes of mature heterosexual love, childbearing and ageing. Only Henry James among American novelists was sufficiently adult to be spoken of in the same breath as Flaubert, Balzac and Tolstoy. Such an elevation of adolescence seemed doubly confirmed to Fiedler by the arrival of the Beats, whose work, the longevity of which may have surprised him, is examined in this book. Fiedler's anxiety, in some respects a variant of T. S. Eliot's gloom over popular culture, elided the fact that the American tradition included themes, styles and achievements that were simply other, as regards the tradition of *Middlemarch* and *Anna Karenina*, rather than being perpetually doomed to lose in some kind of transatlantic competition.

The extended consideration given to George Lippard's masterpiece *The Quaker City* (1845) in chapter 4 is a case in point. This Gothic city-satire, in many ways the begetter of all modern horror, *noir* thrillers and Tarantino-style camp splatter, was the best-selling American novel of its day and one that issues from specifically American experiences of urban change. At points like this, when the dissident young male becomes the American archetype, there is no difficulty in mapping a literary terrain where, for all the vastness of space, the same signs recur, like neon logos on a long drive west. American literature remains nostalgically in thrall to its dominant imagery; the myth of the West followed hard on its actual settlement, and the journey from independence has been a sentimental one, notwithstanding the nation's ready acceptance of violence, institutional or casual. But there is more than a compelling nostalgia at work in the recycling of male myths of frontier, of youth, of walks on the wild side. While the emphasis on masculine risk taking has in one sense marginalized female American writers, it has also, as with all cultural marginalization, honed the critical edge of their work: Harriet Beecher Stowe's *Uncle Tom's Cabin* (1852), arguably the national epic and definitely its most internally influential work of literature, gains scope and analytical power in part from refusing the sentimental magnetism of such myths (see chapter 4). Meanwhile Melville offers the example of a male writer exploring themes of masculine risk taking, but with a critical and demystifying edge that makes him an American paradigm, although his reputation has boomed and crashed (see chapter 3).

A brief examination of work by a writer not mentioned otherwise in this study may help to show how the adversarial or unplaceable nature of writing becomes a characteristic, rather than the antagonist, of a history of American literature. 'The Yellow Wallpaper', by Charlotte Perkins Gilman (1860–1935), was first published in 1892. Its narrator is a young married woman, driven mad (to cut a short story shorter) by chauvinist psychiatry. Her husband John, like her brother, a physician of good standing, enforces a regime in which work, and specifically writing, is forbidden. Sequestered in the nursery and in a life without stimuli, the woman begins to let her mind dwell to the point of hallucination on the room's yellow wallpaper, whose sprawling patterns 'confuse the eye...and when you follow the lame uncertain curves for a little distance they suddenly commit suicide – plunge off at outrageous angles'.[2] In an obvious displacement of the woman's own suicidal plunges of mood, the wallpaper becomes a self-administered Rorschach test, the vertiginous writhings of whose '"debased Romanesque" with delirium tremens' (9) only serve to confirm her estrangement. The squiggles are clearly related to the words of independence and complaint that she is not allowed to commit to paper, just as the figure she begins to see skulking in the design is a projected *alter ego*, a sister-writer caught in the bars. 'And she is all the time trying to climb through' (15). At length, the attempt to climb out of the nursery prison, the impending threat of madness getting in, and vengeance on the male physician combine. The wife locks herself in, throws the key out. The husband breaks in and, in a significantly 'female' display of behaviour, faints on seeing her crawl around the room insane and intoning '"I've got out at last"'(19).

The tale is a product of the 1890s, the great decade of horror stories with social ramifications: Henry James's *The Turn of the Screw*, with its related theme of ghostly projections by a female protagonist who is denied fulfilment, Stoker's *Dracula* and Wilde's *Picture of Dorian Gray* are products of the same period. Gilman's tale was kept in print by the enthusiasm of horror writer fans such as H. P. Lovecraft and August Derleth in the decades prior to its retrieval as a feminist allegory. In 1913 Gilman declared explicitly that she wrote the story 'to save people from being driven crazy' (20) after an eminent specialist in 'neurasthenia' had forbidden her to write or work for a period of three months following a depression that his ministrations pushed towards complete breakdown. As a horror story, it has some of the floridly Gothic aspects of the *fin de siècle*. These are counterbalanced, however, by that flatly explanatory note 'Why I Wrote "The Yellow Wallpaper"'. Just as a number of 1890s texts anticipate the birth of Modernism as much as they mark the end of the Romantic and Victorian traditions, so Gilman's tale contains at least two aesthetics, one the curving sub-Romanesque *trompe-l'oeil* effects of the crumbling mind's efforts to paper over cracks, the other the aesthetic of the writer as distinct from the narrator. The terse, indented sentences point towards the Imagist brevity of the new century, whereas the writ(h)ing on the wall signals the impasse of traditional imprisonment for woman's intelligence.

Yet Gilman's proto-Imagist aesthetic may be unconscious, to use the psychoanalytic vocabulary nascent in the 1890s, the period of

Freud's first writings on hysteria; it may be a side-effect, or even an imprisoned aestheticism railing for freedom from the ideological rationale for writing the story given by its author years later. There is no way of taking the tale that can contain all these salient aspects in a logical relation. It cannot even be argued along the deconstructionist lines fashionable twenty years ago that the only way of including them all is via a reconceptualization of literature as meaning everything, anything or nothing at all, depending how it is turned in the light of reading, for then Gilman's 1913 note would have to be excluded as an example of the 'intentionalist fallacy', one of many shibboleths passed to deconstruction by its godfathers among the New Critics.

Dramatically speaking, the story has an effective ending. In another sense its terminal blurring of categories – the man who behaves like a woman, the imprisoned crawler who declares herself 'out at last' – keeps up an unending dialectic of implosion/explosion, rather than supplying a real conclusion. A reader could dwell on the sexually suggestive term 'smooch', applied more than once to the whorls of decoration, to further multiply the whirl of layered meaning. And yet this very resistance to any interpretation that does not immediately shift to take a counter-interpretation on board runs deep in the grain of American literature. In chapters 2 and 3 I draw out its workings in the *oeuvres* of Hawthorne and Melville. Irony, cut loose by emigration from the culture that had established limits within which to interpret it, grows wild in American literature, a literature written in everyone's second language, where misunderstanding is at once a daily fact of life, a pitfall to be avoided at all costs in the building of a society, and food for fiction and poetry.

The importance of mass immigration cannot be overstated, and a dialogue with the most important recent contribution to American studies in this area, Philip Fisher's *Still the New World* (1999) is carried through the second half of this study. In order to remain United, the States have had to impose by subtle and unsubtle means a cultural sameness wholly bound up with the capitalist provision of services and consumables. The American way depends on surrender to capitalism, with all its inequalities, crashes and ideological impositions, as a 'natural' state. America can feel, and has always felt to some, like Paradise Found, but it is Paradise$^{\text{TM}}$. Thus the paranoid junkie's flight from the dragnet of the law at the opening of William Burroughs's *The Naked Lunch* (1959) describes perfectly any visitor's sense of the eerie uniformity in American life, coast to coast and wall to wall:

But there is no drag like the U.S. drag. You can't see it, you don't know where it comes from. Take one of those cocktail lounges at the end of a subdivision street – every block of houses has its own bar and drugstore and market and liquorstore. You walk in and it hits you. But where does it come from? Not the bartender, nor the customers, nor the cream-colored plastic rounding the bar stools, nor the dim neon. Not even the TV.[3]

This is America, *tout court*, the source of its sameness invisible as gas. To Philip Fisher there is no such thing as American culture, culture being an Old World 'set of practices and beliefs that are stable over time and passed on from generation to generation'.[4] A recurrence of creative self-destruction has replaced the vertical bequests of culture with the innovations of technologically inventive capitalism in a country where 20 per cent of the population move in any given year. What is made in America exists in order to be rendered obsolete. Yet in moving, the maker-consumer finds that uncanny, yet curiously comforting – indeed *heimlich* – replication of which Burroughs is such an acute observer. The bartender in Reno has a different accent from the one in New Jersey, but it is the same bar, and as he steps forward to ask what'll it be, he is the same bartender. Rod Serling's TV series *The Twilight Zone*, the photographs of O. Winston Link, the novels of Philip K. Dick and Stephen King discussed in chapter 4 – all give off this air of reality as replica. It is all uncannily like home, but not home; *heimlich* yet *unheimlich*, to revive Freud's term for the uncanny. The experience is of being, to use a Scots term, outwith America, even while travelling inside it. The literature lays claim to what it can never fully inhabit, and the indeterminacy of settled meaning in Hawthorne's novels or Gilman's tale metaphorizes at a profound level American national identity.

One of the most engaging novels of recent years, *Accordion Crimes* (1996) by E. Annie Proulx, offers a fictionalized history of immigrant America held in sequence by an accordion passed from hand to hand among its characters. Like a damaged accordion, a person can find parts of their past history 'dissolved by the acid of circumstance and accident', and yet be patched up in order to play an American tune.[5] A more genial writer than Burroughs, Proulx reaches an entirely compatible form of literary irony from a different set of starting-points, as in this account of a Polish immigrant trying to make a home in the un-homely United States:

Hieronim had heard the story again and again from his mother of how his father had landed at Castle Garden and a month later was in

Chicago working in the Armour meat-packing plant, living as a boarder with a Polish family in Armour's Patch, this trained pharmacist, but he could neither read English nor speak American and the immigration inspectors marked him down as illiterate. In this way Hieronim learned that to be foreign, to be Polish, not to be American, was a terrible thing and all that could be done about it was to change one's name and talk about baseball. (364)

Proulx's nice distinction between the reading of English and the speaking of American not only gets to the heart of certain immigrant experiences, but has resonance for some of the diverse materials discussed in this book, particularly in chapter 5, where Harry Smith's *Anthology of American Folk Music* (1952, 1997) is treated as historical literature. I am in no doubt whatever that Smith's *Anthology* is a crucial work of twentieth-century America, and my failed attempt to find a more specific and apt term than 'work' cuts straight to the reasons why. The *Anthology* is, among other things, a collection of musics, a book, a diachronic history of the culture of the South, a testament to the persistence of British in American literature, an exercise in hermetic epistemology evoking the English Renaissance but composed by a follower of Aleister Crowley, a postmodern moment in which the artist and critic merge in the figure of the fan, and a box. Ignorant of the box, which was about to make its first appearance, Louise Bogan wrote wistfully in a survey of American poetry:

> I have thought that 'popular art' – so-called – should be brought into some relation with the more formal arts. An anthology of poetry which included 'popular songs', ballads etc., along with 'serious' and formal poetry (the two kinds of expression being printed without any lines of demarcation between) would, it seems to me, be extremely interesting and valuable.[6]

Repeating this quotation during the course of his study *The American Poetry Wax Museum* (1996), Jed Rasula adds that '[n]early half a century later, this remains a project in limbo' (65). Harry Smith's *Anthology* was reissued in the year following publication of Rasula's book. While my conscious decision to place Harry Smith at the centre of this book does not go all the way to filling the gap pointed out by Bogan and Rasula, I hope to have questioned those 'lines of demarcation' between 'popular' and 'formal' literature, and between the literatures of poetry and of popular music, and in ways that seek to define cultural value, rather than simply celebrating a range of demotic material in an anti-canonical spirit. The *Anthology* is not as hybrid as it may at first appear, in the sense that American literature is precisely the expression of hybridity, seeking new forms and serving diverse purposes, at one in that respect with the Declaration of Independence and other texts examined in this book.

Lines of demarcation have also been breached by the serious attention paid to Stephen King. He is the most popular novelist in the world, a fact that would invite comment and analysis even if his novels were dross, which they are not. King is a lightning-conductor for American disquiet, an essentially Republican and sentimental Cassandra who horrifies before he reassures, testing small-town values and backwoods resilience to the limits of destruction before reaffirming their enduring superiority over the unsentimental metropolis, the foreign, the alien. His work also reaffirms the American Gothic tradition of Lippard and Poe, while openly recycling plots and images from popular films and comics. This has of course been read as a weakness in his work, but, without special pleading, it can be said to be a *modus operandi* characteristic of writing of the United States that sets it at a remove from European models. The same stories, figures and tropes cross the decades. To take an example, avant-garde poetry and the novels of Stephen King would seem at first to inhabit different universes, but each shares an amiable relationship with its literary forebears, in distinctively American ways. Allen Ginsberg, nothing if not the standard-bearer for a new poetry, at least at the time of *Howl* (1956), constantly invoked, wrote like and even looked like a fifties poet from the previous century, Walt Whitman. Every American poet via Pound down to Ginsberg and the so-called Language poets is compelled to reaffirm a link on the page with the revolutionary grandfather. In Europe, by contrast, the avant-garde formations of Dada, Futurism and Surrealism were not on speaking terms with each other, never mind the past. The principle of supersedence that Philip Fisher diagnoses in American society at large is actually *opposed* in its literature by a move towards ahistorical and sentimental embrace.

The canon is disrupted in order to be reaffirmed with extended boundaries by such groupings as the Language poets, with whom this history closes. Readers who object to this choice will no doubt also bridle at the assertion that the work of Ashbery, O'Hara, Creeley, Wieners and the other writers sampled in Donald Allen's *The New American Poetry 1945–60* comprise a second American Renaissance. Let them bridle. The importance of this grouping was evident to me from the time I read their work in the 1960s and 1970s, and the passage of time has only served to bring Ashbery and now O'Hara to a canonical status, where some of the other Allen-generation writers will follow. Compendious as it was, Allen's anthology paid scant attention to African-American writers, and I hope that the attention paid in this book to Stephen Jonas in particular will help redress the balance, not merely in the cause of balance, but by virtue of the strengths of his sadly neglected writing.

I decided at an early stage to ignore the American theatre. It would have been easy to include it, if only because the interesting American playwrights could be counted on the fingers following an accident with a bacon-slicer. No matter that one of my most memorable nights at the theatre was at an off-Broadway performance of Sam Shepard's *The Curse of the Starving Class* in 1989, or that I could have written with pleasure about Tennessee Williams or David Mamet. The same is even true of Israel Zangwill, whose play *The Melting-Pot* (1909), which famously deals with immigration and assimilation, also contains my all-time favourite stage direction: '*He plants his feet voluptuously upon the floor*'.[7] But the more vibrant and long-standing connection lies between the literature of America and its popular music, and it is in this emergent area of study that my account has a contribution to make. It may also be the case that the relative weakness of the American theatre tradition (the multi-art, hybrid cinema being a different matter entirely) is in some subtle way bound to the diffusion of a culture of performance in American life. The performative aspects of politics, group and individual identities, and the inculcation of behavioural norms are a recurrent feature in what follows. America *equals* theatre.

This, at last, is because America was invented rather than discovered, its identity subjected to ceaseless redefinition by its new arrivals. Its essence is no essence, but a movement along the spectrum of contradiction sketched in this introduction. American literature is massively inclusive, but dissident and adversarial; obsessive, full of violence, yet pearled with nostalgia and sentiment; addicted to the new, but condemned to repetition; a mirror for its own culture of self-replication, but hybrid by nature; Paradise, but Paradise[TM]. Famously, at the close of F. Scott Fitzgerald's *The Great Gatsby* (1926), Nick wanders down to the beach alone at night, and watches the moving glow of a ferry-boat across the Sound:

And as the moon rose higher the inessential houses began to melt away until gradually I became aware of the old island here that flowered once for Dutch sailors' eyes – a fresh, green breast of the new world. Its vanished trees, the trees that had made way for Gatsby's house, had once pandered in whispers to the last and greatest of all human dreams; for a transitory enchanted moment man must have held his breath in the presence of this continent, compelled into an aesthetic contemplation he neither understood nor desired, face to face for the last time in history with something commensurate to his capacity for wonder.[8]

In order to be lived, let alone 'understood', that unprecedented, paradisal 'something' had to be written. Mine is a polemical history of that writing.

# 1

# Maps and Legends

## The uneasy construction of American identity

It is not entirely clear where America might be located. A glance at the atlas does indicate a sizeable chunk of the earth. More importantly, America's economic world-dominance – long-established and increasing its lead as I write – has made of it something monstrously ubiquitous, ineluctable, the giant mote in everyone's eye that skews perspective, prompting the apprehension that one's own space might be out of kilter, behind the times or in some way second-rate. The majority of world-citizens, in one sense outside America, are never beyond its reach. The Scots – who have had to deal cagily over the centuries with a small but domineering neighbour – habitually use 'outwith' where the English use 'outside'. Unlike the English word, 'outwith' can never be a noun, but can point in a more mobile way to a position of exclusion that can still include proximity and recognition. The Scots term speaks more precisely to our relationship with what Abraham Lincoln termed 'the last best hope of earth'. We are all outwith America. If this is the bitter-sweet effect of cultural imperialism, whose powers of seduction have proved far more successful than the Pentagon in capturing hearts and minds, its most curious aspect, and one which this book and this chapter in particular will trace, lies in the expression by Americans themselves of being both without and within, of being perpetually outwith, America.

'The Whole', as the British commander General Amherst was led quite correctly to observe of North America in 1763, 'is an Immense

Extent.'[1] America has reconfigured its immensity not only through
the addition of territory to the south and to the west, but by what
Alexis de Tocqueville thought of as the lack of a horizon, a crucial,
almost viral identification with restlessness and remaking that flickers
at every turn of the republic's cultural history. Secreted like a germ
aboard the *Mayflower*, 'manifest destiny' was coined in 1845 by
journalist John L. Sullivan as a formula signifying his nation's right
'to overspread the continent allotted by Providence for the free development of our yearly multiplying millions' (305). Now it is the
perceived and manifest destiny of millions of Americans to maximize
the free development of the self through psychotherapy, New Age
occultism, jogging, crime, stocks and bonds, a move to the suburbs or
some other personal analogue for the expanding frontier. A recent
*New York Times* special on 'The Way We Live Now' suggests that
America's self-image is that of a giant recreational vehicle, perpetually
rerouted and going round in circles, but one whose drivers are happy
in their mobile unhappiness:

> In therapy-speak, we Americans like *to give ourselves permission*....
> *Why not go to town? Why not move away? Why not marry out? Why
> not? Why not? Why not?*.... We wonder who we are – what does it
> mean to be Irish-American, Cuban-American, Armenian-American? –
> and are amazed to discover that others wonder, too. Indeed, nothing
> seems more typically American than to obsess about identity. Can so
> many people truly be so greatly confused? We feel very much a part of
> the contemporary gestalt.[2]

Whether or not this is the way individuals live now, this is certainly
characteristic of The Way We Write Now for the American press:
smugly comfortable in 'our' discontent, massaging our problematic
hyphens, the alchemy of our prose turning the golden proclamations
of the seventeenth, eighteenth or nineteenth centuries into something
leaden yet horribly creamy. What does 'the contemporary gestalt'
actually mean, in the passage quoted? Nothing: it isn't there to
mean, to refer outwards, but to help maintain the circulatory system
of restless self-importance. America is the itch the world can't scratch,
Americans themselves least of all, and the perpetual motion, the
obsessing and picking at identity gets no nearer the heart of an
undying cliché, the American dream, but has become part of the
dream itself. Without the dream, the itch, the obsessing, America
might simply be locatable as that 'Immense Extent' the globe shows
us, huge but securely defined. A real place: but one, as they used to say
of Canada, with too much geography and not enough history.

America must always be partly elsewhere for American experience to be itself. This twist in being there was caught by the poet Robert Creeley, who in an interview contrasted his experience with that of his friend the German writer Rainer Gerhardt, by way of a line from the poetry of Walt Whitman:

> 'You know, even during the worst moments of Hitler's regime,' he [Gerhardt] said, 'when I wrote or said anything it never occurred to me I wasn't writing for all of Germany. Not writing to it, but as a person of it. Never thought of myself as separated. No matter how obviously shattered the country was, I was always all Germany.' And I said, 'Well, you know, in America, I can't think of a single person who would ever presume or think that he or she was all America.' You know, 'I hear America singing' – and that's as close as you'd get to it. It wouldn't be 'I am America singing' – it would be 'I hear...'.[3]

Whitman in one sense incarnates, in another sense typifies, by remaining outwith, without but listening to America. These are the voices and sounds of a country that has no centre, that kept moving its capital, that is striated by competing allegiances to race, region or city, that formed an uncivil union through a civil war, and that changed its boundaries almost overnight to take in states the size of France or Germany. A concept more than a country, America has to be thought in order to be lived.

# Alone with America

It has been remarked that the eighteenth-century journey towards revolution was a sentimental one, and depictions of the pursuit or loss of happiness, of independence after Independence, have frequently had a slick and airbrushed quality even when they image melancholy and failure.[4] Andrew Wyeth's painting of Christina, all wild hair and yearning, the marooned lives and gas stations of Edward Hopper, and the Pop self-portraits of Andy Warhol differ in obvious ways – yet all are secretly comfortable with alienation, at home with loneliness. Their mysteries are easily decoded. All could be renamed *Alone with America*, to pick up a phrase that recurs in American literary history (for example, as a well-known title by Richard Howard) but which originated in a Puritan sermon by Samuel Danforth. All are in keeping with the final page of Fitzgerald's *The Great Gatsby*, with the movie industry, sentimental to the core, and with the irresistible seduction of America's greatest cultural triumph, its popular music – the alluring sadness of the blues and its offshoots. Nothing could sound so alone and yet as consoling in that loneliness as the Miles Davis of *Kind of Blue* on late night radio.

Of course some seek aloneness, while many have it thrust upon them. Another contributor to the *New York Times*'s exercise in navel gazing offers this placebo, familiar yet galling to millions: 'the willingness of many Americans to accept the widening income gap, despite their moral reservations about it, grows out of a deep and abiding national conviction: whatever differences fortune may have dictated between people, where it really matters all of us are of truly equal worth'.[5] This offers rather more consolation to those who give than to those who must take such dictation. And where is this place where equal worth 'really matters'? Topeka? That mobile home the heart, no doubt. Personal generosity and collective indifference to suffering run equally deep in the American grain, and sentimentality is a good cover for capitalist depredation. (Anyone seeking the inside story here should consult a little-known masterpiece from the age of Fisk, Gould and Commodore Vanderbilt: *The Book of Daniel Drew*.[6]) The American dream persists, not because it can be realized, but because it continues to index deprivation; and condemnation to the pursuit, rather than the achievement, of happiness. The immigrant's dream of a fresh start in Eden, as old as the first settlers, is alive today for the Mexican construction-worker without a Social Security number, whose own ascent may rapidly find its glass ceiling, but whose youth and labour power help build atriums and swimming pools for those who really own the city on the hill. In fact, 'American' was never an appellation accorded the indigenous population – the 'Tawny Pagans' of Nicholas Noyes and Cotton Mather – but always referred to immigrant settlers. The obvious is one place in which to uncover the truth about America: it is from the changing but for ever wounding gap between the owners and the owned, and from the fundamentally immigrant culture of the United States, that the sense of hearing America singing, rather than occupying it contentedly, issues. America is glimpsed most clearly in the gaps: between incomes, races, urban spaces, different laws in different states. Professional sport now exists chiefly as a trigger to a certain kind of conversation the real function of which is to paper over these cracks.

American literature is what happens when the aporias and impasses in the culture become problematic, and are articulated by individual writers or the micro-communities we call coteries or avant-gardes. A gulf between rich and poor, and vanguard movements, may of course be found in European and other literary history. The American difference stems from the intertwined emergence of the radical and the conservative from the same Puritan tradition, and an ensuing tension between, on the one hand, individualism, and on the other a yearning for absolution and absorption through an epical, republican ideology, both running to extremes of purity not characteristic of European writing.

## Making a republic

The republic is continually claimed and reclaimed through polemic and counter-attack. The vast majority of American literary classics from the time of Hooker and Wrigglesworth through *Uncle Tom's Cabin* to *The Naked Lunch* are, among other things, pieces of social criticism, and the jeremiad is a characteristically American form. One of the traditional aims of American prose has lain in the use of words to cut through what the fourth President, James Madison, termed the 'cloudy medium' of language, in order to establish limits and liberties firmly (Gustafson, 44). The paradoxes as well as the clarities of this aim are a consequence of the Fall from one of the American Edens, that of Puritan theocracy. Without God's help, the mind becomes the only instrument we have with which to understand mind, and language the only medium with which to improve language.

The Declaration of Independence, to which I shall turn shortly, is a classic of Enlightenment humanism, and its emphases on equality, social unity and progress do not free it from the toils of these post-religious circularities and paradoxes. The document was, as its main author Thomas Jefferson noted, 'intended to be an expression of the American *mind*' (my emphasis).[7] To persevere, to take aim from mind to expression and strike through the cloudy medium, forging a direct prose that could not be twisted or misunderstood, was vital to a revolutionary society authoring a Constitution. The impetus had been vital to the persuasiveness of Thomas Paine's *Common Sense* (1776), and would remain intrinsic to Lincoln's great speeches, also orienting the style and intention of such writers as James Fenimore Cooper, whose *The American Democrat* (1838) and late allegories of truth and deception such as *The Crater* (1848) grip the attention more than his lugubrious Leatherstocking tales. (The tradition had a continued, if attenuated, life in the twentieth century, finding its exemplars in writers such as Ernest Hemingway.) A countervailing tradition of writers as divergent in other respects as Henry James and Herman Melville broadened the spectrum of serious possibilities for a new form, the novel, through what Judge Joseph Story, as attentive as Madison to the Constitution, had called the 'elasticity' of words (Gustafson, 50). Both traditions can combine in a third, the vernacular classic, the dissident reclamation of America through particularities of voice. Here the paradigm is Mark Twain's *The Adventures of Huckleberry Finn* (1885). It is surprising how firmly and rapidly all these traditions lead us back to the debates about the Constitution, and the implementation of the Declaration of Independence on the ground.

All forms of democracy are slanted and shot through with contradiction. The American version is remarkable for, and has retained its resilience through, building in risk. The essential dependence on a single document authored largely by one man, Thomas Jefferson, is a risk unique in history. The tripartite division of government into executive (the White House), legislative (Congress) and judiciary (the Supreme Court) – again, Jefferson's idea – may generate what Richard Hofstadter terms 'a harmonious system of mutual frustration', but it also separates powers so as to empower, ensuring (at least in theory) the containment of abuse (Brogan, 217). Aided by a horizontal separation of powers between the federal and state governments, a constant mobility and dialectical receptivity is intrinsic to the system. From the outset, there was genuinely an attempt to recognize, to contain of course, but also to represent, a Babel of competing voices. America's striking out as a separate nation is founded, in a multiple sense that puns on democracy and description, in a crisis of representation. In fact, crises of representation link every significant American development from the abolition of slavery to Abstract Expressionist painting.

## Representative words

The most authoritative recent contribution by a scholar to an understanding of the republic's perpetual return to its founding debates and documents is undoubtedly Thomas Gustafson's *Representative Words* (1992). Gustafson's enquiry into the politically synecdochic or representative inflection of American words and their classical sources is the most compendious of the revisionary accounts of the American canon to appear in recent years. Among many *aperçus* is this comment on *Moby-Dick*: 'The novel convenes a congress of representative voices to counter Ahab's single-minded voice'(32). The democrat Melville was also a pessimist even before the Civil War, and his 'congress' is wrecked, leaving Ishmael as the only speaker, afloat in that most terminal house of representatives, his 'coffin'. As the Declaration of Independence is the key American canonical work – largely non-fictional – so *Moby-Dick* is its largely fictional counterpart. The resemblance between a literature department syllabus and the hierarchies of political representation in the USA is neither a coincidence nor a conceit of my own. It goes to the essence of the democratic American intention: 'In the American republic, the people do not write the laws that govern them, but are granted the opportunity to *select* through elections *the authors* of their laws' (my emphasis, 27). Though Gustafson does not draw out all the implications of his own formulation, his choice of words remains instructive. In this fundamental concern over the selection of authors we may recall Thomas Paine's statement that 'the moral principle of revolution is to instruct, not destroy' (249). The process of representation in Congress is deeply bound to the canon, the founding Declaration, and to a selection of 'authors' by those who are learning America, those who stay the course. America has to be thought in order to be lived, but for both to happen, it had to be written. But before Jefferson's words, there was the Word.

# The Puritans: Cotton Mather, John Winthrop, Nathaniel Ward

America was invented, not discovered. Unable to take the measure of what their eyes showed them, its inventors decided to read their own backgrounds, religions and projections into its vast, enigmatic spaces, conquering through symbol and trope as much as by violence:[8]

'America' denoted far more than the Italian entrepreneur, Amerigo Vespucci, whose falsified sightings, once published, claimed the terra incognita for the Spanish throne. 'America' entitled a carnival of European fantasies. It meant the fabled land of gold, the enchanted Isles of the West, springs of eternal youth, and 'lubberlands' of ease and plenty. It verified theories of 'natural man' and 'the state of nature.' It promised opportunities for realizing utopia, for unlimited riches and mass conversions, for the return to pastoral arcadia, for implementing schemes for moral and social perfection. Columbus thought that it had been the actual site of Eden. Later explorers and settlers, translating the myths of Biblical geography into the landmarks of Renaissance geo-mythology, spoke of America as a second Eden, inhabited by pagan primitives (or perhaps the ten lost Hebrew tribes) awaiting the advent of Civilization and the Gospel Truth.[9]

Of course, the transplanting of mixed Hellenic and Hebraic tropes and legends via European imperialism produced hothouse exotics from cultures that were themselves noticeably hybrid. To view the motley European states as hungry wholes in search of a fragment to boss around is to modernize and falsify the dialectic of colonialism. (A reversed view, of fragments in search of a whole, would show a partial truth.) America could only be forced to 'verify' the Edenic or second-Edenic possibilities its plunderers wished to see by the hallucinatory agitation of power, myth, rhetoric, fact and metaphor into a spinning wheel that could roll over contradiction and inconvenient obstructions posed by the weather, plague or Indians. This process would be worried to perfection by the Puritans, whose errand into the wilderness as the model army of Christ marching to New Canaan, had itself begun in acts of dissidence in old England even before migration cut the last ties to feudal, monarchical and other hierarchies. These acted as brakes on Puritan radicalism and the unfettered capitalism, introspection and metaphorization that – following the false start at Roanoke – their new invention of New England would make possible. The Puritans 'took possession first by imposing their own image on the land, and then by seeing themselves reflected back in the image they had imposed. The wilderness became their mirror of prophecy' (35).

And they were, after all, the latest, best hope of Protestantism, that had applied radical surgery to the necrosis and hypocritical materialism of the Catholic Church and its illegitimate claims on the space between the human and the divine that the Protestant avant-garde knew to be for the individual to sort out. The 'Right Christian' (orthodox Nonconformist) would advance through prayer, a correct interpretation of event and Charity (acts of Christian love) nearer to a 'proper Expansion', full spiritual development in accordance with Scripture. A stumbling-block for these militant readers as they toiled in the darkness of sin, the shadow of predestination and the bright Boston light, lay in the fact that America is nowhere mentioned in the Bible.

This is perhaps the most important of the many paradoxes that Puritan ingenuity made negotiable through metaphor and rhetoric. It may be instructive to look briefly at the way these circles are squared in the work of Cotton Mather (1663–1728). In part because of the popular association with witchcraft and the panic at Salem, Mather is a writer patronized and avoided even by those who quote him. Nevertheless, his *Magnalia Christi Americana* (1702) is, as Tony Tanner remarks in a useful comparison with the habitual veilings of Hawthorne's Miles Coverdale in *The Blithedale Romance*, 'almost a founding volume for America'.[10] The ambitiousness and frenzied eloquence of Mather's writing supply a particularly vivid instance of the Puritan need to explain, interpret, metaphorize and close – preemptively, wherever possible – the gaps between biblical prophecy and lived actuality, between invention and experience.

The Puritans have often had a bad press, even as their writings have been reappraised, and sometimes precisely because their influence persists. The cause lies partly in a historical distance from present-day observers, who are wont to feel that their predecessors on the earth must have led simpler lives and exhibited more *naïveté* than themselves. Although the beliefs and practices of the 'Saints' evolved over two centuries, and show all the tension, variety and contradictions of any articulate society, they seem particularly vulnerable to parody. Several reasons in particular suggest themselves. First, although they did not wear hats like steeples, did not abjure alcohol, could in certain circumstances divorce, were not all suspicious of scientific progress and did not loathe music – Cromwell had supported an orchestra, and the first performance of an Italian opera on English soil was managed by Puritans – it is the case that the more vigorous Protestant traditions on both sides of the Atlantic have always drawn solace from pouring cold water on human pleasure. H. L. Mencken's gibe that the Puritan is a meddler driven by the fear that someone, somewhere, is enjoying himself, amuses by virtue of its partial truth.

Mather's writings about poetry certainly display a mean-minded hatred of pleasure. (His own verses are broken-backed.) However, his criticism can still cause the hair on the back of the neck to rise, not least because it is when the prose becomes most sulphurous that another sort of poetry begins to bubble up:

> Be not so set upon poetry, as to be always poring on the passionate and measured pages. Let not what should be sauce, rather than food for you, engross all your application. Beware of a boundless and sickly appetite for the reading of the poems which now the rickety nation swarms withal; and let not the Circean cup intoxicate you. But especially preserve the chastity of your soul from the dangers you may incur, by a conversation with muses that are no better than harlots.... Ovid's Epistles...deserve rather to be thrown into the fire, than to be laid before the eye.... [T]he powers of darkness have a library among us, whereof the poets have been the most numerous as well as the most venemous authors.[11]

'[T]he powers of darkness have a library among us.' It is superb prose (excerpted from *Manuductio ad Ministerium*, Mather's 1726 handbook for divinity students) and admirably precise, even when the rhetoric of menace is cranked high on the dial; that 'engross', for example, or the nasty Homeric allusion, typical of Mather in the cool precision of its targeting just where the prose itself seemed liable to explode. But then, Mather *likes* poetry. It is the playwrights who really get it in the neck, exciting from its lair New England's prose at its most madly beautiful, howling for revenge on a world that just won't conform, its manic orality verging on glossolalia – inevitably so, as the anxiety always latent in Mather comes close to voicing its real self-hatred, and the desire to be exactly what it excoriates. Having praised Arthur Bedford, whose monument to folly *The Evil and Danger of Stage Plays* (1706) lists 'near seven thousand instances' of impious proclivity drawn from plays written over a five-year period, Mather's mood leads him to the heights of outrage:

> [The plays] are national sins, and therefore call for national plagues; and if God should enter into judgement, all the blood in the nation would not be able to atone for them. How much do I wish that such pestilences, and indeed all those worse than Egyptian toads, (the spawns of a Butler, a Brown, and a Ward, and a company whose name is legion!) might never crawl into your chamber! The unclean spirits that come like frogs out of the mouth of the dragon, and of the beast.... As for those wretched scribbles of madmen, my son, touch them not, taste them not, handle them not: thou wilt perish in the using of them. They are the dragons, whose contagious breath peoples the dark retreats of death. (686–7)

Would that the American theatrical tradition had ever lived up to his accusations! Once again the biblical allusions are as thoughtful and precise as Mather's overarching rhetoric is hectic: the 'plagues' of frogs, 'Egyptian toads' and 'blood in the nation' threaten a reversal of the Mosaic exodus from slavery under the English pharaoh to the American Canaan if these 'wretched scribbles of madmen' are allowed to spread their contagion. The emphasis on the oral is suggestive – the breath, the mouth, the frog popping out of the dragon, the unclean and hidden recesses of the Word. Cotton Mather had to deliver young women from satanic possession as a routine part of his day job. It may be that the identification of possession in others, manifested in words, allowed a ventriloquial release of guilt and anxiety over the mind-bending and revisionary functions that the preacher himself was forcing language to perform. Following a bravura enumeration of the sesquipedalian portmanteau-formulae of Indian 'Lingua', Mather reminisces: 'I know not what Thoughts it will produce in my Reader, when I inform him, that once finding that the *Daemons* in a possessed young Woman, understood the *Latin* and

*Greek* and *Hebrew* Languages, my Curiosity led me to make Trial of this *Indian* Language, and the *Daemons* did seem as if they did not understand it' (506). Easily mocked, such a passage is replete with historical pathos for its clear admission, and its equally evident absence of awareness, that it was the New England witch-finder who brought the demons with him in the dark hold of his craft, the desires that lurk in the below-decks of the mind.

Here then lies a second reason why the Puritan mind is so vulnerable to parody. Our present-day perspective is one in which Freudian watchfulness and a readiness to deconstruct are habitual. We are all now, to draw a phrase from the *Magnalia*, 'the Children of Unperswadeableness', and the irony of a historical formation as attached to self-scrutiny as the Puritans betraying a lack of self-awareness yields easy pickings (177). Political correctness is a weapon that can be turned against the Puritans, but it is itself a modern variant of their own suave hypocrisies. A more honourable ground on which to question their extremism stems, of course, from the twentieth century's repeated experience of 'witch hunts', mass coercion by government and genocide. Modern liberalism has, understandably, invoked hysteria in Salem and authoritarians clad in black as rhetorical armoury with which to attack McCarthyites, Fascist book-burners and other pernicious agents. Even a text as important in reviving intelligent interest in the period as Perry Miller and Thomas H. Johnson's 1938 anthology of Puritan writing backed away from certain texts and authors, describing Cotton Mather as 'a case for a psychiatrist', when a more instructive project might have lain in tracing the lines of descent from Mather's manipulations to ECT, fables of therapy and the mysteries of the couch (46). Unsurprisingly the editors do not dwell on the events leading up to the witchcraft trials of 1692, when an outbreak of satanic manifestations led to mass incrimination, imprisonment and the execution of twenty 'witches', including two dogs. Miller and Johnson prefer to lay stress on the undeniable richness and variety of Puritan writing and progressive thought. (Mather himself wrote supporting inoculation, against considerable resistance.) Of course, the chosen ground on which to vilify Puritanism from a modern perspective is often so muddied through ignorance of church history that the wrong people come under attack: there have been four centuries of Muggletonians, Independent Methodists and Particular Baptists – to mention only some of the more prominent of the dissenting groups, all of whom are then branded 'Puritan', despite their differences of temper and constituency, by the children of unpersuadableness. Few people now want to know that so many people then believed, and believed so intensely.

They believed that Scripture was the living word, divinely author-
ized, and that a close reading of the Bible should be matched by a
constant readiness to interpret signs, whether they issued from self-
analysis or from the external world. John Winthrop (1588–1649),
English-born leader of the American Puritans, writes in his account of
a meeting of synod in Cambridge on 15 August 1648, that the sermon
was interrupted by a visitor:

> [T]here came a snake into the seat, where many of the elders sate behind
> the preacher. It came in at the door where people stood thick upon the
> stairs. Divers of the elders shifted from it, but Mr. Thomson, one of the
> elders of Braintree, (a man of much faith,) trode upon the head of it, and
> so held it with his foot and staff with a small pair of grains, until it was
> killed. This being so remarkable, and nothing falling out but by divine
> providence, it is out of doubt, the Lord discovered somewhat of his mind
> in it. The serpent is the devil; the synod, the representative of the
> churches of Christ in New England. The devil had formerly and lately
> attempted their disturbance and dissolution; but their faith in the seed of
> the woman overcame him and crushed his head. (142–3)

The appearance of a snake in church would have posed few difficulties of interpretation to an audience whose interpretive skills were
perpetually on red alert. Nevertheless, the passage is instructive for its
clear example of the habits of mind, essentially habits of reading, that
the seventeenth-century settlers applied to their New World. The
American promised land was itself a readerly concept, an invention
requiring constant reminders that nothing falls out 'but by divine
providence', so that the contingent, the new, the other could immediately be integrated into a theology, one that Sacvan Bercovitch has
defined as 'a radical troping of Christian tradition to fit the fantasies
of a particular sect. Considered as ideology, it was a mode of consensus designed to fill the needs of a certain social order' (Bercovitch, 32).
The aim of Puritan rhetoric remains the same, whether considered as
a justification of the ways of God to men or as a means of social
control; it is to collapse the difference and distance between signifier,
signified and referent, between individual need and social direction,
between invention and reality. Its instinctive rhetoric is one of overarching and conflation. A tension in the dialectic between the Calvinist doctrine of predestination and the concept of free will serves both
to keep the interpreting consciousness on constant alert and to remind
that one day all gaps will be bridged, between history and allegory,
prophecy and territory, the local and the universal. On that Judgement Day eschatology will be proved on the pulses, as society and the
individual are drawn up to face the audit of eternity.

The rhetoric of conflation had to work particularly hard to leap over doubt when faced by setbacks as various as the absence of America from the Bible, the restoration of the monarchy in London and attacks by Indians at home. Ultimately the narratives of predestination and of immigrant experience deny each other. Given the competing pressures, it is amazing that Puritan ideology was able to evolve, and did not simply vanish in schism. Hence, in part, the heightened importance and the heightened rhetoric of the sermon form – which spells, among other things, social control from the pulpit – and which could, by turns, allay or provoke a sense of crisis, either resituating setbacks within providence and promise, or agitating the mismatch between those concepts and hebdomedary experience so as to whip discrepancy into line with a master-narrative of progress.

A good sermon was also, and is also, a powerful personal statement. It can include elements of confession, the recounted experience of conversion, and thus a personal testament to revelation. It begets, and does not merely anticipate, the 'spilt religion' that T. E. Hulme saw in Romanticism, and beyond that the epiphanies of Modernism which are themselves in an extended sense Romantic. Just as the poetry of John Milton may be read everywhere in William Wordsworth, so the New England pulpit and divinity school produced, even as they were challenged by, Ralph Waldo Emerson. Freed from the shackles of European hierarchies, the settlers and their descendants lost mind-forged as well as iron manacles (as Blake well understood), and modernity was in conflicting senses their aim, their bequest and their undoing. Even in its most avowedly anti- or post-religious texts, the modern is never free of structures and tropes that bespeak Christian, and specifically Puritan, influence.

There is no need to rehearse the well-known arguments and analyses of canonical texts that stress such inheritances, from W. H. Abrams's *Natural Supernaturalism* to late Derrida. Perhaps more contentiously, I would suggest that even in such hallmarks of postmodernity as the methodological alternation between restriction and openness to chance procedure, we can detect the Puritan willingness to move from the local to the universal in a single breath. A clear example is offered by the music and other productions of John Cage (1912–1992), whose avant-gardism seems at first sight to spell the end and unpicking of music, a trajectory typical of the ultra-modernist *via negativa*. But Cage shows a benign Puritan influence. Partly it is his liking for industriousness, and for ingenious construction in performance-spaces almost bare of material. But throughout his career, whether in the polemical care with which echoes of the European

tradition are deracinated in the *Music of Changes*, or in the alternation between free will and prefixed restrictions placed on the performers of *Concert for Prepared Piano and Chamber Orchestra*, or in the
austerity and sustained introspection of a late masterpiece such as
*Fourteen*, Cage shows the Puritan vision of the sounded note in
relation to the overarching plan, the Puritan fascination with interpretation, the self-confidence necessary to thinking the world entire –
and above all, that marvellous Puritan daring, to do it all from
scratch.

As a coda to this brief consideration of the men in black, the
writings of Nathaniel Ward (1578–1652) alone rebut the reputation
of niggardly minds and unimaginative piety. Like Winthrop a participant in the formation of the Massachusetts Bay Company and later a
contributor to the framing of State law, he came to New England after
being silenced by Archbishop Laud in 1634. Ward has an instinct for
the striking image: 'to authorise an untruth, by a Toleration of State,
is to build a Sconce against the walls of Heaven, to batter God out of
his Chaire' (Miller and Johnson, 229). The self-awareness of his
defence of New England (writing as the 'Simple Cobler of Aggawam'
– an Indian translation of Ipswich), reminds us that even Winthrop's
most famous address was for European consumption, and that, as
with much later American literature, a selective retention of Anglophone ties contributes to the effectiveness of the writing:

> We have been reputed a Colluvies of wild Opinionists, swarmed into a
> remote wildernes to find elbow-roome for our Phanatick doctrines and
> practises: I trust our diligence past, and constant sedulity against such
> persons and courses, will plead better things for us. I dare take upon
> me, to be the Herauld of *New-England* so farre, as to proclaime to the
> world, in the name of our Colony, that all Familists, Antinomians,
> Anabaptists, and other Enthusiasts, shall have free Liberty to keep
> away from us, and such as will come to be gone as fast as they can,
> the sooner the better. (227)

Persona is allowed to take over, the better to let wit flow: 'My heart
hath naturally detested foure things: The standing of the Apocrypha
in the Bible; Forrainers dwelling in my Countrey, to crowd out native
Subjects into the corners of the Earth; Alchymized coines; Tolerations
of divers religions' (228). As words mutate into proto-Joycean neologisms – 'a multimonstrous maufrey of heteroclytes and quicquidlibets'
(232) – Ward's own verbal quodlibet becomes so giddy as to blur
certainty as to where exactly parody, self-parody and serious criticism
find their limits. Is it only differing and preferable, modern notions of

what constitutes misogyny that make his Puritan attack on women's fashions so jarring, while it amuses?

I can make myself sick at any time, with comparing the dazzling splender wherewith our Gentlewomen were embellished in some former habits, with the gut-foundred goosdome, wherewith they are now surcingled and debauched. We have about five or six of them in our Colony: if I see any of them accidentally, I cannot cleanse my phansie of them for a month after. I have been a solitary widdower almost twelve years, purposed lately to make a step over to my Native Country for a yoke-fellow: but when I consider how women there have tripe-wifed themselves with their cladments, I have no heart to the voyage, lest their nauseous shapes and the Sea, should work too sorely upon my stomach. (233)

So unlike Mather in so many ways, Ward still excels in that disturbing doubleness of coolly precise imagery shot out by hot invective. Although in persona, the forthright criticism disturbs by virtue of the evident presence of irony; but one with uncertain limits. And it is a Puritan rigour over text turned to a proto-deconstructive extreme that has Ward write, in a casual aside that is also one of the most compelling summaries of the ideology of anxiety that characterized the Colony, and his times: 'Take away the least *vericulum* out of the world, and it unworlds all, potentially, and may unravell the whole texture actually, if it be not conserved by an Arme of extraordinary power' (231).

It is not always clear where 'power' in the writing of the period has become so 'extraordinary' as to be able to afford to laugh at itself, and where it is a case of modern unpersuadableness lighting on unconscious humour. It would be inhuman not to derive callow enjoyment from this diary entry of John Sewall of 26 May 1720: 'About midnight my dear wife expired to our great astonishment, especially mine' (391). On a (one presumes) happier day a quarter of a century earlier, Cotton Mather, standing as a guest in the Sewalls' kitchen, was led to muse aloud that 'more Ministers Houses than others proportionably had been smitten with Lightening', at which moment, as if to serve him right, a freak storm of hail 'as bigg as pistoll or Musquet Bullets' smashed all the windows' (512). In eschatological terms all Puritan writing is comedic, as all versions of the Christian message may be said to be comedic, the Fall and the Crucifixion succeeded by the Resurrection. Yet none of it is freely amusing. Comedic by virtue of the understanding that there can be no incongruity, no human pratfall or *bouleversement* that is not redeemable at last, because nothing falls out but by divine providence, never amusing because incongruity and discrepancy can never persist long

enough in that policed linguistic state for irony to crystallize as an
intellectual position, and so develop the strength to posit an alternative. The 'Arme of extraordinary power' – which is the Church, the
State, the *doxa*, at root the Word – makes sure of this through its
conflationary inclusionism, its paranoid overdetermination of symbolism and the necessity for right interpretation and explanation.
While the Word would not lose any of its 'extraordinary power' as
the colonies grew and moved toward independence, the source of that
power would be viewed increasingly as human legislation working for
purely human ends.

## Thomas Jefferson: *The Declaration of Independence*

Studies of the world turned upside down, by Christopher Hill and
others, demonstrate that capitalism was the defining trajectory, if not
the basis, of English Puritanism. The New Englanders, the colonials
who (briefly) called themselves Puritans, were sufficiently free of residually feudal practices and other forms of cultural mortmain to
establish the Massachusetts Bay Company and move ahead in a race
where America has subsequently almost always seemed the clear
winner. The colonials were nationalist only potentially, and as a result
of their avant-garde prominence in the same economic development.
Just so, the struggle for freedom from England in many ways replicates
the tenor of the struggles for expanded representation and liberty
common across Europe, and that were to climax in a new Eden and a
new Fall, in France. That said, the colonials' self-invention in terms not
only of increased dynamism and modernity, but by the light of scrip-
tural promise to a 'chosen people', confers a distinct social identity.
Aptly termed 'universalist-exclusivist' by Sacvan Bercovitch, this increasingly specific identity would, once its own impetus to revolution
became clearer in the mirror of prophecy, never fail, or gain the tragic
inflection of the European insurrections. This, in part, for the obvious
reason: the enemy lay without and not within. The French condemned
themselves to a sanguinary tiering of society, unable to let go a feudal
model that had not been levelled, but merely decapitated. By contrast,
the travails of 1812 would only consolidate the gains of the American
Revolution whose past lay literally elsewhere.

American separatism would shrug off its biblical sense of providence while still requiring a textual guarantee. It is amazing that
Thomas Jefferson (1743–1826), on this occasion bounced into
authorship by the absence of Adams and by Franklin's indisposition

through gout, should have produced a document which transcended so compellingly and with such untarnished longevity the grievances that catalysed it. Despite the failure to grasp the nettle of slavery and despite the Civil War that would eventually follow, the Declaration of Independence is the textual guarantor that the Eden of America has yet to experience its Fall.

To Jefferson and to the universalist-exclusivist tendency, an important feature of the document's drive for change stemmed from its disdain for originality. It was intended, in the words of a letter penned the year before his death and quoted already, to be an expression of the American mind:

> Not to find out new principles, or new arguments, never before thought of, not merely to say things which had never been said before; but to place before mankind the common sense of the subject, in terms so plain and firm as to command their assent, and to justify ourselves in the independent stand we are compelled to take. All its authority rests then on the harmonizing sentiments of the day. (719)

To Jefferson's deliberate echo of Thomas Paine might be added such writers of the day as Jean-Jacques Rousseau, harmonized in a clear-headed liberalism whose poise and optimism stem historically from the promise of a 'renovated Earth' that Mather had written of in his *Theopolis Americana* (1710) as 'not something *new*', but rather a destiny awaited (Bercovitch, 84).

It is that sense of a final unveiling rather than a new beginning which allows Jefferson, paradoxically, to begin without preamble: 'When, in the course of human events, it becomes necessary for one people to dissolve the political bands which have connected them with another. . . '. In quoting the most famous and the most effectively representative sentences in political history, I follow the practice of italicizing words struck out by Congress, and setting in capitals those inserted by it:

> We hold these truths to be self evident: that all men are created equal; that they are endowed by their Creator with CERTAIN [*inherent and*] inalienable rights; that among these are life, liberty, and the pursuit of happiness; that to secure these rights, governments are instituted among men, deriving their just powers from the consent of the governed; that whenever any form of government becomes destructive of these ends, it is the right of the people to alter or to abolish it, and to institute new government, laying its foundation on such principles, and organizing its powers in such form, as to them shall seem most likely to effect their safety and happiness. (Jefferson, 22)

No matter that the Declaration of Independence lapses into whinge-
ing. No matter that its unconvincing attempt to blame King George
personally for all the blunders of Parliament risks a declaration of
continued dependence, reverting to a transatlantic 'family romance'
of filial rebellion sandwiched by protestations of maturity. No matter
that it degenerates into a list, a fault that (aided from other sources)
would be bequeathed to American political poetry from Whitman to
Pound and Ginsberg. No matter that the list of unjust measures
wrought on America since the Intolerable Acts includes protests –
for example, concerning the Quebec Act – which don't stand up. No
matter that these and other skewings of Whiggery-pokery have been
filleted by more competent historians than I. Or, let all these things
matter: for they will matter only to a particular constituency. The
power of the Declaration's best passages matches the enormity of the
fact of Independence. The Declaration trumps reservations by its
capaciousness, a hospitality and liberalism whose rhetorical antece-
dents lie in the instinctive habit of conflation, of the local and the
universal, addressed earlier in this chapter.

Jefferson thought, mistakenly, that Congress had ruined the document by its alterations. As with the work of all committees, many of
the agreed alterations moderate tone so as to guard the collective
back. Thus Jefferson's insistence on the necessity to 'expunge' an
outmoded system of government becomes the necessity to 'alter',
with its hint at preserving the possible good things about the old, in
the new. More crucially, phrases are deleted that are open to a charge
of excessive conflation, that strike too Edenic a note, or sometimes
both. A proto-Emersonian iconoclasm recurs – not least in the references to 'happiness' that Jeremy Bentham and other commentators
thought silly, but that have come to be invoked most frequently – and
in the picture of a people prepared 'to right themselves by abolishing
the forms to which they are accustomed' (22). The second half of the
following, that concludes a paragraph blaming King George for
'REPEATED [*unremitting*] injuries and usurpations', was however,
deleted: 'To prove this, let facts be submitted to a candid world [*for
the truth of which we pledge a faith yet unsullied by falsehood*]'(23).
Yet unsullied – the truly Edenic note – yet how Emersonian and how
radically *authorial*, to assert the truth of facts not from their place in a
shared or external world but from the 'pledge', the verbalization of
intention, of 'a faith', the risked belief in something beyond, to come,
not quite here; outwith or without. There is in America's eternal
return to its founding tropes something forever young, but, as with
the figures around Keats's Grecian Urn, at the payment of a price:
though America may be 'near the goal', Americans can never, quite,

occupy that space wholly. But then words never quite reach the things and states to which they point. A word can never *be* its object, but only signal it. The world's most authored nation lives out, in a questionable paradise, the limits of language.

And of course, to return to Nathaniel Ward's warning, unpick the least *vericulum* and the whole may 'unravell'. 'We hold these truths to be self evident': well, if they are self-evident, why must they be 'held', asserted? But these are deconstructive quibbles by comparison with the glaring omission of a major section of the citizenry from equality and the pursuit of happiness. The Declaration of Independence does use the words *'transportation'* and *'slavery'*, *'a market where MEN should be bought and sold'*, but intends by them an indictment of impressment and removal of the kind that would befall Melville's Israel Potter in the novel of that name. Thus, following the cold refusal of the South to consider emancipation of the slaves, the silence on this issue from the Declaration constitutes (as Jefferson, who predicted conflict, foresaw) the first shot of the Civil War.

## Jefferson's conservatism

It is not the case that Jefferson himself emerges unsullied from these disagreements. To put it at its best, Jefferson wanted to free the slaves in order to be free of them. He would in time be a supporter of the Colonization Society, and the aim of removing black men and women to Liberia or Haiti. This eagerness to bid farewell to the least fortunate of his fellow-Americans (though my term is an anachronism, most documents of the time equating 'negroes' with 'cattle') was not matched in his own backyard. One of the principal slave-holders in Virginia at the time of drafting the Declaration, Jefferson preferred in certain respects to foresee a democratic future, rather than to act so as to ensure its more speedy arrival. No one hearing his Inaugural Address in 1801 would have deduced, had they not known already, that slavery had ever existed in the colonies or the new nation. These hypocrisies have been well documented, and are capped, at the time of writing, by the results of scientifically analysed DNA, making it likely that the nation's third President fathered up to six children at Monticello by the slave mulatress Sally Hemings.

In such ways the tropes of symbolism were to be unravelled by irony, which in the discourse of conduct is hypocrisy, the gap between saying one thing and doing another. In 1791 Thomas Jefferson wrote an amiable response to Benjamin Banneker, a free black from

Maryland who had achieved modest advancement as a mathematician, clockmaker and astronomer, and whose gift of an almanac to Jefferson constituted a rebuke over the latter's reluctance to hasten changing times:

> Nobody wishes more than I do to see such proofs as you exhibit, that nature has given to our black brethren, talents equal to those of the other colors of men, and that the appearance of a want of them is owing merely to the degraded condition of their existence, both in Africa and America. (508)

Jefferson promised to pass the almanac on to the academician Condorcet as a kind of four-leaf clover. By contrast, in his one published book, the *Notes on Virginia*, Jefferson muses as to the source of black pigmentation, querying whether it issues from the skin, the blood or the bile, but noting that, whatever the source, 'the difference is fixed in nature'. White is superior to black in both essence and appearance:

> Are not the fine mixtures of red and white, the expressions of every passion by greater or less suffusions of color in the one, preferable to that eternal monotony, which reigns in the countenances, that immovable veil of black which covers the emotions of the other race? Add to these, flowing hair, a more elegant symmetry of form, their own judgment in favor of the whites, declared by their preference of them, as uniformly as is the preference of the Oran-utan for the black woman over those of his own species. (256)

The next chapter will be concerned with tales and poems of the changing, imprisoned or veiled body, defined by difference, by violence or desire, and the veilings of aesthetic and ideological form. In conclusion, it is interesting to note that in 1774 George Mason warned that providence might 'avenge upon our Posterity the Injury done a set of Wretches, who our Injustice had debased almost to a Level with the Brute Creation.... As nations cannot be rewarded or punished in the next world they must be in this.' During the War of Independence, Abigail Adams, John Jay and many others feared that unless slavery were abolished, so Americans' 'prayers to Heaven for liberty will be impious'.[12] To adopt the phrasing of an English poem of the time concerning Paradise and the Fall, these were ancestral voices prophesying war. The conservative and liberal traditions in America are intertwined down to their shared root in Puritanism.

# 2

# American Literature and the Body Electric

## The American Renaissance

The next two chapters, and part of chapter 4, are concerned with the major American writers of the nineteenth century. Edgar Allan Poe's work comes in the main from the decade 1835–45. At the other extreme, the crowning achievements of Henry James's long literary career are often held to be the works of fiction, travel and autobiography he published in the early years of the twentieth century. Between the two, the writings of Hawthorne, Melville, Emerson, Whitman and Dickinson cluster at mid-century, so much so that in his influential overview *American Renaissance* (1941), F. O. Matthiessen was able to focus on the period 1850–55, the years of *Representative Men*, *The Scarlet Letter*, *Moby-Dick*, *Leaves of Grass* and Thoreau's *Walden*. Matthiessen's assertion that '[t]he great attraction of my subject was its compactness' was complemented nonetheless by a wealth of historical background and literary detail.[1] His aim in part was to demonstrate the relevance of Shakespeare to Melville, of Milton to Hawthorne, of Hopkins to Whitman – the point being that to make these historical pairings would not work to the discredit of the American side, whose achievements were now to be reckoned as comparable. Notwithstanding the quantity of literary criticism emanating from the universities post-Matthiessen, the most enduring examples of American criticism have been authored by its poets and novelists: for example, T. S. Eliot's essays on the Elizabethans, Charles Olson's book on Melville and James's book on Hawthorne, examined in this chapter. Exceptions include work by academics such as Harold Bloom and Geoffrey Hartman, but there the focus is as likely to be the English Romantic poets as their American successors, with whom Matthiessen's study deals.

The term 'American Renaissance' – immediately resonant, immediately questionable – passed into general currency, so that an important account of the period by David S. Reynolds, *Beneath the American Renaissance* (1988), still finds it useful, while overturning many of Matthiessen's postulates. Reynolds argues that the canonical writers of the ante-bellum years produced classics out of an engagement with popular culture of exactly the sort that Matthiessen (and Eliot and Bloom) dismiss as irrelevant or trashy. Reynolds's book embodies the most convincing argument to date that the *oeuvres* of Emerson and Whitman are the outcome of immersion in a culture of discursive practices, rather than the autotelic masterworks of individual minds alone with America.

The opposite view, that these authors and books are 'hard, isolate, stoic', can be found in a survey that has been repudiated since it was first published, but from which the subject and its scholars have never quite been able to escape: D. H. Lawrence's *Studies in Classic American Literature* (1923).[2] Lawrence's account was meant to prick and irritate. It succeeds. The extremism of the polemic has made it vulnerable, as most Modernist polemic became vulnerable in the harsh light that the catastrophes of the Second World War, and its cultural and political consequences, shed on poses and attitudes struck in the 1920s. Like most significant works of or about American literature, the book addresses a European as well as an American audience, and it is the proximity of Lawrence's prophetic tones to the rhetoric of European fascism that make his aggression so troubling: 'We may have to smash things. Then let us smash' (145). 'I say, let the old guns rot. Buy new ones, and shoot straight' (152). A hatred of women and their emancipation comes through without apology: 'Give her the great slap... Oh, woman out of bounds is a devil' (100). Lawrence claimed to celebrate the unmediated life of the body while hating reflective consciousness, an impossible posture for any human being in possession of his or her faculties to maintain, but particularly contradictory for a writer. In any case, Lawrence is all buzzing, angry mind, and suffers from a Puritan fear of the body: 'The evil thing that all daytime love-making is, and all sex-palaver' (81). (An impartial cosmic observer might note that, just as the European siesta has not lost favour, so the American hotel industry has not crashed.) As with Eliot, Pound, Yeats and Lewis, Lawrence's overview of history is the weakest side of his work, vapid myth making about cycles, heroes and anarchy that frequently disconnects itself from reality: 'The next era is the era of the Holy Ghost' (85).

And yet it is the precise nature of these (and worse) absurdities that enables Lawrence, through a principle of perversity worthy of Poe, to stage an account of the American Renaissance which is true to its pronouncements of messianic yet slippery individualism. All these writers go out of their way to provoke, and risk rejection. Here is Emerson: 'The doctrine of hatred must be preached as the counteraction of the doctrine of love when that pules and whines. I shun father and mother and wife and brother, when my genius calls me.'[3] Whitman: 'What blurt is this about virtue and about vice? / Evil propels me and reform of evil propels me, I stand indifferent.'[4] Poe: 'I took from my waistcoat-pocket a pen-knife, opened it, grasped the poor beast by the throat, and deliberately cut one of its eyes from the socket!'[5] That Emerson is also the poet of the blowing clover and the falling rain, that moments of radiant benignity shine from every leaf of Whitman's grasses, that the cruelties of Poe's 'The Black Cat' can be contextualized as the ravings of a Gothic persona, serve only to increase the irritant factor. If there is nothing these writers won't say to get a reaction, there is nothing they won't retract, instantly. As Whitman famously observes in *Song of Myself*: 'Do I contradict myself? / Very well then I contradict myself.' (Whitman, 246). It is the gamble on caprice, the daring, that Lawrence catches, for it echoes the most interesting trajectory of his own incomplete skills. That is why, even if so much of his book is limited by his personality and times, the core idea, put straightforwardly in the preface, is still arresting, and demands consideration from any serious student of these writers: 'The European moderns are all *trying* to be extreme. The great Americans I mention just were it' (Lawrence, 4).

# Hawthorne

If reading needs to pay heed to radicalism and wilful perversity in writing of the American Renaissance, it needs also to query the degree to which that radicalism is bravura in a nation of rising importance, and the degree to which traits from the eras of revolution and even Puritanism continue to drive the achievements of the ante-bellum years. Here the work of Nathaniel Hawthorne (1804–64) claims attention first, through its overt recourse to the colonial period as scene or subject in novels such as *The Scarlet Letter* (1850) and *The House of the Seven Gables* (1851), and in a number of short stories.

'Young Goodman Brown' in the tale of that name steps into a wild dream of a witch meeting, involving the good citizens of Salem Village; in the 'Legends of the Province House' superstition claims that the ancient governors of Massachusetts still walk abroad: Hooper is buried in 'The Minister's Black Veil' he would neither explain nor remove in life.

In *The House of the Seven Gables* old Matthew Maule suffers the loss of his land to Colonel Pyncheon, a giant in the local legislature, and then, found guilty of witchcraft, curses his tormentor from the gallows with the prophecy that 'God will give him blood to drink'. This sanguinary prediction comes true, and at the climax of the novel, is visited on his descendant, the hypocritical Judge Jaffrey Pyncheon as the past works itself out on the present. A portrait groans and drips blood; papers of ownership are lost and found after years. Houses glare like faces: 'The aspect of the venerable mansion has always affected me like a human countenance, bearing the traces not merely of outward storm and sunshine, but expressive, also, of the long lapse of mortal life, and accompanying vicissitudes that have passed within.'[6] This bears comparison with Poe's House of Usher and its 'vacant eye-like windows' (Poe, 317), the whale's jaw portal to the bar of *Moby-Dick*'s Spouter-Inn, or the hotel in George Lippard's *The Quaker City* (1845): 'a monster-building, with some hundred windows varying its red-brick face, in the way of eyes, covered with green-blind shutters, looking very much like so many goggles intended to preserve the sight of the visual organs aforesaid: while the verandah...might be likened to the mouth of the grand-edifice, always wide open and ready to swallow a customer.'[7] Extravagance and black humour link all these anthropomorphic images, but the inflections differ. Lippard's is a popular fiction that celebrates with an unstable blend of reform agenda and sensationalism the vitality of the expanding city. Poe's seeing house will collapse in the adjacent tarn, thereby collapsing distinctions between physical and mental, sanity and insanity, in an aesthetically perfect moment of self-destruction characteristic of its author. Hawthorne uses a rhetoric of conflation typical of the colonial period, in order to make a palimpsest of that period and the present. Even the name 'Maule' suggests the self-lacerations of Puritan guilt culture, as in Cotton Mather's shuddered aside during the period of Spectral Evidence that 'we are hotly, and madly, mauling one another in the *dark*' (Mather's emphasis: Bercovitch, 106). Moreover, at this time to 'church-maul' meant 'to try before the church'. The present is pinched, mauled, shadowed, overhung by the past, as was Hawthorne's personal history. Descended from Major William Hathorne, who crossed the

Atlantic with the charter of the Massachusetts Bay Colony, his great-grandfather sat as a judge in the witchcraft trials. Such an imprisoning history proposes to the modern mind a psychoanalytic as well as a cultural perspective, confirmed by the themes of guilt and struggling conscience in *The Scarlet Letter*, and traced by Frederick Crews in a bench-mark study of Hawthorne, *The Sins of the Fathers*. Of all these writers, Hawthorne seems at first the one bound to the past.

## Hawthorne and James

And yet there are problems with this interpretation of Hawthorne. In fact, there are problems with any interpretation of Hawthorne that does not pay heed to the contingent nature of interpretation itself. Henry James observed trenchantly in his 1874 study, the first such, that although the older novelist possessed in an adequate degree 'the historic consciousness', he makes the 'mustiness and mouldiness of the tenants of the House of the Seven Gables crumble away rather too easily. What Hawthorne designed to represent was not the struggle between an old society and a new, for in this case he would have given the old one a better chance.'[8] The New England background is a component which the fictions incorporate, rather than one on which they lay a detailed stress, so that Salem and the grim past are pressed into service for literary ends, rather than signposting topics to which the texts are a conduit. Hawthorne is the republic's first major novelist not because he is absorbed in region and history, but because he had the powers of detached expression necessary to a more subtle and allegorizing use of the pictures they call up. Thus James confers on Hawthorne the appellation 'the most eminent representative of a literature', making clear his intention to stake a claim for an achieved *national* literature, not a regional phenomenon (319).

James's attitude to both that region and those days is one of heavy condescension. His bestowal of 'the lonely honour of a representative attitude' (320) on Hawthorne is oxymoronic by virtue of the unfinished condition of the society that produced him. Most 'attempts at social recreation in the New England world some forty years ago' were marked by 'lonely frigidity', and the 'great desire for culture' prevalent in the drawing-room so far exceeded the resources available that '[s]mall things were made to do large service' (371), the example given being a soirée including the young Hawthorne, at which copies of Flaxman's illustrations of Dante, the gift of a Harvard professor, constituted the 'evening's entertainment'. For Henry James, this period of communitarian self-reliance had far-reaching consequences, including Emerson's stress on 'the duty of making the most of one's self' (382) in a situation where 'introspection, thanks to the want of other entertainment, played almost the part of a social resource':

> In the United States, in those days, there were no great things to look out at (save forests and rivers); life was not in the least spectacular; society was not brilliant; the country was given up to a great material prosperity, a homely *bourgeois* activity, a diffusion of primary education and the common luxuries. There was therefore, among the cultivated classes, much relish for the utterances of a writer who would help one to take a picturesque view of one's internal possibilities, and to find in the landscape of the soul all sorts of fine sunrise and moonlight effects. (383)

This is at root a devastating critique of Emerson, to whose acuities James was not blind, but whose Romanticism and iconoclasm form an antithesis to the traditions of European society, and in particular the English novel, with which James had elected to settle. It is particularly telling because it immediately appears to take in writers such as Emily Dickinson, whom we now value, but whose work James would not have known. I would argue not that the critique is correct, but that the fear or the possibility of its being so hovers in the margins of what American Renaissance writers saw in themselves, catalysing in the main a double-or-quit intensification of emphasis: on selfhood, on moments of mystical union with nature, on the tearing down of tradition, on extravagance of image or narrative or attitude – above all, on originality. These writers are made a group in a paradoxical sense, by their insistence on self-reliance and separation; all share 'the lonely honour of a representative attitude'. Rejecting Puritan guilt and the selective vision of Enlightenment rationalism, they reorient Puritan and Revolutionary insistence in modern directions, and their paradox of a group-individualist identity became a genetic inheritance for American literature, including the Beats, Black Mountain and San Francisco Renaissance poets whom Lawrence did not live to see, and whom he would have abhorred but recognized as the latest settlers in Whitman's 'wide, strange camp at the end of the great highroad' (Lawrence, 179).

## The Scarlet Letter

So far I have argued that Hawthorne's use of the New England scene and its past were involuntary subject-matter to the extent that he used what he knew, but were above all *chosen* materials from which to forge an American achievement in the increasingly important form of the novel, so as to stand comparison with European developments. Although James mixed patronage with praise, he wrote at a later date with his own projects to further, and with a sense of accelerated progress in novel writing that verged on a modern avant-gardism, fused in his mind (uniquely, in the period preceding the Yellow Nineties) with an attachment to London. The question of what Hawthorne was doing by his own lights ought to be, but is not, easily settled. According to Julian Hawthorne's memoirs of his father, when asked how one of his best short stories, 'Rappaccini's Daughter' was to end, he replied 'with some emotion' that he had no idea.[9] The prefaces to the novels (which James continually praises) are part and parcel of the fictions they broach, and concepts such as that of the romance, highlighted in the exordium to *The House of the Seven Gables*, are evasive to a fault, which may precisely index Hawthorne's sense of writing as engaging the interest through its transitions – from realism to allegory, portraiture to speculation, tragedy to comedy – rather than through any settled authorial position.

The Scarlet Letter (1850) epitomizes this fluidity and artifice, while seeming initially to deny it. After all, this is the first significant American novel to have passionate love as its theme, played out in the relationship between Hester Prynne and Arthur Dimmesdale, the tortured preacher. The couple are preyed on by her husband, dissector of psyches Roger Chillingworth, and attended by young Pearl, the fruit of adulterous union. There is a vehement alternation at this period of American culture between books that were intended for, or could be read by, children and those that most certainly could not. The classics of the nineteenth century fall on both sides, but *The Scarlet Letter* fell so definitely in the second category as to trouble reviewers, who scented a dangerous French influence abroad in the New England woods. They need hardly have worried, for the most unbuttoned moment in the narrative is that at which Hester shakes free her luxurious tresses, and the effectively impotent Dimmesdale does not even kiss his beloved at his moment of 'Satanic' exhilaration in the forest. Meanwhile Hester sews and forever re-embroiders in the gorgeous colour her life so utterly lacks, the emblem of her shame. Her scarlet letter stands, of course, for adultery, but once again reviewers dreading reminders of the un-virtuous part of Rousseau's *Nouvelle Héloïse* could sleep easily, for adultery is nowhere mentioned, let alone enacted. Indeed, all the crucial incidents are firmly in the past, but no attempt to read the text as a 'historical novel' will work, for, as Leslie Fiedler observed in his *Love and Death in the*

*American Novel* (1960), 'Hawthorne's gestures at indicating the social backgrounds and historical contexts of his characters are half-hearted and unconvincing, a bow towards realism. And his book is finally dream-like rather than documentary...evoking the past as nightmare rather than fact.'[10]

At the time Fiedler's book appeared, the expatriate British film-maker Alfred Hitchcock was making great (perhaps the greatest) cinema out of individual American pasts portrayed as nightmare rather than history, and the orchestrated obsessions of *The Scarlet Letter* can perhaps be heard with greater clarity when set alongside *Marnie* (1964) or, even more, *Vertigo* (1958). Here passionate and life-threatening obsession is played out against a deep-focus American landscape, and the sublime blend of Bartók, woodnotes wild and saccharine that is a Bernard Herrmann score. 'Actors in a dark hallucination', to return to Fiedler's terms, the quartet of protagonists are 'aptly moved by a guilt as hallucinatory as themselves' (499), the sorrowing and mythical Chorus of a primal Fall from the American Eden. Inevitably the scarlet letter also stands for America, amid a myriad alternatives; for there is no provocation that cannot be stated or retracted in a moment, yet no escape from signs and interpretation, emblems and the close reading of character, type and word. What Tony Tanner memorably termed the 'atmosphere of sadistic semiology' in the novel's neo-Puritan paranoia over the unpicking of each *vericulum* is also apt for its reminder of Sade's own fictions, terrible verbal machines grinding their way through the dictionary of human delights/torments with inexhaustible patience on a trajectory to nowhere (Tanner, p. xvi). Even the novel's generally forgotten subtitle, *Notes of a Decapitated Surveyor*, conveys a sense of auto-castration, submission to some kind of mechanical or dream-life. We are as far from George Eliot's *Middlemarch* (1870), with its comforting appendix relating what happened to these 'people' in after years, as it is possible to get. No wonder Sophia Hawthorne, on hearing her husband read the novel to its conclusion, suffered a blinding headache that went on for days.

## The Blithedale Romance

Hawthorne appears to have sleep-walked his way into *The Scarlet Letter*, unsure in advance of its likely length or final form. By the time of his most complex and successful novel, *The Blithedale Romance* (1852), he appears to have learned not so much to move beyond his

Gothic settings, repressed narrators and jarring shifts from realism to allegory, as to deploy them more confidently, in a kaleidoscopic representation whose shifting layers include satire and suspicion. Once again, the writing anticipates cinema in general and Hitchcockian obsession in particular, and the section where the protagonist Miles Coverdale, a retentive voyeur, returns to the city and begins spying on the neighbours in the opposite tenement anticipates *Rear Window* (1954). The climax of the novel, at which the feminist Zenobia is first drowned, and then accidentally skewered, anticipates the autoptic tragicomedies of David Lynch and a thousand horror movies in which curvaceous young women who take liberties must be punished.

Just prior to that climactic incident, the unseen Coverdale attends a satanic pageant in the woods, where 'a concourse of strange figures', including 'an Indian chief', 'a Bavarian broom-girl', 'a negro of the Jim Crow order', 'a Kentucky woodsman', 'a Shaker elder' and a 'renowned old witch', mingling with 'grim Puritans' and 'Revolutionary officers with three-cornered cocked hats', are led to dance by the strains of a 'horned and long-tailed gentleman' playing a fiddle.[11] A representation of American democracy as devil-driven role play, comparable to Melville's microcosm of his countrymen in the crew of Ahab's *Pequod*, the scene anticipates horror films (*City of the Dead* springs to mind) in which an American backwoods community turns out to be run by some secret masonic–satanic compact whose operations are threatened by the unseen interloper. We know that Hawthorne was influenced by the Gothic fictions of Charles Brockden Brown and Ann Radcliffe, but there is more than that in play here. Hawthorne was also a lifelong addict of popular fiction, newspapers, pseudo-scientific and hoax literature, and we might see in Henry James's caricature of a social circle bursting with rectitude but short of entertainment a wilful bourgeoisification of a rather more multi-layered cultural milieu, one in which 'low' and 'high' culture enjoyed a more ongoing and dialogic – indeed, a democratic – relationship.

After all, *The Blithedale Romance* features a 'magnetic lady' with overtones of P. T. Barnum, the impaling of a drowned woman, an engagement with the kinds of radical feminism associated with Margaret Fuller and the Seneca Falls conference of 1848, while the main narrative satirizes the utopian Brook Farm, a commune in which Hawthorne was briefly a participant in 1841. Just as the past was never really given much of a chance in its struggle with the present in Hawthorne's preceding novel, so Brook Farm/Blithedale is attacked from the outset for its hypocrisy and pretension. Talk of synchrony with the rhythms of nature is soon replaced by schemes to undercut the market-gardeners of Boston, 'getting the advantage over the outside barbarians in their own field of labor' (47), and Miles Coverdale, whose very name includes the theme of veiling so insistent in this book, catches flu at the commencement of the proceedings, and spends the first third of the novel not in honest toil, but in bed.

One who will never fit anywhere (and no simple analogue for Hawthorne, as Lawrence assumed), Coverdale is an 'unreliable narrator' with nothing left to rely on, as the opening to the second chapter shows:

> There can hardly remain for me (who am really getting to be a frosty bachelor, with another white hair, every week or so, in my moustache), there can hardly flicker up again so cheery a blaze upon the hearth, as that which I remember, the next day, at Blithedale. It was a wood-fire, in the parlor of an old farm-house, on an April afternoon, but with the fitful gusts of a wintry snow-storm roaring in the chimney. Vividly does that fire-side recreate itself, as I rake away the ashes from the embers in my memory, and blow them up with a sigh, for lack of more inspiring breath. Vividly, for an instant, but, anon, with the dimmest gleam, and with just as little fervency for my heart as for my finger-ends! The stanch oaken logs were long ago burnt out. Their genial glow must be represented, if at all, by the merest phosphoric glimmer, like that which exudes, rather than shines, from damp fragments of decayed trees, deluding the benighted wanderer through a forest. Around such chill mockery of a fire some few of us might sit on the withered leaves, spreading out each a palm towards the imaginary warmth, and talk over our exploded scheme for beginning the life of Paradise anew. (37)

The fires of youth are contrasted with 'frosty' age through the image of a literal 'wood-fire' at which Coverdale warmed himself on his first visit to Blithedale. But winter storms still roared behind renascent April: and both kinds of flame are long burnt out. With a disturbing delicacy the scene shifts ever further into mind and away from matter, finding no Wordsworthian bastion against time inside the workings of consciousness, but rather pruning memory of its verdant hopes, and finally tearing up the thought of mind's having roots in any reality more substantial than 'imaginary warmth' and 'exploded schemes'. As a literary type, the Old Bachelor had in any case become so *déjà vu* by Hawthorne's time, thanks to Addison, Sterne, Franklin, Freneau, Washington Irving and a host of imitators, that the unctuous amiability of the narrator's self-presentation should sound a warning signal from the outset. Under the covering veils of Coverdale's rhetoric of reminiscence lurks a cold, starving rage with nothing on which to feed. The Fall from Paradise is still endured *as* a Fall, even when 'Paradise' is seen to have been merely a concept, a consolatory strategy that shielded the credulous from a clear view of their own meaningless nakedness, a condition bordering on idiocy, where hands are stretched to warm themselves at non-existent fires.

Hawthorne is obsessed by wood, as in this passage, and the book is packed with branches, leaves, trunks, logs, chairs, paper. This fireside opening needs to be set against a passage from late in the novel when Coverdale, the 'profane intruder' at the forest pageant, now fleeing 'like a mad poet hunted by chimeras', stumbles over a heap of logs chopped for burning:

> In my haste, I stumbled over a heap of logs and sticks that had been cut for fire-wood, a great while ago, by some former possessor of the soil, and piled up square, in order to be carted or sledded away to the farm-house. But, being forgotten, they had lain there perhaps fifty years, and possibly much longer; until, by the accumulation of moss, and the leaves falling over them and decaying there, from autumn to autumn, a green mound was formed, in which the softened outline of the wood-pile was still perceptible. In the fitful mood that then swayed my mind, I found something strangely affecting in this simple circumstance. I imagined the long-dead woodman, and his long-dead wife and children, coming out of their chill graves, and essaying to make a fire with this heap of mossy fuel! (219)

Despite its Gothic colouring, the passage does not finally belong to that genre, but is closer to the kind of note struck by Dickens when using a fantastic image to stand for the pathos of human effort faced by the frustrating hand of death. Gothic – the full-on horror from beyond the grave stuff – offers in one sense a rather cheerful account of events; Christian, however perversely, in its refusal to picture death as the final end, while prancing skeletons, ghosts and vampires are figures of misrule in children's games and popular culture. Hawthorne shows an interest throughout his novel in the transformations of wood from budding to human use, abandonment and decay, seeing in its history the incontrovertible facts of death, of special pathos in a land marked out as Paradise in the hard lives of farmers and deracinated utopians alike. In Poe, to whose tales I turn next, death is generally the be-all, though not always the end-all. Hawthorne's melancholy humour is less shrill than Poe's, and never as dark as that of his friend Melville, who gave this as parting encomium to a drenched Captain Ahab, about to be shot out of his boat, and snared in the coils of his own harpoon: 'The ship! The hearse! – the second hearse! ... its wood could only be American!'[12]

# Poe

Edgar Allan Poe (1809–49) has always had a bad press. He began as a poet, though the slim volume *Tamerlane, and Other Poems* (1827) got no press at all. A complex history of debts and difficulties stretching back to abandonment by his actor-father hung over Poe's career as an editor and writer of squibs, reviews and the short stories for which he would gain posthumous recognition. He was an intermittent success as an editor of the *Southern Literary Messenger* and *Graham's Magazine*, in which were published such 'tales of ratiocination' as 'The Murders in the Rue Morgue', generally considered the first detective story. Poe, however, drank – particularly it would seem at times when a public display of inebriation was most likely to damage his career prospects – and the degree to which he suffered from either alcoholism or undiagnosed ailments exacerbated by binge drinking has never been determined conclusively. His sensitivity to imagined as well as real slights, always well developed, appears to have ripened into persecution mania at the time of his death from 'congestion of the brain', in suspicious circumstances. A libellous obituary notice by Rufus Griswold buried his reputation.

The revival of interest in Poe began in Paris with the poet Charles Baudelaire, whose renderings of Poe's tales, the *Histoires Extraordinaires*, *Nouvelles Histoires Extraordinaires* and *Histoires Grotesques et Sérieuses*, appearing between the 1840s and the 1860s, comprise the most influential translation of a work of American literature. Baudelaire also wrote what is still the most penetrating essay on the nature of Poe's appeal, initiating a legacy that would include illustrations by Redon and music by Debussy, and adapted the erotic attributes of Poe's narcotized and towering manikins for the apostrophized belles in such poems of his own as 'La Géante' and 'Les Bijoux'. The French took to Poe, and the usefulness of his tales of terror to the Surrealists, together with the influence of curiosities such as 'The Domain of Arnheim' and 'Landor's Cottage' on Raymond Roussel and then the *nouveau roman* of Alain Robbe-Grillet, to which was added in the 1960s the celebration of all these texts by Jacques Lacan, Roland Barthes and other theorists of the sign, ensured that, from the viewpoint of French and Francophile criticism, Poe has stayed perpetually in fashion.

In the United States, by contrast, the legacy has been a popular one, though with results that are more complex aesthetically and culturally than Poe's academic detractors would wish to concede. The eight film versions of Poe's work directed by Roger Corman enjoy perennial appeal, and made Vincent Price, who portrayed the various *hommes fatales* in mock-Elizabethan sonorities of the Donald Wolfit era, a household name. While Corman's adaptations make very free use of the text, they maintain a curious fidelity to the mixture of fantasy, humour and funereal eroticism that gives the writing its savour. Even technical deficiencies, such as Corman's cost-cutting use of the same footage of burning timbers across all the films, are in keeping with Poe's own insistent use of repetition. The gleeful adoption of the author of 'The Raven' by America's carnival of the demotic is appropriate, given that no major writer of his time was more involved in popular culture on a daily professional basis than Poe, who dreamed of a success he would only gain post-mortem. It is also ironic, in that no writer of his time was more opposed to democracy and ideas of social progress. His pedantic murderers and drug-addicted scholars of Fichte and Glanville are oneiric versions of an elite the republic had failed to produce except in the fragile example of their creator, whose tightrope walk towards a pure aestheticism gave him, to twist James's phrase, the lonely honour of a *non*-representative attitude.

James attacked Poe's reviewing as 'pretentious, spiteful, vulgar' (367) in the Hawthorne study, and fourteen years later could summon only a passing nod to the subtlety and inventiveness of the tales (686). Matthiessen in *American Renaissance* exudes an almost palpable relief that the dates of Poe's productions exclude him from the book's focal years, conceding that in any case the tales lack, in his view, 'the moral depth of Hawthorne or Melville' (p. xii). Passed from James to Matthiessen, this is the kind of emphasis whose British version we see in the criticism of F. R. Leavis, influential in the growth of English Literature as a university discipline. By these lights the novel – at least the grown-up kind epitomized by *Middlemarch* or *Portrait of a Lady* – can bring a finer ethical tuning to the reader's life, can replace Scripture in the desert of post-Darwinian modernity and teach us how to live. To give due attention to either the complexity or the deficiencies of such a position would lead this chapter from its path, but whatever view is taken of that era of criticism, Poe's tenets, essentially principles of lyric compression derived from Coleridge, and the results, beautiful in form and weird in content, fall foul of it. Poe's writing teaches no one how to live (though the tales contain some interesting hints for the more intrepid designer of domestic interiors).

The equation of morality with 'depth' in writing rests on a number of assumptions that must remain unexamined if it is to succeed by its own lights. Hieroglyphs and their connection by syntax are in themselves depthless – a view with which Poe plays presciently. The kinds of depth which Poe is most drawn to *depict* are those that cause vertigo:

> We stand upon the brink of a precipice. We peer into the abyss – we grow sick and dizzy. Our first impulse is to shrink from the danger. Unaccountably we remain. By slow degrees our sickness, and dizziness, and horror, become merged in a cloud of unnameable feeling... It is merely the idea of what would be our sensations during the sweeping precipitancy of a fall from such a height. And this fall – this rushing annihilation – for the very reason that it involves that one most ghastly and loathsome of all the most ghastly and loathsome images of death and suffering which have ever presented themselves to our imagination – for this very reason do we now the more vividly desire it. (Poe, 829)

What distinguishes this excerpt from 'The Imp of the Perverse' from comparable episodes in Whitman's poetry or Melville's fiction (mast-top vertigo in *Moby-Dick* springs immediately to mind) is that in their work the love of dialectic and the fluid conceptions of identity constantly generate alternative positions, alternative 'depths'. Poe has only one position: he is in love with women, in love with death, and wants both in one. The hysterical ejaculations of his narrators when faced by a Ligeia, Morella or Madeline returned from the tomb come not from the desire to have sex with a corpse, but rather from the wish to make love to a woman who is living, but *who has recent and palpable experience of death*, and who can therefore transmit through bodily excitement knowledge of life's shadow-companion, constant but teasingly silent, who will otherwise remain unknowable until, abruptly and beyond the limits of expression, one knows nothing but her. Hence Poe's stress on second wives, daughters, likenesses. The end is always signalled in the appearance of the woman prior to the onset of her fatal malady and its exciting aftermath: Ligeia's 'emaciated' charm, the 'elasticity of her footfall' and 'music of her low sweet voice, as she placed her marble hand upon my shoulder' (263), give her all the charm of a reanimated corpse – drop-dead gorgeous, one might say – even before the *coup de théâtre* of her bandaged and tottering resurrection in the bedroom. '[S]he let fall from her head the ghastly cerements which had confined it, and there streamed forth, into the rushing atmosphere of the chamber, huge masses of long and dishevelled hair; *it was blacker than the wings of the midnight!* And now slowly opened *the eyes* of the figure which stood before me' (277). His dead ringers always come home, and won't let a little solitary confinement stand in their way. Poe liked happy endings.

Poe's spoof 'How to Write a Blackwood Article' includes a tale-within-a-tale, 'A Predicament', whose protagonist Psyche Zenobia endures sundry mishaps including the loss of her eyeballs after a giant clock-finger presses on her neck. Ensuing decapitation by the minute hand leaves her in a philosophical quandary as to whether personal identity resides more in the body or the head. David Reynolds argues that here Poe's parody of sensationalist tales more vulgar than his own aims to generate 'a distanced, stylized laughter... which exaggerates popular black humor until it becomes absurd. Poe makes it clear from the start that he is parodying the directionless sensationalism of his day, for he devotes the first half of the tale to the portrait of a Philadelphia woman who gets information from a magazine editor on how to write "*bizarreries*", or popular tales filled with pointless rant and sensationalism' (Reynolds, 526). The problem here is that the tale is hardly more bizarre in its fusion of *grand guignol* and farce than such non-parodic efforts as 'Berenice'. Indeed, the conundrum as to whether the identity of Berenice lies more in her body or her teeth, which the narrator has unkindly removed, parallels the 'Predicament' of the eyeless Psyche. Moreover, the advice given by the Philadelphia editor comprises a repeated, albeit comic, echo of Poe's own recipes, down to an injunction to quote in foreign languages and adopt a 'tone metaphysical'. Most tellingly of all, the editor advises the neophyte hack to 'Put in something about the supernal Oneness. Don't say a syllable about the Infernal Twoness' (Poe, 283). All of Poe's plots and intellectual trajectory do indeed tend towards the supernal Oneness, the final union of self and other in death. In this respect he is the heir of Shelley, rather than Coleridge, and like that poet chafes at all restrictions, which are identified with the 'Infernal Twoness' of dualism. Everything will disclose its pattern, and everything will fit, but only in the grave. This is why the conclusions of the tales, often so explosive and disintegrative, are also so neat. The zigzag crack in the wall of the House of Usher is matched by the crack in Roderick Usher's sanity; and as his sister, returned from the tomb, embraces him, both die of shock, and the house collapses at once into the adjacent tarn as if it had never been.

Reynolds's argument that popular culture matters more to the antebellum writers than has been admitted is unassailable, if a little blunted by his determination to make the pattern of their involvement with that culture identical in each case. Hawthorne, Emerson, Whitman, Dickinson, Melville and Poe are all shown to be sustained by contact with popular forms, but they must all climb free of this very contact in order to become themselves, in what is finally a twist on the old James/Matthiessen thesis that writing must have moral depth in order to gain literary height. Any other thesis would have been profoundly threatening to James's urging respect for a maturing national literature, and Matthiessen's urging a comparable respect for the new discipline of American Studies. What distinguishes Poe and the rest from their inferior contemporaries is not the superiority of their morals, but their superior abilities as writers.

Poe is in two senses a curious writer, a specialist in freakishness but a seeker after truth. He wants to know the true relationship between mind and matter, self and not-self, being and nothingness. Even his erotic curiosity, his wanting to know woman inside and out, feeds into this larger testing of phenomenological limits by running to verbal extremes. Poe wanted to transgress, not simply from the desire to shock or to excite himself, but in order to find out where limits, if they exist, truly lie. This attachment to phenomenological enquiry revisits in some measure the epistemological questing of English Romantic poetry, re-centred in the body: the body constricted ('Loss of Breath', 'The Premature Burial'), tortured ('The Pit and the Pendulum'), dismembered ('The Man Who Was Used Up', 'Berenice'), duplicated ('William Wilson'), pushed to extremes where its limits and true identity could perhaps become legible, or be shocked into speech ('Mesmeric Revelation', 'The Facts in the Case of M. Valdemar'). Of course, the desire to shock is real, is among other things exactly what it seems to be, and the attempts at rehabilitation by writers such as William Carlos Williams, sympathetic to Poe's misunderstood and misrepresented situation, can ultimately do him as big a disservice as Matthiessen, and through that same queasiness about taking a horror writer seriously. Williams protests too much: 'Poe was NOT, it must be repeated, a Macabre genius, *essentially* lost upon the grotesque and the arabesque'.[13] The prejudice at work here is one that would regard any writer interested in 'the grotesque' as 'lost'. Nor is it the case that Poe's interest in horror was brought about by life's disappointments. Although such tragedies as his young wife's early death can only have consolidated his sense of darkness, that sense is there right from his (still somewhat underrated) work in poetry.

## Electric metaphors, cross-currents

That interest in the body as the site of phenomenological and ontological probing is pushed to a certain stylistic extreme by Poe, but is common to the literary culture of the ante-bellum years, particularly where literature was fed by popular science and speculation. Imagery of electricity and magnetism flows ubiquitously through the writing of the time, making versions of the body electric central to its productions. I draw the term from Whitman's poem 'I Sing the Body Electric', but examples are everywhere: of Priscilla in *The Blithedale Romance*, Hawthorne writes: 'she clapped her hands, too, with great exuberance of gesture, as is the custom of young girls when their electricity over-charges them' (82); while Cousin Clifford in *The House of the Seven Gables* 'would sit broodingly in his great chair, resting his head on his hands, and evincing life only by an electric sparkle of ill humor, whenever Hepzibah endeavored to arouse him' (124). Where Hawthorne diagnoses a latent mischief in the superfluity of energy, Whitman's use of related terms co-opts them into his elastic hospitality of neologism and inner correspondence: 'Stout as a horse, affectionate, haughty, electrical, / I and this mystery here we stand' (190). Overall, change in the nature of recourse to such images follows the evolution of electricity from galvanism to the later nineteenth-century emphasis on illumination.

A brief paragraph on leading lights is called for. Alessandro Volta announced the principles of the first primary battery in 1800, having achieved the provision of a continuous electric current, thus improving on experiments with lightning, static and Leyden jars essayed by Benjamin Franklin among others. Over the next decades inventive efforts were expended in improving on Volta's primitive sandwich of silver and zinc, and by the 1830s the battery had become a practical instrument. In 1820 Hans Oersted had demonstrated that a conductor carrying an electrical current would deflect a compass needle from its natural orientation, and by 1831 an electromagnet had been developed at Yale that could lift a weight of 2,000 pounds; the electromagnet would generate subsequent inventions from the telegraph to the motor. The first cable was laid across the Atlantic in 1866, and in late 1879 the 'wizard of Menlo Park', Thomas Edison, succeeded in making the first electric light. With Edison's display at the International Electrical Exhibition at Paris in October 1881, followed by the first generating station, operating at London's Holborn Viaduct early in the following year, electricity became synonymous with progress and the modern city. In terms of the literary and popular take-up of these developments, three key phases might be hypothesized.

The first employs images of the electric to depict a connection between the previously isolated or disparate. An example: in the 1770s, when patriot leaders began to lay stress on the libertarian aspects of Puritanism for propagandist purposes, certain Puritan practices were reintroduced briefly, including the fast-day ritual.

Thomas Jefferson noted that 'the effect of the day thro' the whole colony was like the shock of electricity, arousing every man & placing him erect' (Bercovitch, 162). Given more space, we might pause over a variety of undercurrents here, but the galvanizing and linking of the inert is of chief importance. By the time Abraham Lincoln describes Jefferson's words in the Declaration of Independence as 'the electric cord' that 'links the hearts of patriotic and liberty-loving men' (Gustafson, 265), the idea of a sustained current of sympathy has replaced the earlier metaphors of jerky and fitful galvanism. In this second, historical phase the newly understood association of magnetism with electricity feeds into both depictions of class and society and interpretations of emotional attraction and repulsion. In synergy with the hypotheses of pseudo-sciences such as mesmerism and phrenology, this would help shape a speculative literature that includes tales by Poe such as 'The Facts in the Case of M. Valdemar' and texts by Whitman and George G. Foster to which we will turn shortly. The third phase, in which electricity becomes synonymous with modernity and urban progress, does not generate such a provocative literature.

## Science and modernity: the horror film and capital punishment

Popular entertainment of the twentieth century would wreak sardonic revenge on the opportunities for social control made possible by not only urban lighting, but all advances in science and technology. For example, in Mary Shelley's original novel of 1818, the means by which Frankenstein brought his trophies of the charnel-house back to life were glossed over. Universal Studios, for whom James Whale directed *Frankenstein* (1931) and *The Bride of Frankenstein* (1935), put electrical paraphernalia for drawing down the lightning and galvanizing corpses at the centre of the action. ('Look Fritz, I have harnessed the lightning!') In *The Bride*, much the more complex and beguiling of the two, the doctor goes on to invent the field telephone. Such anachronistic and comic changes to Shelley's novel may work so as to parody the spasms of male intellectual libido, thereby making the mad scientist laughable but also comprehensible to an audience who could not understand Albert Einstein's equations, and who had been told by Sigmund Freud that they could not understand themselves either. The Whale films use state-of-the-art special effects, but do so in the service of a half-nostalgic, half-mutinous return to the mid-nineteenth-century atmosphere of Poe, Lippard and Foster, where exciting invention, libidinous cross-currents and pregnant metaphor circulate widely through a culture of speculation. All these writers – perhaps all American writers – have something of P. T. Barnum about them, and the artifice of the Hollywood studio was, so to speak, a natural development, and cinema the electric novel.

Dr Pretorius, a kind of Volta to Frankenstein's Edison in the 1935 film, is shown playing with his creations, homunculi in historical costume that try to escape from their jars, a clear adaptation by cinema of the kind of trickery and showmanship associated with Barnum and the travelling show. For a while the little people get out of control and start to fight or fall in love, their squirming carnival life at once a 'bottom-up' fantasy of subversion and a story of contained misrule where little lives are rounded with a sleep. Like all effective cinema of the fantastic, and like the hysterical fictions of the mid-nineteenth century which it echoes deliberately, the film doesn't really know what it thinks because it thinks so many things at once, spilling and containing its energies in vivid and somewhat poetic images. The subversive imagination in America, like many forces for good, would be dammed for a while by the gross and static signifiers of modern horror – the Camp, the Bomb, the Wall – on the eve of whose birth Whale directed his films.

It would not be right, however, to assume that the American *vox populi* is always synonymous with benignity. For example, America – in certain states, at certain times, for certain crimes – retains the electric chair, a particularly cruel and a particularly spectacular form of execution. Death by this means does not come rapidly, and its approach is heralded by appalling bodily changes. It is particularly bad news for the obese, who do not conduct electricity at all well. Despite – or perhaps precisely because of – these factors, it is a spectacle which prison staff, reporters and, latterly, relatives of the victim's victims have been known to attend. No one has as yet suggested pay-per-view TV executions for the delectation of the righteous; but it is, after all, only sixty years since the last public execution in America (a Kentucky hanging, which drew a good crowd). Enthusiasm for the practice is a surprisingly modern phenomenon: Michigan abolished capital punishment in 1846, well before most of Europe, Rhode Island and Wisconsin following inside a decade.[14] A general sense of queasiness at State-sponsored killing coexists not only with an increase in popular support for the death penalty, but with a crucial element of spectacle. I suggest that this degrading practice is an attempt to force the supposedly incomprehensible – generally speaking, a young man who may be guilty of homicide – into the realm of the comprehensible by making him reveal his true identity as a galvanized monster, thereby 'proving' his guilt. Such a transformation would have no meaning without witnesses. The practice of electrocution may actually depend on what seems most to challenge it, the lingering possibility of the victim's innocence, which is then blackened forever by his abominable behaviour after the switch has been thrown. Execution by lethal injection will never go down as well with those who support the death penalty, because its imagery – a hypodermic, a good long sleep – invokes the semiotics of healing and so messes up the spectacle. (As doctors are prohibited by law from killing people, the job is done by paramedics who apparently mess it up in 10 per cent of cases anyway.) More importantly, going for vein over voltage cheats the audience of the revelation of 'guilt'. An echoic association of electricity with revelation may form the continuing appeal of the polygraph, known to be an unreliable instrument in other respects. Finally, the use of electro-convulsive therapy to pacify the mentally ill, a thematic synecdoche for state control in Ken Kesey's counter-cultural novel *One Flew Over the Cuckoo's Nest* (1962), offers a further reminder that American ingenuity in the adaptation of Volta's and Edison's inventions did not stop at cinema and the phonograph.

# Whitman

If we turn now with some relief to the poetry of Walt Whitman, that is not because in his work mutation and reconstruction of the body and the body politic have been abandoned, but because the hypothesizing of new or real bodies beneath the enforced unrealities of society's conformism finds its expression in the optative mood. Following Emerson, who wrote to congratulate Whitman that in *Leaves of Grass* he had produced 'the most extraordinary piece of wit & wisdom that America has yet contributed',[15] the poet strove to identify a poetry of self-realization and achieved personal liberation with the projects of an independent America: 'The United States themselves are essentially the greatest poem' (Whitman, 5), he wrote in the original preface to *Leaves of Grass*, published in ever expanding versions between 1855 and 1892. Unlike Emerson's, his self-realization is not one that leaves other selves behind in order to try its wings, and Whitman's poetry is remarkable for its dramatizations of sympathy and empathy. I stress both, because although moments of empathetic identification with the trials and ecstasies of others are everywhere in Whitman, a posture of standing alongside, with and slightly outwith, stopped 'somewhere waiting for you' (246) is equally characteristic, if not more so. His poem, to return to the arguments of chapter 1, is entitled 'I Hear America Singing', and that slight self-distancing, the mercurial side of Whitman, is as important as the electric cord of empathy stemming from his permission to his own form of negative capability to wander promiscuously.

Walt Whitman, a kosmos, of Manhattan the son,
Turbulent, fleshy, sensual, eating, drinking and breeding,
No sentimentalist, no stander above men and women or apart from
        them,
No more modest than immodest.

Unscrew the locks from the doors!
Unscrew the doors themselves from their jambs!

Whoever degrades another degrades me,
And whatever is done or said returns at last to me.
Through me the afflatus surging and surging, through me the current
        and index.

I speak the pass-word primeval, I give the sign of democracy,
By God! I will accept nothing which all cannot have their counterpart
        of on the same terms.

                                                                    (211)

The current of Whitman's feeling flows differently from page to page, moment to moment, and the contradiction of such jovial and Falstaffian passages by (for example) the statement that 'To touch my person to someone else's is about as much as I can stand' (215) does not so much undermine the first quotation as set both in an imaging of identity which is new, historically, and which is unthinkable outside the project of America, whose citizens' 'deathless attachment to freedom' (6) must necessarily generate an 'unrhymed poetry' with no premature foreclosures of sound, of attachment, of direction, of thought. In the democratic vistas of the *Song of Myself* all lines are equal, and to quote is to focus in one of many directions argument that might be reoriented by the line that follows. This mobility, the product of revision by Whitman, but a begetter of the arts of improvisation in the next century, is powered by trust in a poetics of the horizon rather than the shoring-up of a centre from which poetry makes forays. It is this that makes Lawrence's cartoon presentation of the poet appealing, but a mixture of the well-aimed and the misdirected:

ONE DIRECTION! toots Walt in the car, whizzing along it.
Whereas there are myriads of ways in the dark, not to mention track-less wildernesses, as anyone will know who cares to come off the road – even the Open Road.
ONE DIRECTION! whoops America, and sets off also in an automobile.
ALLNESS! shrieks Walt at a cross-road, going whizz over an unwary Red Indian. (175–6)

As a gibe at American exceptionalism, this is unexceptionable. More-over, Lawrence's critique through Whitman of an imperialist ideology and its capacity to absorb or, failing that, silence all objection is startlingly prescient, and reflects with some accuracy not only the uses to which Whitman has been put, but certain of his views. Noth-ing could shake the poet's idealization of the Union as sacrosanct, a view that led him to oppose the abolitionists as splitters, even though he detested slavery. In other respects, diagnosis of an excess of self-certainty perhaps fits Henry Ford's republicanism, more than Whit-man's, and certainly forgoes any subtle analysis of the links between the two in favour of comedy and polemic, however successful. Where Lawrence entirely fails to do justice is in the risk, the real launch into 'the dark' and 'the trackless wildernesses', the radical use of straight talk in lines such as these, out of the blue and everywhere in *Song of Myself*:

> This is the city and I am one of the citizens,
> Whatever interests the rest interests me, politics, wars, markets,
>     newspapers, schools,
> The mayor and councils, banks, tariffs, steamships, factories, stocks,
>     stores, real estate and personal estate.
>
> (235)

> I do not say these things for a dollar or to fill up the time while I wait
>     for a boat.
>
> (243)

> What is a man anyhow? what am I? what are you?
> (206)

One and a half centuries after such lines were written, the poetry can still sound more a product of our time than Whitman's. His gamble on the 'barbaric yawp' (247) outlasting the drawing-room tones of poets more typical of Victorian America turns out to have been justified, but if we fail to note that the gamble was real, a real risk of absolute failure, we miss perhaps the key component of greatness in American literature.

Genius, or whatever shorthand term seems appropriate to the level of greatness in American literature, is that which by and large antici- pates correctly its own historical aftermath, and which calls from that subsequent history enough of a continuing return to its own innova- tions as to ensure that the original writing survives in its own right, and not merely because of the modifications that later writers were able to pile on its discoveries. Echoes here of the inventor, the better mousetrap and the beaten path are intended, and are quintessentially American. Monastic and other traditions of writing as operative at a social remove belong to Europe and the Old World. There has never been an American writer of note who worked outside the *business* of writing, whatever the final tally. The qualities of apartness in Dickinson (who packed her poems with the bric-à-brac of popular culture), Emerson (whose style draws on popular preachers) or Thor- eau (in demand as a Lyceum humorist) are real, but to be accounted for by other means, and separately in each case. Whitman is a poet of genius, and one who, comparatively speaking, lays the routes to that fact open to inspection, because, more than most of his peers, he was in poetry a popular scientist, willing to make of his imagination a laboratory of what the future might hold. Despite the longeurs, the prolixity, the cranky neologisms and misused foreign words, the wearyingly long lists of persons and occupations with which he is determined to shout his identification, the weaker poems that say too much or that hardly say anything at all, there is no subsequent American poet of significance who has not shared the spirit of Ezra Pound's reconciliation with his predecessor: 'It was you that broke the new wood, / Now is a time for carving'.[16] And as Harold Bloom has shown in some of the most perceptive work done on Whitman (in *Agon* and elsewhere), the bequest includes poets such as T. S. Eliot, who seem most actively to repudiate the reconciliation their work is none the less compelled to make. I do not add that Whitman is a great poet despite the risk of charlatanry, because the broad wink is as integral to his poetry as the open road, the cheerful outward sign of inward risk – important also to Emerson, Eliot, Rothko, Cage, Ashbery – that all of this might be spun out of nothing.

## Whitman and George G. Foster

The cheerful self-introduction in *Song of Myself* paints Whitman as one of the roughs, a regular specimen: 'I, now thirty-seven years old in perfect health begin' (188). This is as important as his more ecstatic modes: 'Press close bare-bosom'd night – press close magnetic nourishing night! / Night of south winds – night of the large few stars! / Still nodding night – mad naked summer night' (208). Even the ecstatic mode may be a regular rhetorical specimen. For example, the same discursive mixture, including many of the same devices, can be found in a book called *New York Naked* by George G. Foster (1814–56):

> Thus I, at the summit of full middle age, standing now at my thirty-ninth birthday, on the highest peak of that everlasting mountain which divides the morning from the evening of life, one side of which lies in fresh and dewy shadow, sheltered from the arid noonday heats, and evergreen and fresh in the exuberance of the glancing streams that flow down its flowery sides – the other basking broad and faint and motionless beneath the fierce beams of the descending sun, its herbage withered, its foliage discolored by the prophetic instincts of a coming dissolution... I have learned to look upon myself as but one atom in the vast amount of mental energy, which is the atmosphere and the sustaining medium of magnetic attraction, holding all things together in the living electricity of the moral world. And so it has happened, that the dreaming poet of sixteen, whose humblest visions were millions of miles above the very loftiest things in this hum-drum, every-day world, has come to be the patient worker at the laboring oar of every-day journalism. The philosophic explorer of the lowest phenomena of life and human nature, in those classes and phases which in the old time had for him no existence; patiently gathering up the fragments, the refuse, of every-day life, he has sought, by the poetical instinct which is the motive power of his existence, to invest them with the brilliant colors of his own imagination, and to embalm them in the amber of his ideal affection.[17]

The premonitions of *Song of Myself* are many and varied, from the stress on the author's age at the time of writing to the emphases on the self as 'one atom' in the vast atmosphere of 'magnetic attraction' and 'the living electricity of the moral world', and the aim to preserve fragments in the 'amber' of idealism and poetic 'imagination'. (The exact date of publication of *New York Naked* can only be guessed. However, it seems certain from biographical and other contextual evidence that publication of the book preceded that of *Leaves of Grass*.)

Foster wrote urban sketches for Horace Greeley's *Tribune*, the reformist New York daily that printed poems by Whitman, the first known review of *Leaves of Grass*, and the famous letter of 21 July 1855 from Emerson hailing the poet's achievement. Foster's distinction lay in transferring the genre of metropolitan exposé catalysed by Eugène Sue from a Parisian to an American context. *New York by Gaslight, New York in Slices* and *New York Above-Ground and Under-Ground* are among his other forays into 'local colour'. The opening of *New York Naked* is characteristic of the genre in its protestations of slumming it, prior to a gloating descent, nose pinched between fingers, into the infernal depths. It is also characteristic in never using one phrase where two will do, and although there are searing exposés and novels from the period that could be termed pornographic, Foster's New York appears in generally decorous attire, with much attention trained on the opera box and the well-turned ankle. Here again there is a kind of affinity with Whitman, in whose work prolixity and admiration of physique also feature. Moreover, there are references in Foster to local figures of importance, such as the campaigner Mike Walsh, who were also known to Whitman. Nonetheless, chunks of the text could have been translated from accounts of any city. A climactic section on 'Lewd Women' is led, despite its promises of impending indecency, to the decent conclusion that 'poverty is the chief determining cause which drives women into prostitution in England and America, as in France' (64). Indeed, the book is caught between the agendas of sensation and reform, a duplicity amounting to a generic category in itself at this period. Tones of condemnation strike out at random, depriving the text of any consistent line, as when Foster broods on the 'Miserable . . . condition of the foreign population of this great city!', whom he describes as 'huddled together, writhing like loathsome reptiles, in a pestilential and noxious atmosphere', all of which forms, however, a 'terrible rebuke' to 'a society that thus remorselessly refuses to recognize so many and such helpless [*sic*] of its members' (122). But it is such an abrupt swerving of attitudes, together with a mix of vatic prophecy and Broadway snapshot that Whitman also claims as his own, turning into a philosophy of contradiction what in Foster is merely confusion.

Most Whitmanic of all, *New York Naked* lives up to its title courtesy of 'the voice of God, pleading now and persuading with most seductive eloquence the advent of the happy days to come, when mankind, released from these soiling and disgraceful garments in which it is now swathed and swaddled, shall rise up in the purity and simplicity of its naked body, and fill all the universe with its anthems of love and joy' (34–5). Hardly as effective as the bathing sequence in *Song of Myself*, this naturism is still in the key of Whitman's prefatory address to the 'goodshaped and wellhung man', whose Adamic qualities shine futuristically in the 1855 preface (Whitman, 26). This kind of prophesying is there also in such questionable utopians as Thomas Lake Harris – and would be bequeathed in time, ironically, to D. H. Lawrence.

The purpose of my juxtaposition is not necessarily to claim as a historical fact Foster's influence on Whitman. Primarily it demonstrates that they shared the same discursive milieu in the old New York of Charlie Pfaff's beer cellar, Greeley's deadlines, the b'hoys and the g'hals, opera, utopian theory and issue-driven campaigning. It becomes clear by these lights that early efforts such as *Franklin Evans* (1842) and 'The Fireman's Dream' (1844) are not aberrations, but essays in popular genres that lead directly to the maturation of Whitman's rhetoric in a more inclusive and fluid credo. Whitman's importance does not in any way cut him loose from the city sights and language he shared with George Foster, but indexes his ability to combine, distil and transmute the discursive flow and spillage of a society in perpetual transition, which the writings of his less able contemporaries could only leave haplessly to pool and stagnate.

# Dickinson

Emily Dickinson (1830–86) claimed never to have read Whitman. He had never heard of her. Nor in many respects are their poems related other than by antithesis; where Whitman writes as a 'kosmos' and as 'one of the roughs', disgorging epics of the future and identifying with a whole nation, Dickinson was a recluse, publishing only eleven of her 1,800 poems during her lifetime, and boxing her arch and elliptical miniatures in verse-forms that look like fractured hymns. And yet from the 1890s, when her work began to gain attention, comparisons were made between the two by reviewers who caught the driven, transgressive energies of her poetry. The comparison has been developed further by feminist critics such as Sandra Gilbert and Agnieszka Salska, who see in the contrasting forms of independence characterizing the two poets a renegotiation of sexual politics from an alienated but progressive consciousness. Whitman risked failure by gambling on the future. So in a different sense did Dickinson, through what Vivian R. Pollak has termed her 'cult of non-publication'.[18] Where traditional close readings of her poetry and her contribution to women's writing emphasized fierce introspection and spiritual autonomy, more recent criticism has attempted with varying degrees of success to reinsert Dickinson into discursive practices as a participating, and not a marginal, member.

James bestowed on Hawthorne the lonely honour of a representative attitude, while Poe had thrust upon him a simpler kind of loneliness.

Dickinson in one sense positively courted a non-representative – indeed, an unseen – position: 'I'm Nobody,' as one of her most famous lyrics begins. Her loneliness becomes representative if we see in it a self-conscious intensification of the invisibility urged by a patriarchal culture on women in general. Her refusal to publish is self-denying, demure, silent, as a daughter of the house should of course be. Her poems offer extended evidence that women, according to the canons of the patriarchy, can't think straight. To claim and then work with, employing irony, positions that were otherwise going to be thrust upon her anyway is partly true of Dickinson's poetry as it would be partly true of many female writers. This situation would persist, as witnessed by Sylvia Plath's exploitation a century later of the roles and mythical stereotypes – mother, medusa, strip-tease artist – waiting for her and revised by her, in the iconography of post-war Britain. Plath's *Ariel* is distinctively a book out of London in the early 1960s, as brash and clear in the outlines of its images ('Am a pure acetylene / Virgin / attended by roses') as a Triumph Spitfire or a photo by David Bailey.[19] (Plath's poems, with their black humour, deliberate bad taste and lyric sheen need to be rescued from her admirers as much as her detractors.) If James was right in his criticism of New England life in Dickinson's day as a culture lacking finish and sustenance, then hers would be a solitude at the opposite extreme from Plath's culture-saturated milieu. Dickinson on this reading is one who took, and helps readers take, 'a picturesque view of one's internal possibilities', finding 'in the landscape of the soul all kinds of fine sunrise and moonlight effects' (James, 383). The poet becomes thereby an intense instance of a general cultural condition.

The poems can easily be made to illustrate the case:

> There's a certain Slant of light,
> Winter Afternoons –
> That oppresses, like the Heft
> Of Cathedral Tunes –
>
> Heavenly Hurt, it gives us –
> We can find no scar,
> But internal difference,
> Where the Meanings, are –[20]

The note of Protestant dissent, the equally Puritan emphasis on the scrutiny of 'Meanings', and most of all the instinctive tendency to internalize, the turning of light and the season into 'internal difference'; all these aspects echo a self-consistent history of Puritan,

Revolutionary and Romantic ways of phrasing and seeing of the kind this book has advanced. They can also be used to prove James's criticism, in that this is so evidently a poem spun from nothing, from the passage of light across landscape and some invisible flicker of mood. Taken on its own, the poem appears to have issued from a world with no social depth beyond the traditions mentioned. We are in as profoundly subjectivized a world as that of a tale by Poe, with at times analogous sensations of vertigo, yearnings for the perverse, hallucination of strange new worlds, the rushing of air in the chamber, and the doting on oblivion:

> I felt a Funeral, in my Brain,
> And Mourners to and fro
> Kept treading – treading – till it seemed
> That Sense was breaking through –
>
> And when they were all seated,
> A Service, like a Drum –
> Kept beating – beating – till I thought
> My Mind was going numb –
>
> And then I heard them lift a Box
> And creak across my Soul
> With those same Boots of Lead, again,
> Then Space – began to toll,
>
> As all the Heavens were a Bell,
> And Being, but an Ear,
> And I, and Silence, some strange Race
> Wrecked, solitary, here –
>
> And then a Plank in Reason, broke,
> And I dropped down, and down –
> And hit a World, at every plunge,
> And Finished knowing – then –
>
> (128–9)

The 'Boots of Lead' and the giant 'Ear' are out of fairy-tale, and verge on Surrealism; the oppressive repetition of 'beating', 'treading' and words such as 'strange', 'creak', 'Box', 'Silence' and 'solitary' speak of nightmare and the confinement of the tomb. The dashes at the ends of lines and the ambiguous 'then' signal both the end, loss of consciousness, and something more open-ended, a sequel or entry to new worlds beyond words. As distant in tone and image as the poem is from an ecstatic and sexualized piece such as the one beginning 'Wild Nights!' (set memorably to music by the contemporary composer John Adams), the Paradise motif, vertigo and hallucination are as important to the latter poem's 'Rowing in Eden' as they are to the first. Once the portals of articulate subjectivity are opened, there is no end to the sunrise and moonlight effects that the nerves, the pulse, the conundrum of being alive can set going.

And why not? An emphasis in post–1960s criticism on literature as product, as consumable, as there to be situated historically, and thereby liberated from suspect categories of opacity and inwardness, misses both the tenor and the terrain of much poetry since the Romantic era. Just as the sonnets and lyrics of a later poet such as Edna St Vincent Millay (1892–1950) are nothing without their fervour and high drama, a keyed-up emotionalism that demands empathy in order to work, so the pensive and forlorn clarities of Sara Teasdale (1884–1933) are the cooler enactment of an inwardness which contemporary criticism skirts, or about which it feels guilty. Lyrical emotionalism is not solely the province of women poets (as the work of Millay's inheritor John Wieners shows), but the privileging of historicization over a reading empathetic to their neo-Romantic, musical emotionalism does particular disservice to these lyric poets.

The most telling critique of Dickinson's work might not be James's, but one that includes James, along with Millay and indeed the general tendency of post-Romantic writing. Oscillation between epiphanic moments at which the self seems omnipotent in its visionary compass and moments that threaten vertigo and annihilation; a consciousness elastic enough to identify with a nation, suddenly imprisoned by a word; of these *The Golden Bowl* and *The Ambassadors* are as characteristic as Dickinson's poetry. A materialist criticism might summarize such phenomenological expansions and contractions as the liberal imagination, and question their configuration of consciousness and politics, or the lack of it. For example, what Donald Pease terms 'the hypertrophy of narcissistic impulses'[21] has arguably been producer of both American imperialism and American romance. In 1971, Quentin Anderson argued thus in a book called *The Imperial Self*:

I believe that the habit scholars have of calling Emerson misty or abstract, calling Whitman a successful charlatan, calling Henry James ambiguous, are but ways of referring to an inchoate perception of the absolutism of the self which is described in this essay. This absolutism involves an extreme passivity, which is complemented by, must be complemented by, the claim of the imperial self to mastery of what has almost overwhelmed it.[22]

Anderson was writing at the time of America's imperial muscle flexing in Vietnam, where it had no business to be, and where it lost the war. The concept of 'mastery' was therefore particularly suspect at this time, and while no credible analysis could equate the imperial raining of napalm on South-East Asia with the poems of a nineteenth-century writer calling herself 'Empress of Calvary' (Dickinson, 299), such a dispassionate rereading of the American canon as Anderson's is useful for its questioning of the relationship between artistic and political action. An imperial ego within the culture that distances itself, with distaste, from an imperialist foreign policy while still finding its validation from an economy built on the latter is a cultural reality in twentieth-century America, as it had been in Victorian England. However, this in itself does not force all American literature that uses the first-person singular to collapse into a guilty sameness.

Of course, there are particular texts or moments for which Anderson's critique becomes true, but 'mastery', particularly 'mastery of what has almost overwhelmed it' is hardly adequate as a summary of what goes on in the construction of, or readerly reactions to, *The Blithedale Romance*, 'Berenice', 'Song of Myself' or *The Awkward Age*. The fluctuations and qualities Anderson describes are simply movements of the consciousness along a light to dark spectrum of a kind familiar in English Romantic, French or Russian Symbolist, and much twentieth-century literature in German or Spanish (for example). If all these literatures are ahistorically the same (which they are not), then any self in literature is the 'imperial' self.

One interesting facet in James's doubt about sunrise and moonlight effects lies in its painterliness, rather than a self-evident literariness. In American painting the history of such effects is one of their transition from a landscape to an abstract tradition, a history worth bearing in mind when reading lines such as these by Emily Dickinson:

> Inebriate of Air – am I –
> And Debauchee of Dew –
> Reeling – thro endless summer days –
> From inns of Molten Blue
>
> (98–9)

The capitalization of 'Molten Blue' makes this more than a charming conceit on the intoxications of summer, and can legitimately be read through painting such as Mark Rothko's, which would continue the American tradition begun in its Renaissance of letting bold images of the outer world stand also for internal possibilities and 'internal difference, / Where the Meanings, are –'. As another poem notes, in this tradition of the new 'Experiment escorts us', and his stimulating company will not let 'Axiom' get a look in (715).

Elsewhere Dickinson's poetry abjures abstraction, and packs its lines with imagery axiomatic to the culture. Many poems combine images drawn from crime and horror, from the 'lonely Houses off the Road / A Robber'd like the look of' (238) to 'The Cordiality of Death – / Who drills his Welcome in –' (237), the 'Guns' and 'Dungeons' of 'They put Us far apart' (228) or 'My Life had stood – a Loaded Gun –' (369). In the poem beginning 'One need not be a Chamber – to be Haunted –', a body electric with fright fails to see that inner horrors are the worst:

> Ourself behind ourself, concealed –
> Should startle most –
> Assassin hid in our Apartment
> Be Horror's least.
>
> The Body – borrows a Revolver –
> He bolts the Door –
> O'erlooking a superior spectre –
> Or more –
>
> (333)

I am not at all sure that this is the self's expression of mastery over what has almost overwhelmed it, so much as a reminder that the self always has the power to paralyse itself by opening up its own ability to race to multiple conclusions. Nor is it likely, as with the discursive mix in the themes of *The Blithedale Romance*, that a piece so packed with images from popular culture (so firmly the case that all recur in *film noir* and modern Gothic) could have issued from a writer who was reclusive in anything but the physical sense. Dickinson's culture, her times and its tastes, speak in the lines, which are also so witty, as is much of her writing; and wit, though it depends on originality, depends even more on recognition. Heuristic in the questions they enable the reader to broach, Dickinson's poems in themselves are calculated performances whose every neologism and idiosyncrasy is calibrated precisely by their performance-artist. No poet could conjure so precise yet oneiric a phrase as 'Doom's electric moccasin' and not know exactly the contours of the path she had so confidently broken.

# Emerson

We have seen how versions of Eden are exiled to the realm of death by Poe, predicted as a future community by Whitman, abandoned as unsafe by Hawthorne, glimpsed by Dickinson. Twisted, projected or regretted, Paradise and the ways in which America can or cannot be mapped on to it form the driving aspiration of literature in the ante-bellum period. And so we come to Ralph Waldo Emerson (1803–82) for whom the paradisal aim was a kind of professional inheritance. Descended from a line of New England churchmen, and himself ordained minister of Second Church, Boston, in 1829, Emerson in one sense abandoned his calling after only a few years in the pulpit, in another sense brought it to fruition. To Henry James, writing in the late 1880s, Emerson '*was* the prayer and the sermon: not in the least a seculariser, but in his own subtle insinuating way a sanctifier' (James, 253). Although the furore caused by his address to the senior class, Divinity College, Cambridge, on 15 July 1838 resulted in his being banned for decades from speaking at Harvard, it is precisely Emerson's intellectual anarchism, his cosmic self-reliance, that leads Harold Bloom in an important essay of 1982 to argue that '[t]he mind of Emerson is the mind of America' and that his work *is* 'The American Religion', an eminence achieved precisely by the work's canon-ization as literature.[23]

Emerson was in overlapping but also differing ways a seer. In the Divinity School address he lamented the withdrawal from church attendance, the 'signing off' as it was called, of people in parishes where no strong influence had succeeded the Puritans' 'austere piety' which Emerson links to their 'longings for civil freedom' (Emerson, 87). However, his role as seer is the opposite of nostalgic, and his signature chafing at restriction, that drive to burst into full occupancy of a spiritual emancipation to which the world is nothing but hints and signals, powers his writing from the opening sentences of *Nature* (1842):

> Our age is retrospective. It builds the sepulchres of the fathers. It writes biographies, histories and criticism. The foregoing generations beheld God and nature face to face; we, through their eyes. Why should not we also enjoy an original relation to the universe? Why should not we have a poetry and philosophy of insight and not of tradition, and a religion by revelation to us, and not the history of theirs?...The sun shines to-day also. There is more wool and flax in the fields. There are new lands, new men, new thoughts. Let us demand our own works and laws and worship. (7)

'We' are humanity, and Emerson's demand as a neo-Christian is really for a third Testament which would declare all debts to a Mosaic tradition of sacrifice amortized, and at last permit humanity a guiltless celebration that returns us to the springs of revelation (accompanied, doubtless, by newly baked bread rather than anything more Dionysiac). But among humanity's tribes the American stands *primus inter pares*, and *Nature* is the third great American manifesto for an original literature, along with Melville's review of Hawthorne's *Mosses* and Whitman's preface to *Leaves of Grass*, to which Emerson became a vital sponsor. If the lesson Emerson would drive home is one of separateness and self-reliance, it is not bound up with stoicism, let alone rights won in gun smoke. The seer sees in unexpected ways, as the most famous passage in Emerson's work, also from *Nature*, shows vividly:

> Crossing a bare common, in snow puddles, at twilight, under a clouded sky, without having in my thoughts any occurrence of special good fortune, I have enjoyed a perfect exhilaration. I am glad to the brink of fear... In the woods we return to reason and faith. There I feel that nothing can befall me in life, – no disgrace, no calamity, (leaving me my eyes,) which nature cannot repair. Standing on the bare ground, – my head bathed by the blithe air, and uplifted into infinite space, – all mean egotism vanishes. I become a transparent eye-ball; I am nothing; I see all; the currents of the Universal Being circulate through me; I am part or particle of God. (10)

While it would be incorrect to see in Emerson's drive to American autosalvation a mere echo of the English Lake Poets, it would be foolish to deny the partial resemblance of tone (ecstatic, incantatory) and philosophical tenor (yearning for unity in Nature) between the Romantic poets and the 'sage of Concord'. It is a complex, and not a coincidental, affinity. If a phrase from the passage quoted such as 'glad to the brink of fear' together with the general theme seem to recall moments of youthful optimism in Wordsworth's *Prelude*, echoes of Coleridge and of De Quincey's troubled depiction of that poet in relation to opium, dreams and the nightmare etchings of Piranesi perfuse the opening pages of Emerson's key essay 'Experience' – without, be it noted, finding acknowledgement there.

Of course there are tones available to Emerson that could not be found in the English poets. Emerson wrote in his Journals – as readable for their Yankee cut to the chase as for their drive towards the Supernal Oneness – that 'A man must have aunts and cousins, must buy carrots and turnips, must have barn and woodshed, must go to market and to the blacksmith's shop, must saunter and sleep and be inferior and silly.'[24] The sentence is made memorable by the unexpected turn it takes; that 'saunter' shines out. And as in Wordsworth, the conspicuous unemployment of sauntering that is in reality latent work produces some brilliant sketches of the woods, the seasons, the changing air. More important, however, than the surface affinities between these sketchers of nature is the turn their thinking takes when the desired union with the larger world is balked. To Wordsworth we enter this world 'trailing clouds of glory' only to ask whither 'the visionary gleam' is fled as the dissociations of maturity socialize the individual they expel from childhood's Eden.[25] To Coleridge, Paradise is available only in glimpses paid for in the guilt of addiction to its 'milk', and the conclusion to 'Kubla Khan' is a wistful comedown: 'Could I revive within me / Her symphony and song, / To such a deep delight 'twould win me, / That with music loud and long, / I would build that dome in air.'[26] Could I, 'twould, would: the conditional tense undermines the visionary drive of the poetry, a canker in the rose or, to use the terms adopted by Paul de Man in his critique of Romantic rhetorics, allegory within symbol.[27] In attempting to establish more firmly the relationship between Emerson and the English Romantics, we need to see what happens when being 'part or particle of God' or becoming 'a transparent eye-ball' collides or has somehow to be reconciled with the world of aunts, carrots, turnips and (not to mention darker or more difficult places) the 'blacksmith's shop'. Is Emerson's writing braced to meet opposition, deflation, unperswadeableness? Or is this too a case where, to return to Nathaniel Ward's classic American anxiety, to unpick the least *vericulum* is to risk unravelling the whole?

If *Nature* does not address these questions explicitly, it provides a blueprint of characteristic feints and manoeuvres that would recur throughout Emerson's writing. He concludes the paragraph quoted above, with its audacious eyeball and credal affiliation to the 'uncontained and immortal beauty' of nature as follows: 'In the tranquil landscape, and especially in the distant line of the horizon, man beholds somewhat as beautiful as his own nature' (10). And so it is the ever-moving dawn of the horizon, the promise of no limits, that leads us on. And coupled to that mobility is no fusion with nature, but rather a moving mirror in which post-Enlightenment 'man' can view his own best features. The next and penultimate paragraph of the essay invokes 'the suggestion of an occult relation between man and the vegetable'; while turnips and carrots are not specified, 'the waving of the boughs in the storm' is prized for its 'effect' – a key swerving away from unity with, to use of, nature, and one confirmed by the analogy of 'a higher thought or a better emotion coming over me'. The world outside the self does not draw up the human into itself, but exists as prompter to selfhood's self-bettering – indeed, to the self-made man. Thus are the Yankee and the prophet united, or at least, to reach for a formula from *Leaves of Grass*, wrapped in the flag 'of hopeful green stuff woven' (Whitman, 193). Of course, storms will come, but their buffetings and stresses cannot dislodge the slightest *vericulum* from the American tapestry; for, as the seer says in his final paragraph, donning the overcoat of self-belief, 'Nature always wears the colour of the spirit.' But for any reader sensing in this a crescendo of simple humanism following the vatic overture, there is admonition in the closing sentences which take, as so often in Emerson (whose simplest thought is rescued frequently by powers of expression), an unexpected turn: 'Then, there is a kind of contempt of the landscape felt by him who has just lost by death a dear friend. The sky is less grand as it shuts down over less worth in the population' (11). There is a straightforward thought in this startling conclusion, but it is lifted by the originality of Emerson's phrasing to a point where it is that originality, and not the thought, that will linger in the mind. Emerson is saved by strangeness. Crucial to the seer are powers of saying.

He says so in the Divinity School address: 'Somehow his dream is told: somehow he publishes it with solemn joy: sometimes with pencil on canvas; sometimes with chisel on stone; sometimes in towers and aisles of granite, his soul's worship is builded; sometimes in anthems of indefinite music; but clearest and most permanent, in words' (83). Words were the medium through which Emerson's Americans were to grant themselves permission: to risk themselves in experiment; to start life again from scratch, forgiven by the next and more intense instant; to dethrone all authority; to love themselves; to *be*. To test the words, he trod the boards. On a freezing winter's night, with the snow piled high and more to follow, in some drafty hall calling itself a 'lyceum' in the back of a beyond from which the road out might be impassable, this was no joke for either the speaker or the crowd who put on their over-shoes and braved the sleet after a long day's work in the fields. He was universally described as having a beautiful and a persuasive voice. He had need of it. There is a touch of cynicism but rather more steely professionalism in this Journal entry: 'When a village Lyceum Committee asks me to give a lecture, and I tell them I will read one I am just writing, they are pleased. Poor men, they little know how different that lecture will be when it is given in New York, or is printed. I "try it on" on them; "*The barber learns his trade on the orphan's chin*"' (Linscott, 48). And what they got on the night or we get on the page is the razor-sharp wit of a performance-artist.

'Experience' is a blast of one-liners, worthy of the greatest comedian or, what comes to the same thing, the Blake of *Marriage of Heaven and Hell*: 'A man is a golden impossibility.' 'The wise through excess of wisdom is made a fool' (482). 'There is an optical illusion about every person we meet' (474). 'Everything good is on the highway' (480). 'I am a fragment, and this is a fragment of me' (491). 'At Education-Farm, the noblest theory of life sat on the noblest figures of young men and maidens, quite powerless and melancholy' (478). 'I am ready to die out of nature, and be born again into this new yet unapproachable America I have found in the West' (485). New yet unapproachable: he is without America; it cannot be lived until it has been thought, cannot be thought until it has been written. And of course it was the world of sauntering and the woods, the world of what was always there all the time: 'In the morning I awake, and find the old world, wife, babes, and mother, Concord and Boston, the dear old spiritual world, and even the dear old devil not far off' (480). 'Every roof is agreeable to the eye, until it is lifted; then we find tragedy and moaning women, and hard-eyed husbands, and deluges of lethe, and the men ask, "What's the news?" as if the old were so bad' (472). Emerson's poetry is cranky, unexpectedly thin, liable frequently to spark a great line but rarely a great poem, except in 'Days', 'Blight' and the poems customarily anthologized. The real poetry, his prose, flowed in performance, and was polished for the page.

And of course it is, in the risky sense, all a performance. In a country powered by successive waves of immigrants from diverse cultures, the counterweight to an estrangement let loose by deracination and redoubled by aloneness with America became the new role, the performance of an individual's bread-winning usefulness. Exigencies of the latter might force some unexpected and rapid changes of costume: 'We live amid surfaces, and the true art of life is to skate well on them' (478). This is the open secret of Emerson's 'philosophy'. Emerson here is a long way from Wordsworth and from the skating episode in *The Prelude*, exactly as far in fact as Concord is from Cockermouth. This should not be mistaken for a triumph of style over substance. (If that had been the case, he might have worked harder to make units longer than the single sentence his regular measure.) Emerson should be valued for what he himself termed his provocations, and because what he writes is so often *true*, not only to dull fact but to the unquenchably sentimental and energetic pump of America: 'Never mind the ridicule, never mind the defeat: up again, old heart! – it seems to say, – there is victory yet for all justice; and the true romance which the world exists to realize, will be the transformation of genius into practical power' (492). This sentence sums up Emerson, who begins in the world of the Romantics and ends up sounding like Edison.

# 3

# *Melville*
## Crises in Representation

## Melville and political representation

Synecdochal America is dead. Or at least, the idea that any part might stand for the whole is currently bedevilled by a mutual suspicion among the parts so intense as to make a holistic understanding of 'America' imaginary. It may always have been thus. Or it may have depended on which part was speaking, and what powers or fantasies of representation were in play. Certainly to John Bryant, introducing a collection of essays catalysed by the centenary of Herman Melville's death, synecdochal America as imaged in a particularly vulnerable concept of Emerson's – 'Representative Men' – is defunct:

> Of course, the claim that Melville, or any particular author, is 'representative' is bound to draw fire, for as the nation's canon wars have reminded us, we take a perilous step when we surrender our cultural identity to a set of representative 'classics'. Indeed, the very notion of representation challenges the notion of democracy even as it enacts democracy. In a culture that has always been diverse and always on the brink of disunity, the question of what part shall represent the whole of us has been a continual, in fact biennial, reminder of the fragile status of our political being in what is essentially a perpetually revolutionary society. Who will stand for me? Who *can* speak for me?[1]

Bryant's questions cut to the heart of contemporary American estrangement. There is now significant doubt in America as to whether a body politic really exists. Individuals are of course still sent to a House of Representatives. There is a President (though the majority of those who bothered to vote may have supported his opponent). But just as modern satire from Philip K. Dick to *Toy Story* or the horror film variously exposes the figure of the individual as the self-delusion of a reproducible simulacrum, so synecdoche has shrunk to the reduced status of an essentially fictive trope, unable to sustain the weight of social obligation. Of course the collapse in confidence that has undercut the concept of representative democracy has in no way derailed the operations of capitalism. In a condition where nothing will change that does not suit the agenda of profit seeking, the failure of political consensus leaves only a dialogue between disenfranchised minority groups, held down to a tolerable decibel level by the good manners of political correctness. Like the enlightened but self-denying Bodhisattva of Buddhism, the liberal white male reader of dead, white representative authors refuses to leave the turning wheel of suffering for Nirvana until everyone else's more disadvantaged group has got through. There is a touch of this self-flagellation in John Bryant's apology for the concept of 'surrender ...to a set of representative "classics"', as if to argue for the greater value of one text or corpus over another was somehow sinful. The questionable aspect of canon making has lain historically in the failure of the canon to read its own selections, arguments and preju- dices as other than normal and inevitable. A tendency to prefer and value one thing over another, and on reasoned grounds, is as funda- mental to humanity as breathing.

It is worth noting that such a set of 'classics', however rigid and open to attack from one quarter or another, may still have propaedeutic value. My own generation was introduced to many of the canonical novels of Britain and America via *Classics Illustrated*, cartoon versions of Dickens or Hawthorne, and I cannot believe that any empathy or broadmindedness I might conjecturally possess was hurt rather than helped by reading these comics as a child. *Classics Illustrated* led its readers to take for granted the equal potential to interest of American and British novels, a circum-Atlantic assumption that Herman Mel- ville spoke for eloquently. Also worth noting is the fact, well under- stood as recently as Charles Olson's time but apparently forgotten in the smoke and heat of the canon wars, that Melville's status is a fluctuating phenomenon, as subject to fashion and debate and as attached to specific agendas as any other cultural manifestation. Far from being some immovable idol, Melville had a brief success as the author of *Typee*, went downhill fairly fast in public esteem, was rescued briefly at the time of his death, revived somewhat in the 1920s following the discovery of *Billy Budd*, and, lifted by the differing agendas of the avant-garde poet Olson and his Harvard teacher Matthiessen, brought to a prominence that is real, but seldom put to the test by actual reading outside the demands of a university syllabus.

Melville's writings are not of a kind to which the reader can turn like a homing pigeon in search of rest and the firm terrain of an idealized nineteenth century, before modernity's flood came and drowned realism. The disunity of Melville's textual corpus does not simply predict the current crisis in representation, but implies its recurrent happening, or waiting to happen, right from the struggles for independence to the tensions of the ante-bellum years, from the rhetoric and paradoxes of Union to the proto-modernist *fin de siècle*. No writer of fiction in his century is as prone as Melville to the ludic, the caustic, the filleting of realism for overtly theoretical purposes. Linked by his own ambition, by an essay that will be discussed later in this chapter, and by a whole tradition of criticism to the establishment of a national literature, Melville wrote texts unparalleled in the intensity of their alienation from that nation's characteristic modes of representation. He is as aggressive and as interested in violence as Poe; indeed, *Pierre* (1852) can only be made to make sense by viewing it through the glass of dark Romanticism. It is with *Pierre* and other late books that much of this chapter will be concerned. For further signs that Melville may be the representative writer for the disunity of the unrepresentable and dis-United States, it may, however, be helpful to begin at the beginning, with *Typee*.

## Typee

The title of Melville's first book on first publication was *Narrative of a Four Months' Residence among the Natives of a Valley of the Marquesas Islands; or, A Peep at Polynesian Life*. That *Peep* and its ribald, colonial and anti-colonial associations still warrant scrutiny. My long-lost 1960s children's version undoubtedly failed to address these aspects, and I doubt that it included the narrator's rumination on the whereabouts of the barnacle-encrusted hulk from which he jumps, now perhaps 'tacking twice in the twenty-four hours somewhere off Buggerry Island, or the Devil's-Tail Peak'.[2] Although the centre-piece of Winston Churchill's triumvirate of shipboard attractions – rum, sodomy and the lash – barely breathes its name in Tommo's story, we are embroiled from the outset in a version of the picaresque which trades gleefully in very British forms of innuendo. It is one of the paradoxes of Melville's literary nationalism that he self-consciously wooed the larger Anglophone community, wanting – and at least in *Typee*, getting – a transatlantic hit. The egregiously pro-British appendix to the book, peeping at colonial and saturnalian goings-on in the Sandwich Islands, was no doubt worded with that audience in mind. Elsewhere, double meaning prevails, so much so that at times it runs riot, triggered by salacious incident, but ending in semantic excess well beyond the baggage allowance of the travel-narrative genre.

The bulk of the first chapter is taken up by two such yarns. The second concerns the Island Queen, the beauteous wife of Mowanna, King of Nukuheva, or more precisely her bottom, which, as with many figures in Melville's fiction including *Moby-Dick*'s Queequeg, is illustrated. 'Eager to display the hieroglyphics on her own sweet form', she displays her rump to a boatload of aghast Frenchmen, catalysing their precipitate retreat from 'so shocking a catastrophe' (17). We will return to the Queen's hieroglyphics in due course. The first story, described by Tommo as 'a somewhat amusing incident', concerns the efforts of the Protestant missions to wean the natives of Tahiti and its outlying islands from their heathen ways:

> An intrepid missionary, undaunted by the ill-success that had attended all previous endeavors to conciliate the savages, and believing much in the efficacy of female influence, introduced among them his young and beautiful wife, the first white woman who had ever visited their shores. The islanders at first gazed in mute admiration at so unusual a prodigy, and seemed inclined to regard it as some new divinity. But after a short time, becoming familiar with its charming aspect, and jealous of the folds which encircled its form, they sought to pierce the sacred veil of calico in which it was enshrined, and in the gratification of their curiosity so far overstepped the limits of good breeding, as deeply to offend the lady's sense of decorum. Her sex once ascertained, their idolatry was changed into contempt; and there was no end to the contumely showered upon her by the savages, who were exasperated at the deception which they conceived had been practised upon them. To the horror of her affectionate spouse, she was stripped of her garments, and given to understand that she could no longer carry on her deceits with impunity. The gentle dame was not sufficiently evan-gelised to endure this, and, fearful of further improprieties, she forced her husband to relinquish his undertaking, and together they returned to Tahiti. (15)

However this incident is taken, it is not unequivocally 'amusing', and a certain acidity in the telling suggests that it was not so to Melville, but that discomfiting the reader was in some way to his purpose. The tale is taken forward by a sequence of gaps: between the missionary's and the savages' beliefs, between items of clothing removed unceremoniously, between the euphemism and circumlocution of Melville's chosen style and the assault described, between the natives' preconceptions of divinity and the 'deception' unwittingly practised, and so on. All parties feel decorum has been violated, and Melville's own allegiance is neither to one side nor another but to an almost structuralist sense that encounter between America and the Other exposes the arbitrary nature of the codes by which each side defines itself. It is in the cultural vertigo of not belonging set in motion by the gaps that Melville's modernity lies.

*Typee* is kept on course by a simple narrative threading of incidents along a trajectory from innocence to experience. The narrator jumps ship, 'goes native', and is in two senses captured by the attractions of an unclouded life among allegedly simple people. All the women are beautiful and are really one woman, Fayaway, who 'for the most part clung to the primitive and summer garb of Eden. But how becoming the costume! It showed her fine figure to the best possible advantage' (107). She has 'the easy unstudied graces of a child of nature' (106), and feels sufficiently comfortable with Tommo to permit him the discovery that 'the skin of this young creature, from continual ablutions and the use of mollifying ointments, was inconceivably smooth and soft' (106). Fayaway is a piece of exotic fruit, and yet in the explicit equation that follows one can see Freud's, or rather womankind's, *vagina dentata*, for once again it is the gaps, and not the superficial narrative continuities, that give the writing intermittent depth: 'Her full lips, when parted with a smile, disclosed teeth of a dazzling whiteness; and when her rosy mouth opened with a burst of merriment, they looked like the milk-white seeds of the "arta," a fruit of the valley, which, when cleft in twain, shows them reposing in rows on either side, imbedded in the red and juicy pulp.' Like pubic hair, the hair on her head is 'of the deepest brown, parted irregularly in the middle' (106). Fayaway may look good enough to eat, but given that in the Marquesan dialect the word Typee 'signifies a lover of human flesh' (35), the danger, *sub rosa*, is that she will devour Tommo. Eating people is wrong; Tommo catches the islanders at it: and so he has to leave. Everyone now has fallen from innocence into experience, and the 'child of nature' is shown to possess a potentially uncontrollable, animal side. We see this coming, not only in Tommo's early suspicions that he has fallen among 'arrant cannibals' (35) but in his perhaps less self-aware formulations, as when, driven by a wounded leg to seek the ministrations of a 'Savage Aesculapius', he notes that 'My unfortunate limb was now left much in the same condition as a rump-steak after undergoing the castigating process which precedes cooking' (100).

Readers of the time were taken by the simple romantic allegory in which a young adventurer tarries in a garden of earthly delight, faces danger, and comes home to tell the tale. A more subtly interesting aspect of *Typee* lies in its continual recourse to the grossly unsubtle. *Double entendre* and innuendo of the rump-steak and juicy-pulp variety are so common as to become the chief linguistic means by which human conduct is recorded and understood. Every activity described looks and sounds like something else, invariably something genital. Fayaway smoking tobacco and 'holding in her delicately formed olive hand the long yellow reed of her pipe, with its quaintly carved bowl' looks particularly 'engaging' (160), as she does when, along with other 'sweet nymphs, whose bright eyes are beaming upon you with kindness', she descends on Tommo and gives him a good rub-down with vegetable oil (134), prior to little Kory-Kory striking a light so that Tommo can enjoy what is by implication a post-coital smoke. Lighting up in this context is no mean feat, but an epic of mounting, grasping and rubbing, as Kory-Kory urges his stick into the accommodating labia of a dried hibiscus. 'At first Kory-Kory goes to work quite leisurely, but gradually quickens his pace, and waxing warm in the employment, drives the stick furiously along the smoking channel... the perspiration starting from every pore. As he approaches the climax of his effort, he pants and gasps for breath, and his eyes almost start from their sockets' (135). This, however, is as nothing compared to the unexpected conversion of parts of a bread-fruit tree into a head-dress several pages further on, when 'the elastic sides of the aperture pressed apart, the head is inserted between them' (138) – point taken.

More seriously, this is among the factors complicating *Typee*'s overall 'point', as reading tracks nomadically once levels of insinuation have been breached, here faced by a flood of meaning, here by mute enigma. The Queen of the Islands is decorated with hieroglyphs and is keen for an appreciative readership; shocked by the physical location of her text, its potential admirers withdraw precipitately. The ribald little anecdote is not the gentle overture to Tommo's narrative that it seems, but an early exposure of the impasses in understanding that the depths of the text will posit, paradoxically, as our commonality. Generally his encounter with the Other allows Tommo a return to a blissful toddler state where orality and other areas of need and pleasure are perpetually discovered anew, to be satisfied at once. Sexual innuendo may signify not so much the indulgence of a young

nd Porpheero (Europe) in the turmoil of 1848. Melville's
genuity is undone by his political despair as the narrative
ardi, in the words of Lawrence Buell, 'establishes an
 between the cultures of imperialist Britain and bumptious
l America as social pathologies witnessed from an Olym-
of view'. In this sense Mardi is the first work to typify the
 Melville's maturity, which very frequently deploys rhet-
l to the search for a metaposition from which apparently
lief systems or sets of interests will be exposed as, in Buell's
rror images of insufficiency' (Bryant and Milder, 88). This
ulates the narrative voice of Billy Budd and, more obvi-
thal ironies of Israel Potter, the tragedy of whose protag-
ted in his inability to accept that the republican agenda
s animated by self-interest, in its own way, as that of
oppressor. The problem, wrought to a pitch by the tene-
volence, the almost Wyndham Lewis-like paranoia of The
-Man, is that when the metaposition offers such a radical
f external failure in the body politic, there are internal
es for the body of the text, now a house of cards that can
tumble into scattered obscurity or be put back into circu-
e played once more to lose on America's 'ship of fools'.[5]
g is without peer, but it sent the early readers of Melville
 droves.

ious revolutions in what might be thought success and
the working-out of texts have been responsible for the
Melville as a writer who engages the interest by virtue of
rather than his language. The inextricable linking of idea
ge, concept and style, is amply evidenced in Mardi, as for
 the second chapter, which both anticipates the phenom-
see-saws of Moby-Dick and remains in itself a perfect piece
 It is titled 'A Calm', no joke to a landsman at sea, but a
on that not only 'revolutionizes his stomach, but unsettles
tempts him to recant his belief in the eternal fitness of
d, in short, makes him Melvillean. In this state, 'where
tself seems suspended', the observer testing the reality of
xpanse before him 'grows madly skeptical', and we see the
cern not only of Mardi but of Emerson's essays, James's
d twentieth-century American poetry from Stevens to
he articulation in words of the thinking mind. Thus it is
ing that makes Mardi an advance over Typee that undoes
 as a successful novel in conventional terms. The mind's
g of epistemological boundaries, of what constitutes self,
d the relationships between, is no longer triggered by

man's appetites once freed from civilized constraint, as a return to
younger stages of play with the growing body, its projections, boundaries and apertures. The reverse of paternalistic, the infantilist regres-
sion still patronizes, though this discourse carries continually, if
almost subliminally, questions that lead the reader in a political rather
than a Freudian direction.

Tommo's and his compatriot Toby's flight from the Dolly inaugur-
ates a theme that recurs from Omoo to Moby-Dick and Billy Budd:
the ship is a microcosm of society's hierarchies, prejudices and pressures. Their flight is therefore not an escape into a fantastic alternative, but the opportunity for an understanding of forms of ideology
and subjugation which will happen in the movements of the text more
than in Tommo's lively but essentially unreformed consciousness.
Well treated by the Typee, Tommo and Toby are still hostages of
potential usefulness in barter with the enemy, de-briefed and subtly
interrogated – over, for example, French troop movements, of which
Tommo knows nothing, or about his ability to repair an old musket,
which is non-existent. Tommo does not fully grasp what textual irony
makes clear: that, on board as a wage slave or captured by the
islanders, he is property. The lubricious innuendo that animates the
narrative is to be read as displaying a commodification of the body
over which the subject has scant control. Bodily potential for an
unalienated, free give and take is then displaced into metaphor,
joke, fantasy – the flipside of the paranoid fantasy that bodies will
devour each other.

Ironic similarities between the sailor and the native begin to
emerge. As John Carlos Rowe observes in an important revisionist
and historicist account of the novel:

> Only Tommo's naiveté prevents him from understanding that the ser-
> vitude of a native like Kory-Kory or the sexual favors of Fayaway may
> well be staged in the interests of the community. Such awareness, of
> course, would require Tommo to acknowledge a bond between himself
> and Kory-Kory and Fayaway that is based on their shared condition as
> those required to work for others. It is a connection that Tommo never
> makes, but that Melville's narrative repeatedly emphasizes.[3]

Although there may be a touch of wishful thinking in Rowe's question
as to whether the flight of the Frenchmen from the sight of the
Queen's hieroglyphs constitutes an 'exposure of the unconscious of
colonial domination' (276), his point that an inversion of the classic
scene of recognition in the early pages of the novel prompts us to look
for ironies of (mis)recognition thereafter is astute. Typee's bottom line

restores otherness to all parties as their common condition. Viewed from another perspective as real as our own, we are all aliens. The codes in which we are raised that make us recognizable and individual are arbitrary, and to present them to the Other may be to court derision, incomprehension, assault, shocked flight. The posture of the Queen, which Melville would seem to have adopted *vis-à-vis* his public by the time of the later novels, is a quintessentially human feature.

## Narratives of experience

Melville's Pacific years (1841–4) are amply documented. Shipping out in the whaler *Acushnet*, he spent eighteen months in the forecastle, learning the ropes, before jumping ship in the Marquesas and spending a month among the Typee people. Escape on an Australian whaler, the *Lucy Ann*, saw him embroiled in a mutiny followed by imprisonment in Tahiti, then months of roving, sometimes as a boat steerer. He was briefly employed in a bowling alley in Honolulu. In August 1843 he signed aboard a navy frigate, the *United States*, proceeding via South America and the storms of Cape Horn to dock in Boston Harbor in October 1844. The life-material thus gathered was refashioned in six books, between 1845 and 1851. Of course the life and the work are an echo chamber. At some point while Melville was composing the ending to *Moby-Dick*, in which the *Pequod* and, by analogy, the idea of a United States is swallowed by the indifferent ocean, the *Acushnet* was itself wrecked off St Lawrence Island. However, only the most disingenuous reader would try to read the books today as faithful records of experience. Not only are they full of borrowings or reworkings of travel literature in exactly those areas where Melville had more experience than most – more, for example, than R. H. Dana, whose *Two Years Before the Mast* (1840) had lifted the genre to new heights – but they combine an extraordinary variety of literary and philosophical approaches to truths that are then either exploded or re-presented as forever beyond.

As seekers after truth go, Melville's narrator is for the most part languidly becalmed, but no more conspicuously unemployed than Wordsworth or Emerson. Melville's absorption of Plato, Rabelais, Thomas Browne, Coleridge and other writers during the period of *Typee* and *Omoo*, in combination with his Pacific experiences, opened up new vistas of contradiction and experiment, as well as deeper understanding. While the Platonic concept of knowledge as

recollection resonates in these i[...] revive a Kantian distinction, as h[...] discovery. This made of Melville a[...] through books and life lived on [...] Murray his publisher doubted tha[...] suspected that 'Herman Melville' [...]

In a recent account of philosop[...] Wenke unpicks strand after strand[...] observe evenly that 'Melville's pur[...] its intrinsic futility'. However, rath[...] paradox', this position is shown t[...] the provisional working-out of '[...] ultimately, yet, in the improvisatio[...] of successful fiction unsuccessfully[...] last on the shores of Truth.[4] In thi[...] are all failures, necessitating a new[...]

## Ma[...]

*Omoo*, successor to *Typee*, succee[...] *Mardi*, was a disastrous flop. It i[...] perimeter works, pushing certain f[...] far as they will go, and if it is har[...] chapters without pleasure, it becom[...] those fine sentences with urgency [...] readers of Melville felt from the sta[...] revulsion, in the nineteenth-century[...] sense. The rhetorical switches into t[...] of the blue in the second half of *Pie*[...] destroy the continuities that sustai[...] *Budd* moves from the poetry of exp[...] with an abruptness unsettling to th[...] the exception, a text that needed sor[...] sense of danger and internally ge[...] morselessly gorgeous word-flood.

In terms of political allegory, such[...] *potentia*, for *Mardi* utilizes the c[...] begun in the eighteenth century by [...] order to ask how occidental society [...] East. The narrator Taji is shown the[...] Media, taking in the sights of Domi[...]

(Vivenza) a[...] aesthetic i[...] form of *M*[...] equivalenc[...] postcoloni[...] pian point[...] thinking o[...] orics helpf[...] opposed b[...] phrase, 'm[...] is what re[...] ously, the [...] onist is ro[...] might be [...] the British[...] brous male[...] *Confidenc*[...] diagnosis [...] consequen[...] only either[...] lation to [...] The writir[...] packing, i[...]

Such cu[...] failure in [...] picture of [...] his ideas, [...] and langu[...] example i[...] enological[...] of writing[...] phenomer[...] his mind; [...] things' ar[...] existence [...] the glassy [...] prime co[...] fiction, a[...] Ashbery: [...] the very t[...] its chance[...] questioni[...] not-self a[...]

dramatic action to which it reverts, but has essentially become the ground of that action. Even the experience of the 'positive vacuity' of the calm is a catalyst to thought, and that is the sum of the chapter:

> The stillness of the calm is awful. His voice begins to grow strange and portentous. He feels it in him like something swallowed too big for the esophagous. It keeps up a sort of involuntary interior humming in him, like a live beetle. His cranium is a dome full of reverberations. The hollows of his very bones are as whispering galleries. He is afraid to speak loud, lest he be stunned; like the man in the bass drum.
>
> But more than all else is the consciousness of his utter helplessness. Succor or sympathy there is none. Penitence for embarking avails not. The final satisfaction of despairing may not be his with a relish. Vain the idea of idling out the calm: He may sleep if he can, or purposely delude himself into a crazy fancy, that he is merely at leisure. All this he may compass; but he may not lounge; for to lounge is to be idle; to be idle implies an absence of anything to do; whereas there is a calm to be endured: enough to attend to, Heaven knows. His physical organization, obviously intended for locomotion, becomes a fixture; for where the calm leaves him, there he remains. Even his undoubted vested rights, comprised in his glorious liberty of volition, become as naught. For of what use? He wills to go: to get away from the calm: as ashore he would avoid the plague. But he can not; and how foolish to revolve expedients. It is more hopeless than a bad marriage in a land where there is no Doctors' Commons. He has taken the ship to wife, for better or for worse, for calm or for gale; and she is not to be shuffled off. With yards akimbo, she says unto him scornfully, as the old beldam said to the little dwarf:–'Help yourself.'
>
> And all this, and more than this, is a calm. (670)

The horrors of being becalmed are explored in a range of canonical texts, including Coleridge's *The Rime of the Ancient Mariner*, Conrad's *The Shadow Line* and of course *Moby-Dick*. In all these texts the discomforts of a situation real to the external world are re-created so as to show the discomforts of the mind, which, turned in on itself and away from outside distractions, leads the subject into states of eccentric solipsism that might also, or instead, be the world of a more fundamental reality. I quote at length because it is only through the sense of protracted duration that the passage from *Mardi* can do its work. Here ideas are inseparable from language, the cerebral prison from its tolling cadences, and just as the prose harks back to the King James Bible, so its whispering gallery echoes to the torments of Poe's many incarcerated speakers (the ship-bound Arthur Gordon Pym, most of all) and prefigures in its ironies of a nothingness that has become the whole of being, the darkness, lit paradoxically by black humour, of Samuel Beckett and the existentialist wing of Modernism. The off-key joke about the dwarf and the beldam is deliberate dissonance, the breaking of the improvisations of reverie, phenomenological drift, so that the splendid, futile, but ineluctable, cycle of truth seeking can again begin.

## Melville's middle period

Melville, a great and pessimistic originator, insisted on keeping his distance from Emerson: 'I do not oscillate in Emerson's rainbow, but prefer to hang myself in mine own halter.' Yet he emphasized the lines of descent and influence among writers with a candour that could cheer Harold Bloom, defending the 'brilliant' Emerson from Duyck-inck's charge of being derivative:

> Be his stuff begged, borrowed, or stolen, or of his own domestic manufacture he is an uncommon man.... Lay it down that had not Sir Thomas Browne lived, Emerson would not have mystified – I will answer, that had not Old Zack's father begot him, Old Zack would never have been the hero of Palo Alto. The truth is that we are all sons, grandsons, or nephews or great-nephews of those who go before us. No one is his own sire. (Wenke, 72)

One of the reasons for the canonization of Melville as a founding classic of American literature stems from the sheer brio and vitality with which the evocation of tradition and the suggestion of the new are carried off, as if the centre of everything were this writer, this work in hand. Even the tortures, the shredded nerves and the answering silence of the calm in the passage quoted offer an evocation of what it feels like to know one's self alone in the world naked, yet clothed by the language of 'those who go before us' and those yet to write. It is hard at times to take up the challenge with which Melville terminates chapter 96 of *Mardi*: 'Read on.' Yet, for the reader who does, there awaits chapter 97, perhaps the most extraordinary chapter of this odd book, one in which the later Melville appears to have emerged completely, while simultaneously doing a perfect take, in terms of style, rhythm and cadence, on Thomas De Quincey's *Confessions of an English Opium-Eater*, as unacknowledged here as it was by the Emerson of *Experience*.

In *Redburn* and *White-Jacket* Melville would become to a certain extent his own sire, making a partial return to the action-narrative that had pleased the reviewers. There is something curiously stalled about *Redburn*, and the undoubted magnetism and complexity of characters such as Jackson and Harry seems of an order that Melville could present but not develop. The savage ironies that alienated the novelist from his own day, and that make his work so salient to our multi-cultural but racist times, abound. Speaking of the 'friendly reception' accorded black ship's cooks and stewards in the port of Liverpool, the narrator notes: 'I was surprised that a colored man should be treated as he is in this town; but a little reflection showed that, after all, it was but recognizing his claims to humanity and normal equality; so that, in some things, we Americans leave to other countries the carrying out of the principle that stands at the head of our Declaration of Independence' (222). Americans do, however, continue to insist that all others discard their independence and mimic American declarations, as when, in an otherwise informative account of the impact of New York on Melville's writing, Wyn Kelley asserts that Liverpool cannot possibly be an English seaport:

> The Liverpool sections of *Redburn* appear to most readers to establish the urban themes of the novel. Redburn's wanderings through town, his discovery of vice in the 'Corinthian haunts' of the port, and his attempts to relieve a dying mother and her children in a cellar have been extensively discussed as evidence of Melville's awareness of social ills and his capacity to represent the city and its mysteries. It has, however, not been viewed in the more specific context of New York's urban form, its growth, ideology, and cultural construction as a labyrinth. Placed in that context, Liverpool appears a faithful portrait of New York.[6]

How foolish of me not to have realized, while treading in Melville's footsteps during seventeen years' residence in Liverpool, that I was all the time crossing Delancey!

## Pierre

After *Moby-Dick* Melville produced the novel which has always been the source of most readerly hostility, *Pierre*. Harold Bloom declares flatly that 'despite various modern salvage attempts *Pierre* certainly is unreadable, in the old-fashioned sense of that now critically abused word. You just cannot get through it, unless you badly want and need to do so.'[7] *Pierre* is a weird and jarring experience, and no new salvage attempt from this quarter will overturn the tradition of dislike. My own candidate for a virtually unreadable Melville would be *Mardi*, an adventure so liberated into untrammelled textuality that anything could happen at any given point. By contrast, it is clear from the outset that whatever happens to Pierre is going to be awful, a fatedness which in combination with the protagonist's lack of self-knowledge makes up a narrative strategy that goes back to the forms of Greek tragedy.

As with the novels of Thomas Hardy, or for that matter Melville's tale 'Bartleby, the Scrivener', the invocation of tragedy combined with the failure to achieve it appears to fall within the writer's self-conscious designs, and may be read as pointing to features in modern experience as the grounds for the 'failure'. And, as frequently in Hardy, the narrative scene is awash with cosmic ironies, in the glimmerings of the firelight and the wording of a letter as much as in larger storms and disasters. What Hardy termed in *Tess* 'the ache of modernism' led him to the conscious use of dissonance – in the characterization of Sue Bridehead in *Jude*, and that extraordinary fable of identity *The Well-Beloved*, whose regulation of character by allegory and a quirky aestheticism looks forward to the waning of affect, the rhetoricity and automata of the twentieth century. The opposition between the cloying pastoral of Saddle Meadows into which the pampered Pierre is born and the city of dreadful night to which he travels can be understood as operating in this way, its alleged unreadability a feature of a fable that 'aches' from the inability to abandon that in which it no longer believes. *Pierre* narrativizes the perils of Romanticism, and in its inability to move beyond disillusion with those paradigms, plunges into the darkness of the Gothic, always the dialectical concomitant of Romantic idealism.

The charge of unreadability boils down to the same mistrust of the Gothic that fuelled Henry James's distaste for Edgar Allan Poe. And the Gothic is everywhere in *Pierre*. As the untested protagonist 'passed on beneath the pendulous canopies of the long arms of the weeping elms of the village, an almost impenetrable blackness surrounded him, but entered not the gently illuminated halls of his heart' (75). We know precisely from the insistence that the chambers of his pseudo-aristocratic heart are untouched by 'blackness' that they will shortly be flooded by it, just as we know that the happy campers in the modern slasher-movie are ill-advised to go necking in the woods, where there are bound to be maniacs with chain-saws about. And sure enough, Pierre is about to receive a letter from Isabel, the sister he didn't know he had, whose name is synonymous with 'Mystery' and incest, another fated attachment of Romanticism, and one anticipated by Melville's shouted hints, such as 'much that goes to make up the deliciousness of a wife, already lies in the sister' (12), the theme compounded by Pierre's unctuous and claustrophobic relationship with his mother, whom he calls 'sister', though Melville stresses her essentially patriarchal 'masculineness' (213). (This is a very weird book.) Further Gothic colouring comes from the opposition between the 'dark ravings of the loftier poets' and the 'untutored' Pierre's 'fine-spun, shallow dreams' of a lifelong and bloodless idyll with the spotless Lucy – eventually sucked into the vortex of a *ménage à trois* with Isabel. The latter could be straight out of Poe: as she faints in Pierre's arms, 'his whole form was bathed in the flowing glossiness of her long and unimprisoned hair...She seemed as dead; as suffo-cated'; but while her 'death-like beauty' (134) recalls the prema-turely buried Madeleine Usher, her wild guitar playing recalls Madeleine's mad brother, Roderick. Poesque too is the doting on rancid ideas of the chivalric, set up only to be flushed away by the collective psychosis of the city, home of 'that darker, though truer aspect of things' into which Pierre will be 'initiated' and where he will die (84).

The sick humour of modern Gothic is also marked in *Pierre*, but in its ghastly way superbly judged, the reverse of unreadable. Pierre's first glimpse of a prostitute is unforgettable:

Pierre turned; and in the flashing, sinister, evil cross-lights of a drug-gist's window, his eye caught the person of a wonderfully beautifully-featured girl; scarlet-cheeked, glaringly-arrayed, and of a figure all natural grace but unnatural vivacity. Her whole form, however, was horribly lit by the green and yellow rays from the druggist's.

'My God!' shuddered Pierre, hurrying forward, 'the town's first welcome to youth!' (277)

Worthy of George Lippard and crying out for illustration by Edward Gorey, such a moment of Gothic hilarity at the protagonist's expense is comparable to the final scene in his ancestral home, where, watched by a marble statue of 'temple-polluting Laocoon' writhing in a mess of snakes, Pierre bids a grandstanding farewell to his mother, spins proudly on his heel, trips and falls to the ground (219). It would not be right, however, to suggest that Melville's Gothic is all Gothic skit, an indulgence that, once set going, unaccountably got out of hand. The narrative of Isabel's upbringing by a couple who 'seldom or never spoke' to her is powerful, and in a different key altogether (138). The text's obsessive and explicit return to the term 'ambiguities' is among the devices that keep the reader at a critical distance, asking whether this truly is Gothic – or if it might not best be read as an essay on the

Gothic, one whose analytical tendencies do perhaps become shrouded in claustral lucubration, but whose curiously Freudian and even deconstructive prescience, along with a wealth of striking images, portraits and micro-dramas, still commands attention. *Pierre* is, among other things, a warning about the power of tropes to shape life.

The narrative of Isabel's upbringing is a reminder of the real-life abuses to which Gothic novels allude hyperbolically, while Pierre's hyperbolically innocent upbringing suggests the dangers of a determination to live life according to the rules of fairy-tale. The innocence and lamb-like blitheness that characterize Pierre and Lucy's affections and life in Saddle Meadows before the Fall (incest, the city, self-delusion, violence) are made nauseating not only by Melville's deliberate deployment of lurid style, but by the suspicion that innocence may be *chosen* – as it may be by a very different character, Billy Budd. *Pierre* is saturnine about the family romance of Saddle Meadows in the way that horror as exemplified by David Lynch's *Blue Velvet* delves into the crawling life beneath the suburban surface of Lumberton. Really, everyone knows what's going on; the price to be paid for choosing an innocent or idealistic Romanticism is that you get the dark side, sooner or later, whether you want it or not. And with that, 'the whole man droops into nameless melancholy' (198).

## *Israel Potter* and Melville's later work

Early in *Pierre* there comes an intervention by Melville on the topic of American democracy which is developed by all the late books:

> For indeed the democratic element operates as a subtile acid among us; forever producing new things by corroding the old; as in the south of France verdigris, the primitive material of one kind of green paint, is produced by grape-vinegar poured upon copper plates. Now in general nothing can be more significant of decay than the idea of corrosion; yet on the other hand, nothing can more vividly suggest luxuriance of life, than the idea of green as a color; for green is the peculiar signet of all-fertile Nature herself. Herein by apt analogy we behold the marked anomalousness of America ... and how wonderfully to her, Death itself becomes transmuted into Life. (13–14)

It is easy to tell when Melville starts using irony, hard to locate the point at which such irony stops. The rhetorical moves that produce the conclusion here are so deft as to set reading once again at a critical distance, and the speech is convincing as the stories spun by his Cosmopolitan aboard the ship of fools convince, just prior to his requests for money. The speech bears comparison with the description of America on the eve of battle with British forces in *Israel Potter*: 'intrepid, unprincipled, reckless, predatory, with boundless ambition, civilized in externals but a savage at heart' (561). Melville understood fully that his country was invented, not discovered, and that the invention was perpetually ongoing, with an unflinching acceptance of the inevitability of destruction. Israel Potter thinks he has accepted this, as an optimistic soldier in the Revolutionary wars. His tragedy lies in his failure to see that the burgeoning republic's supposed incarnation in the individual could still view the individual as expendable. Setting out to do battle for his country results only in imprisonment and long-suffering exile, with Israel a 'bondsman in the English Egypt' (602). Returning to New England in 1826, an octogenarian and a broken man, he finds the ruined remnants of his family home, and is recognized by no one. 'He died the same day that the oldest oak on his native hills was blown down' (615). Some of Melville's ironies fall with as heavy a crash, though the cameo appearances in the novel by such figures as Benjamin Franklin, John Paul Jones and King George III are brilliantly managed, and it is fair to say that if *Pierre* has alienated critics by virtue of its opacity, *Israel Potter* has been neglected because its transparency, an equal but different literary achievement, has failed to excite.

Chapters 2–6 of *Israel Potter* rewrite sections of the *Life and Remarkable Adventures of Israel R. Potter*, ghost-written and published by Henry Trumbull in 1824, while Israel's encounters with the famous draw on a variety of sources, including Jared Sparks's 1830s edition of *The Works of Benjamin Franklin*, Ethan Allen's own narrative of his captivity, Robert C. Sands's compilation *The Life and Correspondence of John Paul Jones* (1830), and Fenimore Cooper's history of the United States Navy. A number of source-books are therefore pressed into service so as to create the impression of veracity and extra-textual life. Based on a real-life figure, Israel is made to correspond to the kind of hero common in other nineteenth-century developments of the picaresque novel, but generally not of use to Melville's intellectually laden and riddling allegories. An American loser, Potter is duped by the charisma of confidence men. For example, Benjamin Franklin's blend of mandarin politicking, slipperiness and peasant guile typify the more fluid aspects of the developing American character to which Melville would attend in *The Confidence-Man*.

## The Confidence-Man

Con men, abusers of trust, are a vivid and traditional feature of American cultural history, from the riverboat card-sharper to the quack healer and the spurious clergyman. In American literature these figures are not confined by class, as their European equivalents in the novels of Dickens or Balzac might have been. In fact, the con man has no exact European equivalent, as his serpentine and chameleon qualities can cross boundaries of class by their very nature, so as to become discernible in all spheres of American life from the visionary and the political to the criminal, frequently blurring precisely those categories in order to further the interests of the 'self-made man'. As Tony Tanner notes, this phrase of 1832 is ambiguous, suggesting 'both the independent achievement of success and a more radical act of self-parenting' (Tanner, p. xviii). Serial replication alternating with a functional recasting of the self are shown by Gary Lindberg (in *The Confidence Man in American Literature* (1982)) as intrinsic to New World fluidity, 'linking land boomers and poets, prophets and profiteers' until 'in the general atmosphere of boosterism and mutual congratulation, "America" itself came to exist primarily in the imagination' (p. xviii). Emerson is a visionary of this order, one to whom we are (to use the terms of 'The Poet') creatures of symbol, mystery, metamorphosis, energy and exhilaration; 'America is a poem in our eyes' (Emerson, 465). One of the charms of Emerson's writing is its blitheness, its musical pronouncements that fuse idealism, aspiration as statement of fact and blatant untruth in a beguiling – but by Gary Lindberg's reading of the period, a representative – self-confidence. 'All that we call sacred history attests that the birth of a poet is the principal event in chronology' (451). That is one such amazing statement. The reader of poetry and, above all, the poem of America, is one who must wait like John the Baptist for 'the arrival of a brother' in whom I can have confidence, one who will lead me to 'know what I am doing', who will invite me 'into the science of the real', risking trust in a Christ who may, after all, only be Icarus, or even the shape-shifting Cosmopolitan aboard Melville's ironically named *Fidèle*:

> Oftener it falls, that this winged man, who will carry me into the heaven, whirls me into the clouds, then leaps and frisks about with me from cloud to cloud, still affirming that he is bound heavenward; and I, being myself a novice, am slow in perceiving that he does not know the way into the heavens, and is merely bent that I should admire

his skill to rise ... I tumble down again soon into my old nooks, and
lead the life of exaggerations as before, and have lost my faith in the
possibility of any guide who can lead me thither where I would be.
(452)

If one is to become skilled in 'the science of the real', it would clearly
be better to be a self-made winged man than to trust in another's
transcendently vehicular powers, and it is significant that the two
figures who most resolutely refuse to be duped by Melville's confidence man are Mark Winsome and Egbert, based respectively on
Emerson and Thoreau.

The coldness of such self-reliance, to draw on another Emersonian
watchword, may not be compatible with the social contracts that
make up a body politic. Since the time of Alexis de Tocqueville, the
perception that America is a field without a horizon, its democracy a
ceaseless rushing towards modes of self-transformation, leads to a
sense of the inevitability of recoil into a bounded individual security,
so that, where social trust has vanished, one can at least trust in one's
self. Lawrence's skit on the inflationary rhetoric of the American
Renaissance catches accurately the ways in which a Coleridgean
note of cosmic self-celebration is amplified by Whitman into a national anthem, but misses the stung recoil of disillusion, explored by
Melville in his last full-length novel. Alienation of the citizen from
government, the rejection of representation, goes back to the crisis of
authority that Tocqeville foresaw in the undirected sprawl of American democracy, and shows its anger in senseless acts such as the
Oklahoma bombing, itself allegedly a reaction to the siege at Waco
earlier in the 1990s, when armed government agents clashed with the
eccentrically 'Christian' survivalists of a Texan commune in a characteristically American substitution of fire-power for authority collect-
ively agreed. It is at least arguable that the tripartite structure of
government in America is in hebdomedary reality a contest as much
as a system of regulated checks and balances, a tug of war prolonged by
vested interests and self-interest. Likewise it is at least arguable that the
pillorying of President Clinton for lying about his sexual dalliances, an
over-reaction to many European observers, is not so to Americans, for
whom the moment of retreat from a duping by the confidence man into
an aggrieved and accusatory self-reliance (even at the cost of leading a
'life of exaggerations') is now a reflex action. The recoil, not only from
the representative men but from the unwanted burden of being thought
representative one's self, is bred in the bone even in this nation where to
burn the flag is to break the law and where all schoolchildren begin the
day with the pledge of allegiance.

Thus far, reference has been made to the confidence man in the singular, as if ideas of character prevalent in the novel of Melville's day but represented only rarely in his own fiction had now been allegorized and amalgamated into a representative con man. However, uncertainty hangs over the nature and number of confidence men at work in the novel, from the moment when one who is 'in the extremest sense of the word, a stranger' steps aboard the Mississippi steamer bound for New Orleans (841). On making his way to the lower deck, he notices a placard 'offering a reward for the capture of a mysterious impostor, supposed to have recently arrived from the East; quite an original genius in his vocation, as would appear, though wherein his originality consisted was not clearly given' (841). A crowd gathers around the poster, as if it had been 'a theatre-bill', their appetite for performance implying a susceptibility to deception, though whether the 'man in cream-colors', so Christ- or sheep-like in his 'downy', 'flaxen', 'white' and 'fleecy' mildness is the figure on the poster, or whether that individual is a New York novelist soon to turn customs officer, or someone else entirely, will not be resolved. For one thing it is the first of April. Moreover, a sign at the barber's reads 'NO TRUST' (844). The reader, like the passengers, had best be on his or her guard. Later the novel will contain episodes when more than one con artist is present, or indeed two attempt to fleece each other, as in the central dialogue between Francis Goodman (a likely story) and Charlie Noble (naval slang for a galley funnel). Arguably the man in cream colours, 'quite an original', has viral powers of self-multiplication appropriate to a parasite, but, as Tanner and Lindberg observe, that begs the question of what it is to be a self-made man let loose amid the fluidities of booster culture.

Other oddities abound. The captain of the vessel never appears, and the *Fidèle* never reaches New Orleans. Its final port of call is Cairo, on whose 'villainous bank ... the old-established firm of Fever & Ague is still settling up its unfinished business' (978). At the Illinois junction of the Mississippi and the Ohio, Cairo features also in Mark Twain's *The Adventures of Huckleberry Finn*. North of Cairo lay the 'free' states; to the south, the slave states of Kentucky and Missouri, Arkansas and Tennessee, lay on both sides of the river. *The Confidence-Man* breaks with the novelistic consensus of its day, not least in its overtly fictive play with language, privileged over character and narrative climax. Of course a novel concerned with confidence, trust and judgements about the character and motives of new acquaintances was bound to show a certain degree of linguistic self-awareness, but the *Fidèle* is depicted in terms of the 'pigeon-holes ... and secret drawers in an escritoire', and the level of artifice verges on the Rousselian (847). Yet, even at its most 'wordy', the novel never abandons real issues of citizenship and political representation, containing some of Melville's most powerfully anti-racist writing, as in the pigeon-holing of one who says punningly of himself that 'dis poor ole darkie is werry well wordy of all you kind ge'emmen's kind confidence' (853), cutting to the heart of the book's concern with confidence and the worth of words. A 'half-frozen black sheep nudging itself a cozy berth in the heart of the white flock', the man may of course by his black fleece so neatly reverse the cream colours of the mild Manco Capac as to seem his partner in deceit, or to be his own self-made go-getter. But in this society whose bonds are less powerful than the next man's breath on one's neck, everyone is still in the same boat, and singing out the allegation of his own superior needs, lest supper be withdrawn.

It is therefore horribly appropriate that the one who first casts doubt on the black beggar's lameness as 'got up for financial purposes' should himself be 'one who himself on a wooden leg went halt' (851). This follows a section in which the performative nature of identity under capitalism, a commonplace of twentieth-century critique, is antici-pated by one of the most savagely sympathetic passages in Melville:

> Suddenly the negro more than revived their first interest by an expedi-ent which, whether by chance or design, was a singular temptation at once to *diversion* and charity, though, even more than his crippled limbs, it put him on a canine footing. In short, as in appearance he seemed a dog, so now, in a merry way, like a dog he began to be treated. Still shuffling among the crowd, now and then he would pause, throw-ing back his head and opening his mouth like an elephant for tossed apples at a menagerie; when, making a space before him, people would have a bout at a sort of pitch-penny game, the cripple's mouth being at once target and purse, and he hailing each expertly-caught copper with a cracked bravura from his tambourine. To be the subject of alms-giving is trying, and to feel in duty bound to appear cheerfully grateful under the trial, must still be more so; but whatever his secret emotions, he swallowed them, while still keeping each copper this side the oesophagus. And nearly always he grinned, and only once or twice did he wince, which was when certain coins, tossed by more playful almoners, came inconveniently nigh to his teeth, an accident whose unwelcomeness was not unedged by the circumstance that the pennies thus thrown proved buttons. (850)

As a utilization of irony and literary rhetoric for the purposes of sympathy, this passage is the equal of Blake and Dickens at their most coruscating. Just so, those who are treated like dogs – in 'a merry way', of course – will begin to exhibit a certain canine merriment themselves, just as humans herded into sealed trains could no doubt be read as exhibiting a herd mentality. In one sense of its time, the passage emphasizes the reification of the human individual, whose mouth 'is at once target and purse', anticipating the genocidal projects that would give the next century its questionable shape. Just so, the elimination of great numbers of people with a shared ethnic origin by a shared means – for example, in a gas chamber – would indeed lead them to a notably similar end, that quality of sameness recommending itself to those doing the killing as further, confirmatory evidence of a second-rate, identikit humanity in those no longer able to complain at the course of events. As with Blake, the quality of sympathy underpinning irony is the stronger for its powers of analysis and for a particularly sharp sense of the power of internalized ideology. 'As for their fingers', Melville notes of the crowd eyeing the poster promising a reward, 'they were enveloped in some myth' (841). Melville had written in defence of Emerson and influence that 'No one is his own sire', and personal and social analogues for that literary statement are not absent from his work. The self-made man of the nineteenth century, freed in practice from the social contracts that ensure, however clumsily, that mouths and purses will not be confused, would have no such commitment to integration.

There is insufficient space here to delve further into the secret compartments of this unparalleled and in some respects unequalled novel. A critical paraphrase that even hoped to do justice to the twists and turns of the last two chapters, where all the lights truly go out, would have to quote them in full. At the risk of reductiveness, the bare bones of action and theme in the final chapter of *The Confidence-Man: His Masquerade* might run as follows. The Cosmopolitan makes his way down to the cabins, ostensibly to ascertain whether certain sceptical words quoted by Cream the barber are truly to be found in the Bible, a copy of which, as with today's motel Gideon, is sure to be there, 'a present from a society' (1100). Melville makes the darkness of the state rooms quite literally microcosmic, lit only fitfully by such 'lamps, barren planets' as have not yet been extinguished by those 'who wanted to sleep, not see' – that is, almost everybody in the book. In the middle of the gentlemen's cabin burns an appropriately 'solar' lamp, but it is patterned – perhaps in a merry way, perhaps not – with 'the image of a horned altar, from which flames rose, alternate with the figure of a robed man'. Keeping his lone vigil beneath the lamp sits a snowy old fellow with the 'hale look of greenness in winter', perhaps – to jump the gun – the greenness of one who is about to be fleeced, corrupted or even murdered, in a narrative whose mordant ironies place it somewhere between *King Lear* and *The Naked Lunch* (1099). The Cosmopolitan makes eye contact with the old man until good manners compel him to yield up the Good Book. 'Believe not his many words – an enemy speaketh sweetly with his lips' (1101). Locating these warnings against excessive confidence, the Cosmopolitan professes amazement, and craves illumination; what follows is a key passage:

> 'Ah!' cried the old man, brightening up, 'now I know. Look,' turning the leaves forward and back, till all the Old Testament lay flat on one side, and all the New Testament flat on the other, while in his fingers he supported vertically the portion between, 'look, sir, all this to the right is certain truth, but all I hold in my hand here is apocrypha.'
>
> 'Apocrypha?'
>
> 'Yes; and there's the word in black and white,' pointing to it. 'And what says the word? It says as much as "not warranted;" for what do college men say of anything of that sort? They say it is apocryphal. The word itself, I've heard from the pulpit, implies something of uncertain credit...'
>
> 'What's that about the Apocalypse?' here, a third time, came from the berth. (1102)

The Cosmopolitan protests disingenuously at a passage so calculated to destroy trust, and questions the divisions of the sacred text: 'Fact is, when all is bound up together, it's sometimes confusing. The uncanonical part should be bound distinct' (1102). And yet, if apocryphal text debated at night in smoky darkness would seem to be the Cosmopolitan's natural hunting-ground, Melville's commitment is also to the apocryphal, to a fertile indeterminacy of meaning, not a metaposition that would transcend dialectically the mirroring testaments of sacrifice, but the corrosion that is also luxuriance and wonderful contradiction, the 'anomalousness of America' depicted in *Pierre*. There are no stable meanings in texts, no immutable truths in life, and to seek them is to try to pin the air with a harpoon and risk the un-American death, that of the *idée fixe*. Melville's diagnoses of the failures of trust and the related dangers to democracy run alongside another aspect of his thinking as a democrat, his final commitment to something like the words on Frank O'Hara's tombstone; grace to be born, and live as variously as possible: a commitment to the 'masquerade' and being as a house of fiction.

At this point there enters a boy whose multicoloured fragments of clothing swirled 'like the painted flames in the robes of a victim in *auto-da-fe*' (1103). His steady, comic corrosion of the old man's trust results in the latter's buying from him a traveller's patent lock and a money-belt. He throws in a Counterfeit Detector (the very phrase is ambiguous), thereby generating an anxiety on the old man's part as to the bankable nature of his paper currency that marks his final undoing. Poring over his bills in search of the microscopic 'figure of a goose', it is the old man who is truly reduced to that condition, just as the attempt to read a banknote (or a novel) in search of fixed meaning is to go on a wild goose chase. In the book's penultimate insult to the old man, he scrabbles for a 'Life-preserver', which turns out to be a 'brown stool with a curved tin compartment underneath' (1111), which chamber-pot has, alas, been used. In a crude joke that brings us full circle to the ruderies of *Typee*, Melville has the Cosmopolitan commend the pre-server: 'any of these stools here will float you, sir, should the boat hit a snag, and go down in the dark' (1111). And that is truly where we are. With the smell of excreta lingering in the air, the novel concludes:

> The next moment, the waning light expired, and with it the waning flames of the horned altar, and the waning halo round the old man's brow; while in the darkness which ensued, the cosmopolitan kindly led the old man away. Something further may follow from this Masquer-ade. (1112)

For F. O. Matthiessen, the novel was an 'angrily frustrated satire' that breaks off 'unfinished' (373), 'a distended fragment' (412). A Black Mountain pupil of Olson's, Edward Dorn, revived the man in cream colours for an extended appearance in the guise of the crazed million-aire Howard Hughes in his epic poem *Gunslinger* (1975), which also makes use of the book's action through punning philosophical dia-logue. J. H. Prynne, an English poet who in different ways collabor-ated with both Dorn and Olson, quotes the final paragraph of *The Confidence-Man* as the epigraph to a rhapsodic lyrical sequence of poems, *Into the Day* (1972), whose crystalline complexities suggest new directions for what 'may follow' from the masquerade. The ending is readable as the final snuffing-out of meaning in a hall of mirrors, now closing for the season. By whatever instincts, I cannot read it as other than the prelude to a different kind of snuffing-out. 'What's that about the Apocalypse?'

# Melville's performance

This study stresses performance as intrinsic to American life. The causes of this are multiple, and certainly include the freedom and importance of the entrepreneur in a social space set wilfully at a remove from the vertical strata of European society. In a new country of immigrants where American English is everyone's second language, communication and exchange become theatre, a space into which actors step in their new New World role, the abandoned hinterland of the past and distant origins a second-order reality. We have seen how Melville critiques, and is wary of, Emersonian and other forms of rhetorically powered mystique that might prove to be a confidence trick, yet his own word-spinning, shifting its hues from text to text, is as self-aware and rootless a performance as anything in the literature. Moreover, Melville, while incarnating an America whose readership tired of him after early success, wrote out of a circum-Atlantic awareness, addressing, even as he claimed independence from, the wider Anglophone community. All these slippery and contradictory qualities can be seen to operate in microcosm on 9 August 1850.

A picnic, planned for Friday the ninth, was put off due to the weather, and Melville found himself unexpectedly with a working day in which he produced twenty pages or so on Hawthorne's *Mosses from an Old Manse*, with great enthusiasm and without, it may be said, having read that new book in its entirety before setting pen to paper. What catches Melville's eye is the duplicity and darkness, not generally perceived, at work behind Hawthorne's 'Indian summer sunlight' (1158). Whether this 'mystical blackness' be a foil to the 'ever-moving dawn' of the unfolding tale or something more 'Puritanic' or 'Calvinistic' (1159), Melville declares himself unable to tell, though by now his resentments regarding the critical failure of *Mardi* and his hopes for a national, as well as his own, literature are beginning to combine self-portraiture with criticism of Hawthorne. Suddenly, this quick review of one of Hawthorne's less important productions is also about Shakespeare, and the problem facing an American writer aiming to equal his achievements in tragedy without recourse to the glamour of the past, its rhetoric and heroes. 'Believe me, my friends, that Shakespeares are this day being born on the banks of the Ohio. And the day will come, when you shall say who reads a book by an Englishman who is a modern?' (1161). Here Melville's provocation reverses Sydney Smith's notorious put-down in the *Edinburgh Review* of 1820, remembered since childhood: 'In the four quarters of the globe, who reads an American book?' Reaching to the new developments of the Leyden jar and electricity, Melville writes of the 'shock of recognition' not only that he feels on reading Hawthorne, but that America must feel from the literary consequences and potential of its independence.

The essay three-quarters written, Melville did a strange thing. In what his biographer Hershel Parker (who sees deflected sexuality everywhere) regards as 'an extraordinary display of deflected sexuality', Melville abducted another man's bride.[8] He stole Mary Russell Butler (née Marshall) from her wedding car and set her in his buggy, which the groom (whom Melville had met once) and Evert Duyckinck duly pursued. The escapade was terminated when Melville and Duyckinck demanded the bride and groom's attendance at a friend's masquerade party that night as their terms of release. Unamused, they declined. Keeping up infidel and predatory appearances, Melville appeared at the party dressed as a Turk, turbanned, kitted out with a scimitar, and serving cherry cobblers.[9]

While Parker may or may not be right in assuming that sexual tensions generated by writing the manifesto for an American literature caused Melville to behave badly, there is no doubting that an anxious groom feared for his wife and she for herself in the company of the author of *Typee*, who, in contrast to his later phases of reclusiveness, was a young and aggressively romantic figure, a writer associated with the theme of sexual conquest. It might be suggested without irony, exaggeration or any certainty at all that Melville was intent on re-enacting the abduction of Helen that began the Trojan War and would become a founding moment in the myth-making and symbolic repertoire of Western literature. His action was symbolic, vacuous, misogynistic, impenetrable, childlike, unguessable finally in the depths or shallows of its irony and/or its clumsiness – in short, its performative nature. In a final and definitively American twist to this history of strange performances, the writer's great-great-great-grandson and the most currently esteemed rock performer, the appropriately named Moby, has become the first recording artist to have every track of his latest compact disc (*Play*, 1999) used as background music for a television commercial. Who now buys a CD by an Englishman that is a modern?

# 4

## *'Eden is burning'*
### Literature of the Popular Imagination

### Nineteenth- and twentieth-century affinities

A distinction between high and low forms of art lives on, both in the top-down hierarchies of the Western canon promoted by Ivy League critics such as Harold Bloom and from the bottom-up tradition of cultural criticism intent on situating literature, song and other practices as indices of social deprivation. In the next two chapters it will be argued that either form of division misrepresents the nature and achievements of American popular culture in its liveliest manifestations, from the protest novel to horror and science fiction, cinema and popular song. I begin with George Lippard's novel *The Quaker City* (1845), the most popular novel by an American prior to the appearance of Harriet Beecher Stowe's *Uncle Tom's Cabin* (1852), which book, Lincoln told its author only partly in jest, had caused the Civil War. The effects of war on literature are charted in this chapter. Chapter 5 deals with the literary aspects of the music that emerged from the racial group whose oppression was to continue after what Stowe termed 'our peculiar institution' of slavery had technically been abolished following the victory of the Union.

The commercialization by white musicians of black innovations was, and continues to be, an obvious feature of American tradition that itself constitutes a part of, rather than a liberation from, the oppression of African-Americans. However, an examination of the history of popular music uncovers a complex dialogue through music between various ethnic and regional groups, a reciprocal process of dissemination, sharing and theft that runs from the nineteenth century, through the evolution of recording and the early rags and blues, through to the latter-day folk revival, figures such as Bob Dylan and the commercial ascendancy of rock.

A landmark source for study here is Harry Smith's *Anthology of American Folk Music* (1952, 1997), which throws into question both auteurist and collective models of cultural expression, upsetting thereby the modes of criticism that have battled for ownership of 'American literature'. The place of the *Anthology* at the midpoint of this study is no accident. What has been called Smith's 'memory theatre' is as essential to an understanding of the cultural history of American literature as the work of Melville or Dickinson.[1] The murder ballads, gospel epiphanies, medicine showmen and lyrical vortices to which the *Anthology* beckons the listener, form a dark carnival that exemplifies the central argument of this book. The nineteenth century cannot be read in separation from the twentieth, which its most vivid texts anticipate and on which their posthumous life is a gamble. Meanwhile, the twentieth century alludes to and mirrors a past history outside of whose major wounds and concepts it could not be understood.

The trans-historical persistence of Gothic horror as one of the pleasures of the popular is a case in point. The imagination of madness, of murder and haunting is arguably evoked more vividly in the *Anthology* than in the books and films of the books by Stephen King that have made him the world's most popular novelist. King's ultimately comforting stories, whose secret narrative drive is always toward the containment of horror, are indebted to nineteenth-century forebears whose power to shock is perhaps greater; but, before the spectre is raised of a Gothic Eden of True Horror from which contemporary literature is cast out into commercialism, it should be recognized that those texts themselves knowingly echoed Romantic tropes and images, Lippard's underrated novel being an obvious case. Once again, the centuries are an echo chamber; once again, the Edenic America is hoisted like a flag which turns out to have been woven of corrosive stuff. America was always Eden, but always, to echo Bob Dylan's 1975 song 'Changing of the Guard', Eden burning. Its utopias are dystopias, Brook Farm and Walden the dream that literature has to leave to become itself. This is the central chatter of the machine in the visionary satires of Philip K. Dick, where horror and the jeremiad enter the world of accelerating technological achievement to become science fiction. My chosen texts are in an obvious sense wildly various, and it is not my aim to set everything in the memory theatre whirling so giddily that it implodes to congeal in a new metanarrative of superimposition, where Emerson and Stowe stare through Dylan's shades – though there would be a certain carnival truth in such an American imposition. There is more affinity and compatibility across the range of nineteenth- and twentieth-century American literature than across any comparable banding. Nor would a ludic sense of American literature as a dangerous game mean that all grains of truth were forever lost among the shells beneath the bleachers of cultural studies. The performance of identity as intrinsic to American society is its carnival truth, source of both its hollow, showy politics and its greater (and lesser) books, songs and pictures.

## The Gothic inheritance: George Lippard and *The Quaker City*

There is no more appropriate place to begin than George Lippard's hollow, showy and horribly wonderful novel *Quaker City: Or, The Monks of Monk Hall. A Romance of Philadelphia Life, Mystery and Crime.* Lippard was a friend of Edgar Allan Poe, and dedicated his most famous novel to the memory of Charles Brockden Brown, whose 'Wieland' is as a sombre quartet for strings by comparison with Lippard's manic symphony. He was Byronic in appearance, in behaviour, in prolificity and in dying early (at thirty). A lover of cloaks and velvet, with shoulder-length hair, Lippard travelled armed in case of attack from those opposed to his proto-Marxian but essentially anarchistic politics, who dubbed him a 'pothouse brawler' and a 'redhot locofoco' (Reynolds, p. xvi). His transplantation of Byronic dandyism to Philadelphia signals the meeting of American authorship with exhibitionism: Lippard married by moonlight among the rocks, was prevented from throwing himself into Niagara Falls on his wife's death, and saw visions. He also founded a co-operative movement, the Brotherhood of the Union, aimed at bypassing exploitative capitalism and which, although it dwindled into an insurance group, ceased operations only in 1994. Lippard's multi-directional self-fashioning goes back to the ambiguities of Byron's own multiplicity of personae: acting the jaded Regency buck in the *beau monde* of Beau Brummell; playing the redhot locofoco while parodying the accents of his social inferiors, such as Keats; supplying arms to Greek insurrectionists; cultivating a reputation for satanism and incest, debunking, carousing, swimming, dieting, collapsing the distinctions between play and real life. Refracted in Byron's own personality, these ambiguities replay the tensions of Europe in the wake of the French

Revolution, one of whose indirect consequences, as the Marquis de Sade famously observed, was the tale of terror.

The Gothic castle is itself a perfectly ambivalent symbol, which in part explains its longevity as the most enduring aesthetic icon of the last 200 years. The castle unites vividly the smouldering power of the old and the newly interesting condition of fragmentation. Once Bastille and Palace had fallen, the smashed architecture of feudalism and the aristocratic order began through broken windows to emit mysterious and contradictory significations, being charmingly pictur-esque, a focus for nostalgia and conservative resentment, hauntings, but also for new order and the promise of material change. Gothic begins in a dream version of power relations, in which the cannon's roar is silenced and replaced by the cry of nocturnal visitation, which may be sexual or ghostly, may deny or grant power to the past. Thus the garish image of the 'satanic' Byron would segue into the figure of Count Dracula, another aristo who was (to revive Lady Caroline Lamb's verdict on George Gordon) mad, bad and dangerous to know. The past casts its shadow on the present. And yet the buildings lie in ruins; the aristocracy no longer enjoys real privileges, as the levelling Revolution has made us all equal, at least in theory. The late eighteenth-century cult of the fragment, the taste for ruins and the victories of republicanism are contemporary. Each expresses and critiques the other.

The vitality of these ambiguities as a fructifying source for Ameri-can Gothic is increased by the superimposition of the American house of horrors – the House of the Seven Gables, Shirley Jackson's haunted Hill House, Wes Craven's house on the left, Hitchcock's Bates Motel – over the European castle. Europe had to be shrugged off so that America could become itself, yet Eden could only be declared open on foundations of bloody land grabbing, internally directed genocide, slavery and free-floating Calvinist fears of divine retribution, an ex-cellent and shallow burial-ground for forms of guilt whose accusing fingers stir the soil easily, rising to trouble the living. Lippard's Monk Hall therefore superimposes an American nightmare of foetid burial chambers, trapdoors and the midnight debauchery of a secret society on to a European template, both being haunted by a recessive variety of original (and some perfectly unoriginal) sins. Moreover, Lippard participated in the vogue for exposés of city life deriving from Eugène Sue and Americanized by Ned Buntline, George Thompson, and books such as George G. Foster's *New York Naked*, sampled in chapter 2. Consequently it is not surprising to find the few critics interested in Lippard in some disagreement as to whether his novel should be read as castigating, satirizing, or indulging in the episodes of murder, drugging, imprisonment and revenge that drive the hectic narrative of *Quaker City*.

To Leslie Fiedler in *Love and Death in the American Novel*, Lippard's is a fiction of titillation in the guise of class satire, its pornography 'justified as muckraking' (236). But Fiedler's study is itself haunted by American literary descent from European traditions in which, allegedly, 'the subject par excellence of the novel is love', and in particular mature, heterosexual and passionate love. America had failed to provide this literary negotiation, save in the work of the renegade Europhile, James. 'Where then is our *Madame Bovary*, our *Anna Karenina*, our *Pride and Prejudice*, or *Vanity Fair*?' (p. xx). Instead, America has produced books and authors (*Moby-Dick*, *Huckleberry Finn*, *The Last of the Mohicans*, *The Red Badge of Courage*, Poe and Lippard are the examples given) 'that turn from society to nature or nightmare out of a desperate need to avoid the facts of wooing, marriage and child-bearing' (p. xx).

Writing more recently in an essay entitled 'Nationalism, Hypercanonization and *Huckleberry Finn*', Jonathan Arac has recourse to a different vocabulary and cultural perspective, but is still troubled by the centrality of youth and dissidence, so that, for example, 'one of the most provocative features of *Huckleberry Finn* lies in the fact that its very canonical prestige is connected to the sense that it is *counter* cultural' (Pease, *National Identities*, 19). The formation of a national literature in an act of political parricide was responsible for the elevation of the dissident young male to a position of cultural primacy, one which, far from waning in the twentieth century, would reach a new emphasis in literature and music after 1945. As a redhot locofoco and dandy, Lippard was one more wicked son, a position to which his biographer David Reynolds attempts to bring depth and a kind of maturity by reading into *Quaker City* the reforming instincts its author showed in other, extra-literary contexts, but which in reality are hardly there in the text. What Lippard *does* do in the novel is speak to American city experience, an exercise to which Flaubert or Tolstoy are an irrelevance. While the novel is hardly lacking in sensationalism – it has more deflowerings than a lawn-mower – the violence, archness of tone and other features stem from a worldliness that has its own skills and which hardly avoids issues of civic and psychological life, notwithstanding the absence of an Anna Karenina.

While it is not possible to say with confidence who read the book, its unwillingness to toe a moral line clearly struck a chord, if a dissonant one: 60,000 copies were sold in the first year, and a further 10,000 a year over the next decade, to which American sales were added those of pirated editions with varying titles in England, Germany and elsewhere.[2] The novel has three main plot-lines. First is the seduction by the Byronic rake Gustavus Lorrimer of Mary Arlington, a merchant's daughter, leading to eventual retribution at the hands of her revenger-brother, Byrnewood. Meanwhile, Dora Livingstone, born in poverty but married to wealth, attempts further social climbing through an adulterous liaison with a pseudo-Byron, Algernon Fitz-Cowles, a pretend-aristocrat who dangles royal rank as a reward for getting his wicked way. An ex-lover, Luke Harvey, spills the beans to Dora's previously uxorious spouse, who turns revenger and poisons her in one of the book's pivotal scenes. The latter is typical in its stop-start preference for lingering on morbid detail within a narrative which moves overall at a cracking pace. The third and wildest plot concerns Mabel, illegitimate daughter of the monstrous killer Devil-Bug, and raised by the lecherous clergyman F. A. T. Pyne. The latter drugs and attempts to rape his 'daughter', but is intercepted by Devil-Bug who, minded at first to enact on him the treatment meted out to Marlowe's Edward II, opts instead for torture by tickling. Mabel becomes high priestess of a cult led by the mad magician and pseudo-scientist Ravoni, killed by Devil-Bug, who is himself crushed to death in a semi-suicide that allows him a Pyrrhic triumph as the net closes in.

There are sub-plots involving forgery, the Philadelphia newspaper world, and sundry vignettes and cameos that mingle Dickensian exaggeration with dextrous satire. In its unstoppable brio, relish for violence, amorality and taste for Surrealist effects, it is the begetter of a popular American tradition in which the genres of horror, crime fiction and fashionable satire overlap. Early William Burroughs, *noir* thrillers by John Franklin Bardin, Quentin Tarantino's film *Pulp Fiction* and the novels of Bret Easton Ellis are among the direct and indirect inheritors. As in their work, switchback shocks and brutal juxtapositions are the order of the day, the authorial position a shrug of the shoulders at life's lethal charades, made interesting by the agility with which the narrating voice can jump ahead of the reader in self-awareness and the well-turned, or at least engagingly nasty, phrase. It is important to see that Lippard travesties at an early date forms of 'Victorian melodrama' that would continue to be trotted out for decades, and with a callow humour that is one of the book's saving graces. The rakehell Lorrimer, for example, is a parody as much as a perpetuation of Byronic bad-boy attributes:

> He stood before the crouching girl, a fearful picture of incarnate LUST
> ... His form arose towering and erect, his chest throbbed with sensual

excitement, his hands hung, madly clinched, by his side, while his
curling hair fell wild and disordered over his brows, darkening in a
hideous frown, and his mustachioed lip wore the expression of his fixed
and unalterable purpose. (133)

His utterances subsequent to the deflowering of the hapless Mary are
a parody of *Childe Harold*, Canto III ('I have gathered the fruit, and it
is ashes!' (215)). Later, Fitz-Cowles and a redoubtable Dixie stereo-
type, Major Rappahannock Mulhill, weigh the attractions of a literary soirée at Mrs Tulip St Smith's, their dialogue casting some light on
Lippard's sense of his audience and its reading habits at the time of
Felicia Hemans:

> 'What is to be did?' replied the Major, sticking his hands in his vest
> pockets – 'Cock fightin' or a bear bait, or any thing o' that kind?'
> 'Nothing so refined. You must talk of Byron and Shelley and Mrs.
> Hummins or Hemans –'
> 'Don't know much about Byron, Colonel, but as for poor Shelly –
> Gad! Didn't my next neighbor give him thirty-nine for runnin' off with
> a yellow gal? Shelly was the worst buck nigger on Jones' place!'
> Fitz-Cowles' acquaintance with the literature or the literary cant of
> the day was exceedingly limited, but the remark of the round-faced
> Mulhill was too strong for even his intellectual nerves.
> 'The fellow is a decided jackass!' he muttered, leading the way from
> the parlor – 'I say Mulhill, did you ever read a book in your life?' he
> exclaimed, as he lifted the dead-latch of the front door – 'Did you ever
> read so much as a Magazine?'
> 'Didn't I? Haven't we all them pictur books down south? Steel plates
> in front, depictin' the feelin's of pussies deprived of their ma's, and nice
> love tales full o' grand descriptions of the way young genelmen and
> ladies dies for won another, without so much as leavin' a pocket-
> hank'cher to tell their fate! Read the Migizines? Wot po'try, wot
> sentiment, wot murder, an' madness, an' mush-and-milk, for a greasy
> quarter! Cool me with a julap, by—!' (286)

The sentimental themes and imagery of the popular magazine are to
be subverted and traduced by Lippard's exposure of the real sexual
and criminal life of the city by night, but he will not supplant Victorian kittens and pining lovers by importing realism on Zolaesque lines.
In terms of transatlantic affinities, Lippard's city is a premonition of
German Expressionist cinema, and if 'po'try' and 'sentiment' have
been struck from the bill of fare, 'murder' and 'madness' reheated
from Jacobean as well as Gothic ingredients are definitely on the
menu. The implication is that the exposure of the hypocrisies of the
dominant class comprises an exordium to sensational effects for an

audience whose appetites Lippard understood, and that this is in no sense a novel of reform, whatever the non-literary directions in which Lippard's politics may have led him on other occasions.

'Cool me with a julap ... Kick me to death with crickets!' (286): the Southern Major is mocked for his inability to see that what he takes to be his own natural behaviour and incontrovertible attitudes are acquired, are in reality a *performance* that could be altered. Slavery in this novel is not an issue in itself, but an instance of parochial stupidity in a class unwilling to move with the times. The *Zeitgeist* demands accelerated levels of performance in those intent on success, and causes a raising of the eyebrows at Southern recalcitrance among metropolitan East Coasters more in tune with modernity:

> 'Larkspur, would you like to earn a hundred dollars?'
> 'Jist try me. I'm putty desp'rate now, I tell you. I might accept.'
> 'Could you assume the manners of a Southern planter?'
> 'What d'ye mean? Swear a few big oaths, carry a Bowie knife, and talk about my niggers? I jist could do that, and nothing else.' (214)

Along with the theme of forgery in the novel and Lippard's interest in disguise, such moments, of which there are many, indicate the belief that to exhibit an unselfconscious regional, ethnic or class position is to give yourself away, to be fully understood and hence contained. The lesson of Lippard's Philadelphia is that survival in the city has to be a self-aware performance. The art of life, as Emerson noted, lay in skating over thin ice. Refuse to change, and to perform the changes of selfhood at the going rate, and you are frozen in the icy glare of American capitalism. Again, whatever Lippard's hope for his Brotherhood of Union, his only message as a novelist is to go with the flow. Devil-Bug is undone at last by his sudden access of pity for his illegitimate daughter, his momentary self-betrayal into a world of illustrations depicting forlorn kittens and 'nice love tales'. Elsewhere his catch-phrase 'I vonders how *that'll* vork!', applied to methods of torture and stratagems of all kinds, anchors his identity in a theatricality of knowingness which Lippard barely condemns, for it is his own authorial credo pushed to an extreme of *grand guignol*. As the killer lugs the unconscious Byrnewood down into the pit of Monk Hall for premature burial, his thoughts take a Barnumesque turn:

> 'Ho, ho, ho!' chuckled Devil-Bug, as he stood on the verge of the granite stairway. 'Here's dampness, an' darkness, an' the smell of bones all for nothin'. *Children under ten years half price!* This feller on my shoulder don't move nor struggle. Vonder if he thinks o' the jolly

things we're a goin' to do with him? Buried alive! I do vonders how that
'ill vork!' (306; my emphasis)

Phineas T. Barnum's museum (mentioned in the novel) had opened
three years before, presenting for public delectation a two-headed
calf, a bearded lady, strongmen, dwarves and the array of unfortu-
nates that would in time be portrayed in Tod Browning's film masterpiece *Freaks* (1932). (Indeed, I can just recall these things from the
seaside holidays of my own childhood in the North of England in
the 1950s, by which time the raree show was a thing of the past in the
USA, though instantly revived for literary and cinematic purposes in
the tales of Ray Bradbury or Roger Corman's *X* (1963).) When
Lippard has his Dr McTourniquet describe the two-headed black
child and other trophies of his 'museum' in chapter 6, he is playing
on the taste for the freakish exhibit, though, as his biographer David
Reynolds observes, 'almost every character in the novel is in some
way a freak' (p. xxv), and this larger grotesquerie is a reflection of
Lippard's culture and times.

The pace at which cities such as Philadelphia and New York grew
between 1800 and 1840 resulted in extreme social and personal dislocation, resulting in new forms of mass violence. The period of Jackson's Presidency (1829–37) was one of race and theater riots, church
burnings and the rise of urban gangs: 'riot after riot went howling
through the town', as Lippard notes in the novel (206). The acceler-
ations of social change proceeded at such a rate that a *soi-disant*
realism, with its reliance on sustained modes of representation, and
understanding based on precedent, would have been untrue to experience. If *Quaker City* is a novel of 'sensation', that is, to give the novel its
due, not merely through its author's willingness to supply scenes of
drugging, rape and murder on cynically Barnumesque lines, but because only a novel of sensation could speak accurately to the felt
condition of America's cities. The conclusion of the novel shows an
unexpected subtlety and modernity in this regard by resolving its plot-
lines in a medley of headlines and scandal-sheet reports, all of which
conflict. We are invited, as by many nineteenth-century novels, to learn
what became of the fictional characters in the aftermath of the sundry
dénouements, but cannot do so, for F. A. T. Pyne and Fitz-Cowles are
lauded and excoriated as innocent or guilty in different newspaper
accounts aimed at different markets. Lippard's novel is proto-Marxist
in this regard at least, in showing how the absorption of personal
histories by commercialization renders truth-values obsolete. Once it
gains dominance in society, the profit motive swallows everything,
undercutting the reality of any perception outside its projects.

## The performative nature of American identity

The central plot-line of the novel was based on a real and well-known case of 1843 in which a Philadelphian, Singleton Mercer, killed, but was acquitted of murdering, Mahlon Heberton, who had enticed Mercer's sister into a house of ill repute and allegedly dangled a proposal of marriage as bait to a seduction. Such novelistic triumphs of the popular and sentimental will over the facts of homicide were not rare, and offer further instances of the essentially performative nature of life in the violence of ante-bellum America. Consider the case of Daniel E. Sickles, 'The Congressman Who Got Away with Murder'. On the afternoon of 27 February 1859, a Sunday when many Washingtonians were strolling in Lafayette Square, Sickles, a New York Democrat, looked out of his window and was enraged by the sight of his wife's lover waving a white handkerchief up at her window. Packing two derringers and a revolver, the congressman trailed his prey, US Attorney to the District, Philip Barton Key, to the other side of the park, where, after a protracted and noisy struggle near the White House, Sickles shot his man dead in sight of witnesses. Such behaviour was not unprecedented among Washington polit- icians: duelling had not yet been outlawed, and frequently formed the conclusion to fist fights begun on the floor of Congress. An interloper had pulled a gun on Thomas Benton of Missouri there, a Carolinian pro-slavery representative had thrashed a Massachusetts abolitionist with his cane, and another congressman had recently shot the waiter in a Washington hotel. A year prior to the Key slaying, a Senate committee issued a report noting that 'riot and bloodshed are of a daily occurrence. Innocent and unoffending persons are shot, stabbed and otherwise shamefully maltreated, and not infrequently, the offender is not even arrested.'[3] This of course is still true; while researching this study in Washington, I took my children to the zoo, where a few days later six children were shot. The blind stupidity of America's gun laws (or lack of them) deserves a separate book, though it would be one with a simple message. That said, the ante- bellum tensions in a city such as Washington, defined as well as aggravated by friction between rural, effectively frontier hardship in outlying areas, immigration and urban dislocation, produced a par- ticularly volatile atmosphere. Key, the victim in this case, was the scion of a prominent Maryland family; indeed, his father Francis Scott wrote 'The Star-Spangled Banner'. However, any appeals to outraged patriotism which the defence might have launched as a coda to the evident guilt of the accused were outgunned by Sickles's defence of temporary insanity, the first such to be heard in the American courts. A known killer and a free man, Sickles was shouldered and borne in triumph from the court room. A pamphlet citing biblical precedent and justification for his actions could be purchased outside for a quarter.

The story has a memorable sequel. Sickles forgave his wife, for which he was criticized in the local press. She died young. After, and in part because of, the trial, he held a number of significant posts, including Sheriff of New York County, US Minister to Spain, where he was said to have had an involvement with Queen Isabella II, a second stint in Congress, and for many years chairman of the New York Monuments Commission, from which post he was removed following an embezzlement scandal. The most telling episode, however, comes from his Civil War career, during the course of which he was hit in the leg by a twelve-pound cannon-ball at Gettysburg. Sickles sent his freshly amputated leg to the new Army Medical Museum in Washington with a card reading, 'With the Compliments of Major General DES'. For many years he visited his leg on the anniversary of its amputation. It is still on show in Walter Reed Army Medical Center.

It might fairly be said that, having made an exhibition of himself by the shooting incident, Sickles ended by turning himself into an exhibit. His life was a performance, by which, it should be stressed, I do not mean that he was a fake, but rather, a genuine and in many respects typical incarnation of his times. Nor is his career in its questionable aspects simply a parable of the abuse of power. The lives of the poets in nineteenth-century America were equally replete with dramas of identity changes and radical self-(re)fashioning, of which Sickles's post-bellum ability to manifest himself physically in two places at the same time is exemplary. Henry Clay Work (1832–84), writer of 'My Grandfather's Clock' and other banjo favourites, was a fruit farmer who also invented and patented a rotary engine, a walking doll and a knitting machine. Joaquin Miller (1837–1913) worked as a miner, lived among the Indians, was gaoled for horse theft but escaped, made a profit from the pony express, with which he bought a newspaper, practised law, served as a judge, had success in Britain as a 'frontier poet' in buckskin and spurs, moved into the theatre, became a lecturer, a correspondent for Hearst newspapers in the Klondike, travelled to China to cover the Boxer Rebellion, and planted thousands of trees in Oakland. Such vaudevillian life changes would of course be possible in the twentieth century, the 'American Century', in which the vaunted opportunities for self-transformation and a better standard of living would continue to draw waves of immigrants to Ellis Island. However, the kind of picaresque life narrative sketched in the cases given above was more common in the previous century, and the period preceding the Civil War in particular. Thereafter the pressures of industrialization and commercialization, more socially influential drivers of that conflict than emancipation of the slaves, would enforce kinds of conformity which the flux of pre-Civil War life agitated beyond the reach of control, notwithstanding the hardship of other kinds endured by many citizens.

## Violence, masculinity and popular culture: Dock Boggs

It is worth jumping to the twentieth century to clarify this issue, by looking at the contrasting styles and fortunes of the two musicians represented in the *Anthology of American Folk Music* on whom most critical attention would be lavished, in time: Bascom Lamar Lunsford (1882–1973), whose 'Mole in the Ground' is smoked out later, and Dock Boggs (1898–1971). These men had a Southern background in common – North Carolina and Virginia, respectively – and both sang ballads to a banjo accompaniment. Lunsford's career has something of the nineteenth century at work in its twists and turns: fruit-tree salesman, honey-bee promoter, teacher, practising lawyer, federal worker, reading clerk of the North Carolina House of Representatives. In 1928 he founded the Asheville Mountain Dance and Folk Festival, a version of which is still held, and his work gained increasing recognition. He played for the British king and queen at the White House in 1939, and ten years later laid down an archive of several hundred performances of folk-songs for the Library of Congress. Lunsford was an artist of major importance, range and subtlety; the archive, together with his other recordings, comprises one of the great artistic *oeuvres* of the American Century, albeit one that is insufficiently known. The contrast with Dock Boggs's life and fortunes could hardly be greater.

Boggs worked as a miner for forty-five years, from the time he was twelve. He escaped briefly from the scarred terrain of the Virginian coal camps in the late 1920s, when touring producers from the Brunswick label heard and brought him to New York to record eight blues and ballads, sampled decades later in the *Anthology*. The Depression sank his career just at its inception, and he pawned his banjo around 1930. Boggs was in any case under pressure from the parishioners of his wife's church, who disapproved of music, and who would send him anonymous hate mail when he took up playing again in the 1960s to appreciative college audiences at Newport and other shrines of the Folk Revival. He had an Indian summer, recording for Folkways in his old age. At certain points even mine work was unavailable to him, and Boggs, like many, took to bootlegging, a symptom of strained social fabric in a mountain region so rapidly developed and just as rapidly subjected to market collapse. Boggs's life was profoundly violent. He carried a .38 calibre revolver most of the time, plotted seriously to kill his wife's entire family ('they had a tendency to be overbearing'[4]), and though he had the courage in the end never to kill, went half-way. One brother, two brothers-in-law, several cousins and his teacher died of gunshot wounds. This was life in Virginia in the early twentieth century:

> It was dangerous to get on the highway. People a-shootin' in the road, shooting everyway, carrying guns, everybody carrying revolvers, and they'd shoot to hear 'em pop like you'd shoot firecrackers. I was standing in my own doorway, and a fella down the road, about a hundred and fifty yards, pulled out his pistol and shot, shot right inside of the door. A foot from where I was standing. I emptied my pistol right down where the shot came from. (13)

What caused, he was asked in interview, the temper of those times? 'People were afraid' (35).

That fear is in his voice, not expressed as such, but there in the recoil, the harsh tones of repressed emotion that lead Greil Marcus to describe Dock Boggs's voice as sounding 'as though his bones were coming through his skin every time he opened his mouth' (2). While such encomiums are unlikely to lead to queues at the Folk section of Tower Records, the intensity of the early recordings in particular is unforgettable, the very narrowness of range a telling representation of a society as well as a particular personality. The later recordings show the way that personality might have evolved had the life context been other than it was, and anyone disinclined to take the banjo seriously should listen to Boggs's instrumental 'Coal Creek March', where notes fall like pure spring water on hot skin, and the ethereal beauty of which would have preserved his name even if this otherwise some-what Calvinist entertainer had never opened his mouth to let his bones through.[5]

As with all hard men, musicians included, there is always someone harder around the corner. For those who become inured to the Boggs rasp, there is always the 'high, lonesome sound' of Roscoe Holcomb, truly the Samuel Beckett of country-and-western music. No doubt there lie in some outhouse the mouldering platters of an Appalachian songster whose skeletal austerity makes Roscoe Holcomb sound like Dolly Parton; the point is that, inseparable from the primitivist modernism of these rural musicians, is a deletion or extreme suppression of sung warmth, tenderness or sensual satisfaction. Masculinity was a question of work, drink, discharge in guilty sex or a .38, but otherwise reined in. This is a consequence of the kind of society produced by industrialization, for many a post-slavery enslavement, which is what the Civil War and the succeeding century were about. It is not an ante-bellum manner. Boggs's work – like that of Frank Hutchison, a 1920s player who sings the 'Worried Blues' as if he were outlining varieties of life insurance – or that of most of the white performers represented by the Folkways and Yazoo labels – has few remnants of ante-bellum style. (The *content* of course can be a different matter, drawing on the melancholy fatedness of ballad narratives originating in the Britain of the Napoleonic Wars or even centuries earlier.) These recordings can be contrasted with those of, say, Henry Thomas, the black singer, guitarist and pipe-player. Born in the immediate aftermath of the Civil War, and recording in the 1920s songs he had played and heard in the 1890s, Thomas's music has gaiety, good humour and a certain melodic fluency, though it is built from the same standard chord changes and bending of 'blue' notes, the third, fifth and seventh in the scale, from which Holcomb or Boggs shout the triumph of death and Bascom Lamar Lunsford builds his troubled reflections. The picaresque life was taken by the Civil War, though its masks and motley survived in the side-shows to industrialization that the children of that process would celebrate, just as these things vanished over the horizon into American nostalgia and the eras of the suburbs and the mall.


## Uncle Tom's Cabin


Of course the performative nature of identity in ante-bellum America coexisted with identity erased, in the lives of African-Americans. Harriet Beecher Stowe's *Uncle Tom's Cabin* was the novel that helped bring the bestialization of people of colour in America to public crisis in the prelude to the Civil War. The novel surpassed Lippard's *Quaker City* in popularity, exhausting the first edition of 5,000 within two days of publication on 20 March 1852, and selling 300,000 copies in America and 150,000 in Britain within a year. By the end of that year George Aiken's dramatization was being performed by as many as

four companies simultaneously in New York City, sometimes, so great
was the public interest, in three shows a day. More than a book,
this was, in the words of Frederick Douglass, an attempt to light a
million camp-fires in front of the embattled hosts of slavery, a *roman
à thèse* whose thesis was designed to leak, flow back into and so
redirect the society whose inequalities had brought it into being. In
this sense it is more the national epic than *Moby-Dick* or *The Scarlet
Letter*, texts whose hypercanonicity (to adopt Jonathan Arac's phrase)
rests in part on their permission to imagination as a tenet of American
ipseity. Critically, *Uncle Tom's Cabin* has been neglected or patronized until relatively recently, in the main through Fiedlerian doubts
over its unabashed and repeated use of the sentimental climax, crude
(not that Stowe cared) by contrast with the better European novels,
and so a perilous cause to support in the years when the national
literature was felt to lag behind the Europe that had generated
*Madame Bovary*. However, two points might immediately be made
in defence of the book, registering the use of sentiment by writer or
reader for purposes that in the end are dialectical, and intrinsic to the
success of the work.

The famous scene in which the slave Eliza escapes to freedom,
pursued by bloodhounds across the cracking ice floes of the Ohio
River, became a synecdochic image for the book, reproduced countless times on theatre posters. However, that portion of the tale is
actually short in the telling, a page or so, and does not exhaust by
any means its own sentimental potential. Moreover, it is echoed
subtly at a later point in the novel, when the good-hearted but
compromised Shelby, who has sold Uncle Tom and cannot raise the
money for his 'redemption', muses on the ups and downs of market-
driven capitalism, while smoking his postprandial cigar: 'Once get
business running wrong, there does seem to be no end to it. It's like
jumping from one bog to another, all through a swamp: borrow of
one to pay another ... all scamper and hurry-scurry.'[6] The obvious
dissimilarities between the 'scamper' of fleeing banknotes and a life-
and-death rush across the ice from bondage to safety do not obscure
the underlying parallel, one confirmed by the acidic but resigned
assessment of labour relations under capitalism offered by St Clare
in chapter 19. St Clare is in a dual sense the centre of the book;
appearing only in its middle section, his jaundiced liberalism, acced-
ing to a *status quo* which he is morally and intellectually equipped to
destroy, but to which he sees no practicable alternative, incarnates
precisely the attitudes Stowe saw as winnable to the abolitionist cause
by argument and ethical appeal. 'Born a democrat', St Clare notes the
consistency in his brother Alfred's defence of slavery:

Alfred, who is as determined a despot as ever walked ... stands high
and haughty, on that good old respectable ground, *the right of the
strongest*; and he says, and I think quite sensibly, that the American
planter is 'only doing, in another form, what the English aristocracy
and capitalists are doing by the lower classes;' that is, I take it, *appro-
priating* them, body and bone, soul and spirit, to their use and convenience. He defends both, – and, I think, at least, *consistently*. (237)

At such points it is clear that Stowe's intuitions, if not her demands,
went far beyond even the partial emancipation bought at such cost
by war. Once the least *vericulum* is unpicked, all of Alfred's consistency and all capitalist 'use and convenience' begins to unravel in
the face of unanswerable accusations of imposed social control.
(Note, for example, the coupling of the Southern planter with
the English capitalist, rather than the American capitalist of the
'free' Northern States.) St Clare is the archetypal guilty liberal
whose *mea culpa* makes him first to admit, and last to act on, his
perceptions of an inequality that keeps order in his house and on the
street:

> 'In short, you see,' said he, suddenly resuming his gay tone, 'all I want is
> that different things be kept in different boxes. The whole framework
> of society, both in Europe and America, is made up of various things
> which will not stand the scrutiny of any very ideal standard of moral-
> ity.' (191)

The danger in Stowe's eyes, though she says it nowhere and implies it
everywhere, is that the necessary smashing of one of the boxes will
result in the collapse of the 'frame-work' into an anarchy, or, to use a
term anachronistic to the period, a Balkanization of America. Much is
made of the different weather, architecture and opinions that identify
regions and sects, from Miss Ophelia's stern but ultimately swayable
New England severity to the gorgeousness of fountains and court-
yards in New Orleans, the kindness of Quakers to Eliza and the
Gothic sadism of Simon Legree's crumbling plantation, where Uncle
Tom meekly accepts his violent end. All this, she argues, is already so
disparate that the slavery issue risks splitting the nation irrevocably.
Set against her pulling at the heart-strings must be a registration of
the remorseless rigour with which Stowe pulls to pieces all arguments
for any but the abolitionist position, a rigour which, turning an
analytical screw on issues that are intended immediately to flow out
of the book and into debate and political action, contributes to the
alternation of centrifugal and centripetal rhetorics that forms Stowe's
essential strategy.

There is little point in bringing the values of Flaubert or the English novel tradition into the discussion. If Uncle Tom is a wooden character, and he is, that aesthetic judgement has only limited usefulness. It becomes hard to argue that any characterization in the text is weak or that any incident doesn't work, for such points of resistance or discrepancy only become grist to analysis of the kind that the book exists to raise. If Uncle Tom's meek, Christian turning of the other cheek even under mortal provocation grates, that is more a prompt to questioning the efficacy of personal morals next to political organization than an aesthetic flaw. Likewise, the deathbed scene of little Eva is apt to provoke variants of Oscar Wilde's reaction to the death of *The Old Curiosity Shop*'s Little Nell, on which waif she is indeed based, but the mawkish may actually be fertile ground if seen in the light of the novel's intentions. (A book such as *Uncle Tom's Cabin* makes nonsense of New Critical dismissal of authorial intention – and was consequently ignored by that generation of critics.) When little Eva's end becomes nigh, Tom, Mammy and other, generally Methodist, slaves and domestics gather weeping to hear her bid farewell:

> 'You must be Christians. You must remember that each one of you can become angels, and be angels forever … If you want to be Christians, Jesus will help you. You must pray to Him; you must read – '
> The child checked herself, looked piteously at them, and said, sorrowfully, 'O, dear! you *can't* read, – poor souls!' and she hid her face in the pillow and sobbed. (296–7)

The conscious intentions of the author are not quite guessable here, the Pandora's box of dialectical irony having been opened so widely that this is now text, and its alternative political futures, talking. The emphasis throughout on Christianity and heaven issues, quite reasonably, from the author's own wholly unironic faith – another black mark for New Critics, and indeed the majority of their successors. However, the functions served textually by the afterlife are various, and it provides a vocabulary for the one conjectured realm beyond the temporal where contradictions almost insupportable to bear will at last be reconciled. In this sense Heaven is the final symbol to which no allegory is indigestible; on everyone's and no one's side. St Clare is a drawing-room Shelley with his wings clipped, firmly placed at the end as a mother's boy in a deathbed vision that is his author's sly revenge, though a tremendous tear-jerker: 'Just before the spirit parted, he opened his eyes, with a sudden light, as of joy and recognition, and said "*Mother!*" and then he was gone!' (326). Nor does Stowe have much time for the senator who 'looked after his little wife with a whimsical mixture of amusement and vexation, and seating himself in the arm-chair, began to read the papers' (86). Once the least *vericulum* is unpicked, the horizon of equality becomes limitless yet draws nearer. Perhaps her lack of interest in the dissident young male removed a potential stumbling-block in her creation of a national epic. Stowe's politics are not ultimately those of inclusion and integration. The particular 'docility' of the African is frequently remarked on and exalted in preference to the more sophisticated traits of 'higher and more skilful culture', a residual albeit diminished expression of racism. The aspirations of George, an educated black, are turned by Stowe towards Liberia, in preference to the allegedly 'worn-out, effeminate' context of 'Hayti' (440), a form of international Darwinism whereby the stronger of the liberated slaves might raise some far-off laboratory of a country that does not threaten America towards corporate self-betterment. Jefferson's ambiguous commitments to freedom were still working themselves out on the eve of the Civil War which he had foreseen as a possibility.

# Literature and the Civil War

War is the point at which the discursive push-and-pull of civic life is pushed into an ancillary or underground role while alternative futures are decided by military strategy, and death. The paucity of literary production at such periods of social catastrophe ought not to surprise. The books that war generates are few, and are rarely effective other than as markers to a history which finds its real tenure in the intimate or silent sifting of unrecorded, personal experience. The American Civil War remains fundamental to the history of violence in the nation. It let loose millions of individuals, many of whom had never strayed from a defined locale of home, into an enforced exploration of their country, putting a gun in their hand as it did so. It is the true source of American gun culture.

It is estimated that there are 250 million guns in private hands in the USA today. A further 5 million are purchased annually, mostly by white males in their twenties and thirties. As a result, more than 16,000 citizens are shot dead each year, a quarter of them children. Those like the National Rifle Association who oppose laws aimed at restricting this carnage argue that the right of the citizen to bear arms, enshrined in an amendment to the Constitution in 1791, was crucial to the success of the Revolutionary phase, and remains intrinsic to American identity. Yet the NRA was founded in 1871 by two former Civil War generals in hopes of improving the marksmanship of the average American. Many of their soldiers had reported for duty in the Civil War without ever having owned, let alone fired, a rifle. New research by Michael A. Bellesiles indicates that less than 15 per cent of households in New England and Pennsylvania owned firearms in the period 1765–1790, the period mythologized as the smithy of gun-carrying heroism.[7] Over half these weapons were listed as broken or defective in contemporary records. Individual ownership of a working firearm had no causative link to independence, and in fact became possible only after Samuel Colt had begun to improve the efficacy of the pistol in the 1830s. It was the Civil War of 1861–5 that put guns in the hands of the citizens, linking the assertion of rights and the right to fire.

To examine maps of territory taken, lost and often retaken several times during the Civil War is to see no simple picture of conflict between North and South, but a honeycomb of fluctuating gains and losses whose outcome lay in the balance for the greater duration of hostilities. That brother, famously, was set against brother is not only a large metaphor for civil war, but an index of the miniature and familial realities that this war of contesting concepts set in motion. The war defined the American as a man carrying a gun. Like all wars, it never ended, but was carried on by other means. NRA culture is rooted, unconsciously, in the indelible anxiety generated by the knowledge that the neighbour, the brother, the fellow-citizen had been, and therefore must at some level still be, the enemy. Made possible through industrial manufacture by the likes of Samuel Colt, this culture will presumably only be eroded, if at all, by litigation and other forms of profit strangulation brought to bear on the manufacturers (cf. the cigarette). The culture of enmity, meanwhile, was an immediate consequence of the cessation of hostilities. Lincoln's speeches show it.

The President encountered a myriad problems in setting up a government of reconstruction in occupied Louisiana alone, and, prior to his own demise at the hands of a man carrying a gun, worried in his last public address that civil war, as distinct from the repulsion of a foreign invader, left him with a situation of enmity but no identifiable enemy with whom to negotiate. In contrast to the grave and tolling simplicity of his Gettysburg Address, when the outcome of the war was far from certain, his speech on 11 April 1865 from a window of the White House is evasive, politically slippery, almost of a deconstructionist humour:

> We all agree that the seceded States, so called, are out of their proper practical relation with the Union; and that the sole object of the

government, civil and military, in regard to those States is to again get
them into that proper practical relation. I believe it is not only possible,
but in fact, easier to do this, without deciding, or even considering,
whether these States have ever been out of the Union, than with it.
Finding themselves safely at home, it would be utterly immaterial
whether they had ever been abroad. Let us all join in doing the acts
necessary to restoring the proper practical relations between these
States and the Union; and each forever after, innocently indulge his
own opinion whether, in doing the acts, he brought the States from
without, into the Union, or only gave them proper assistance, they
never having been out of it.[8]

These airy formulations have the sound of a man trying to do his best
in tortuous circumstances. Nevertheless, this is also the voice of an
industrial machine accelerated and strengthened by war quietly
making certain things plain. As a political and economic hegemony
had settled which of the alternative futures would now be imple-
mented, so it had to be accepted which of the alternative pasts had
not, now, ever taken place. The South was to be forgiven and em-
braced on one condition, voluntary amnesia, and the aftermath of
resentment generated by this insistence that the Rebels had fought for
a pseudo-nation would not be brought to reconciliation by such
simple truths as, for example, that the right side had won, that slavery
is illegitimate, and that Southerners had only themselves to blame.

Equally, it would be wrong to read into the conceptualizations of
Lincoln's final speech a reflectively intellectual mood catalysed by the
signing of documents in the Appomattox Court House. The war had
been *ab ovo* a struggle between warring concepts. This was well
understood by writers such as Walt Whitman, who, like Lincoln,
saw the war as a test of the Union rather than a struggle defined by
the issue of slavery.


## Whitman's war poetry


What Whitman liked to call the 'Four Years War' assumed, right from
the firing on Fort Sumter, the qualities of a sacred rite of purification,
and the poet resolved at once to avoid late meals and fat and to drink
only water. This sacral identification of self, country and purification
persisted until, and including, the 'fierce deed' of Lincoln's assassination, which Whitman viewed as the crucifixion of democracy.
Henceforth it would be the Civil War and not the Revolutionary
period in which his sense of America's 'parturition and delivery'

would be located, the Union victory a sign that the nation was 'born again, consistent with itself'.[9] Concepts derived from Christianity and its romanticization in Coleridgean organicism are at work here, realized but also put into question by the paradox of democracy renewed through gun-fire. These issues and anxieties were not, to my eyes at least, resolved successfully in the collection of poems *Drum-Taps* (1865), gathered eventually into the fold of *Leaves of Grass*. (Betsy Erkkila's *Whitman the Political Poet* (1989) offers a contrary view.) These may be, as has been claimed, the best war poems by an American, but that does not in itself say much, and their relative thinness next to the great earlier work is as much to do with the impossible pressures of the subject as with the drain on Whitman's energies incurred by his selfless work in the wards at that time. 'Vigil Strange I Kept on the Field One Night' can be made interesting by importing a modern sense of the poet's homosexuality, 'Come Up from the Fields Father' by changes in literary sensibility *vis-à-vis* sentiment and irony, 'Bivouac on a Mountain Side' (and other poems) by certain presentational affinities with the new technology of photography.

## Cannon-Fire and the canon

In this relative weakness the texts are typical of war literature. Hemingway's *A Farewell to Arms* (1929) is effective in its earlier sections, but quite rapidly becomes a love story so haunted by unconfessed guilts, in Fiedler's apt phrase, that it can only end badly. Literary realism, as so often, fails to convey a convincing engagement with experience as well as more hallucinatory or otherwise disjunctive forms, the catch being that to utilize those forms is to risk reviving the whole machinery of the Gothic genre, which will then dictate the direction that texts take. This is at least arguably what defines the limits, as well as the successes, of Stephen Crane's *The Red Badge of Courage* (1895), the most widely read novel about the Civil War, though one written by a non-combatant. The book's blood-red skies and admonishing corpses, its episodes of panic and disorientation, are ultimately the generic pointers to a young man's *rite de passage* from innocence to experience, terminated at a point where that experience threatens to introduce a complexity that would make it a different kind of text. This is not an American failing, *per se*. The overrated poems of Wilfred Owen and other poets of the First World War are likewise limited, and find their real cultural usefulness at those points in the school English syllabus where it is deemed appropriate to have young readers discover that texts can carry a moral, while telling a story. In much the same way, neat performances such as George Orwell's *Animal Farm* are wheeled out to demonstrate the potential of political allegory, while D. H. Lawrence's 'Snake' and the earlier poems of Ted Hughes offer assimilable parables that test the fluency of schoolchildren or bring succour to university students for whom all else has failed. None of these texts is seriously interesting. Their classic status, their usefulness to the culture, lies in their setting up puzzles that can be solved in simple ways, using approaches that can then be graded for educational purposes. In fact, the *literary* qualities of the text are exactly what have to be broken down and destroyed in order for the task to be completed successfully.

In order to perpetuate itself, the system must adapt and find ways to prize most what could defeat the system. Throughout the second half of the twentieth century students learned to excel by investigating texts such as *Hamlet, The Ambassadors* or *Heart of Darkness* whose value lay precisely in their evasion of any conclusive allegorization. To pull back layer after layer of Conrad's adjectival prose in search of a clearing of narrative certainty was to go on a fool's errand, for at the centre of it all was a shifting hollow, Kurtz, a creature of rhetoric in any case available to the reader only through the hectic pseudo-confessions of a famously unreliable narrator. Relocated in the war-torn Vietnam and Cambodia of the Lyndon Johnson years, *Heart of Darkness* would become *Apocalypse Now* (1977, directed by Francis Ford Coppola) and be made to serve very different purposes.

## *Apocalypse Now* and the Vietnam War

America's myths of itself are fraught with blatant contradictions. American individualism is typical, frontier self-sufficiency a collective trait, and the figure of the dissident young male may stand for a whole culture. Coppola's film uses Conrad's saturnine exposure of the rhetoric and the reality of European colonial behaviour for the reinforcement of all these American self-imagings. We have seen how Puritan sermons worked assiduously and with an instinctive rapidity to conflate categories which, if considered separately, might tend toward civil unrest or a loss of faith in the collective errand. Just so, *Apocalypse Now* is a 1970s sermon seeking such a conflation in its retrospective reading of America's failure to learn from the experience of the French at the time of the Pathet Lao and SEATO, and its ensuing and disastrous interference in the Vietnamese civil war. Superficially the film holds to an anti-war perspective by showing incidents in which youthful panic among soldiers leads to the loss of innocent civilian life, American militarism echoes Nazism, and where drugs and drink blur the bounds of sanity and inhibition so as to undermine sentimental and right-wing stereotypes of honourable conduct and grace under fire. At a more fundamental level the film makes its decisive intervention in an understanding of the war by conflating the sensibilities that had been thought most antagonistic at the time of the draft: the patriotic soldier and the anti-war, hippy protester. The fire-storm of psychotropic drug use and the hallucinatory nature of war merge so as to reunite America's dissident and warrior types in one troubled figure. Made vulnerable, that figure, and therefore his country, can be forgiven in the muddle of a double exposure, for the literate alienation of the first – the Marlow character's poetic monologues, the copies of T. S. Eliot and J. G. Frazer on Kurtz's table – restore profundity to the losing chess moves of the war machine. Once again America has to be written, dramatized, filmed, in order to be.

Coppola's film is a hymn to masculine values of risk taking and self-testing, its vivid evocation of consciousness on the edge a genuine, if politically questionable, echo of Marlow's psychic dislocation on the journey to the heart of darkness. In order to be credible, Coppola's conflation had to be lived. The making of the film was itself conducted like a military campaign under a general gone mentally AWOL; the star Martin Sheen collapsed with a heart attack, the Philippine jungle suffered expensive defoliation in the pursuit of art. The documentation of the film's making in books by, among others, the director's wife, Eleanor Coppola, has contributed to the myth of a psychedelic Vietnam, buttressed by *Dispatches* by Michael Herr (adviser to the movie) and the aura around legendary war photographer Tim Page. *Apocalypse Now* is a masterpiece of cinematography and psycho-drama, by one of the most proficient directors in the history of the American cinema, at least in terms of the breadth of thematic and emotional spectrum his films have covered. Hitchcock's achievement is greater, but his range is less wide. And by terming the psychedeli-cized Vietnam a myth, I am aware that the linking of false Edens and Falls from innocence to experience in the army and the drug world is one of the film's key insights, as well as the site of its final conformism. The trouble is that the motif of the individual pitted against dangers external or psychic restores the film to an archetypal American genre, thereby eliding the need to understand Vietnamese perspectives. To Coppola as much as to Richard Nixon, the Vietnam War was an identity crisis suffered by America, not a catastrophe forced on the Vietnamese.

Not, of course, that the Vietnam War did happen to the many Americans who had no family involved. An air of blankness contributes to both the national failure to understand the war and what is perhaps the country's most effective work of public statuary, the Vietnam Veterans Memorial, cut into the lawns of Constitution Gardens not far from the Lincoln Memorial, the Reflecting Pool and the White House. Here, on walls of polished black granite that each run for 250 feet meeting at a vertex 10 feet high, are etched the names of the 58,191 American casualties of the Vietnam conflict, recorded in chronological order (1959–75). The memorial, designed following an open competition by Maya Ying Lin, then a student at Yale, was initially vilified for its lack of overt reference to military sacrifice, and indeed for its lack of any hieroglyphic or dramatic reference beyond the names listed. Now the public mood has shifted in favour of the memorial's sombre abstraction, and a nearby sculpture of three servicemen bulging with weaponry and waving the Stars and Stripes, built to placate the hawks, looks mawkish. Meanwhile the veterans who attend on Memorial Day have taken to wearing the leathers, beards and studded denim associated with the Hell's Angels motorcycle chapters during the years of conflict, rather than with either the Green Berets or the flower people. In a further act of cultural conflation and recycling, the dog tags, teddy bears and other mementos left by visitors against the granite are collected regularly, and often end up in the nearby National Museum of American History. All these actions – the retrieval, the sculpture, the film – turn America smoothly in on itself, unable to comprehend the reality of a perspective on events other than its own, one massive but baffled clearing-up operation around the Reflecting Pool after the crowds thin out.

*Apocalypse Now* may be said to have succeeded exactly where *The Red Badge of Courage* failed, while occupying the same territory whereby the topic of war becomes catalyst to the true theme of young manhood's rites of passage. Both employ images that, while they are not pure Gothic generically, could not have existed without the Gothic tradition, but Coppola's greater intrepidity and orchestral powers keep the Gothic in play without its threatening to flood the narrative and dictate its stylistic course. As a film about the 1960s it has no equal apart from Donald Cammell's *Performance* (1970), whose focus and iconography are as introspectively English as Coppola's perspective is American. Both films tap the carnival and horror traditions of their native cultures; both are obsessed with superimposing contrary images of manhood to produce a conflation: gangster/pop singer in *Performance* and soldier/dissident in *Apocalypse Now*.

Even in its contradictions, Coppola's film is not disabled, but deepens its parabolic relationship to its times. Ostensibly anti-war, the film's breath-taking use of Wagner's *Ride of the Valkyrie* as accompaniment to the strafing of a jungle village invites collusion, using the pleasures of the switchback ride as bait, while Robert Duvall's unforgettable 'I love the smell of napalm in the morning' and 'Charlie don't surf' became cultural catch-phrases rather than triggers to disgust, the mixture of theatrical dementia and obsession with logistics an echo of Lippard's 'I vonders how *that'll* vork' to the extent that both Barnumize violence. The not-so-secret complicity that *Apocalypse Now* encourages *vis-à-vis* its imagery of militarism exists to blur the distinctions between Right and Left, miming exactly the failure of 1960s radicalism to push its rejection of the parental State to the point of actual fission. As with the proleptic warnings of *Uncle Tom's Cabin* and the Civil War, so with *Apocalypse Now* and its rewriting of the crisis over Vietnam: the conflation has to happen, the Union has to triumph. For ever after, there will be scars, enmity, difference – but in America there can never be a real, political opposition. The defining irony of American popular culture lies in the contradiction between its imagery of explosion and liberation and its final and voluntary containment within a unitary ideology. Now President of the Czech Republic, Vaclav Havel has spoken many times of holding on to albums by the Velvet Underground and Frank Zappa during the darkest days of underground resistance to Soviet oppression, as talismans of audible freedom. But while Havel was truly in opposition to the regime, citizens such as Zappa and Lou Reed were figures of a counter-culture that never truly threatened the State, and were in a sense its best ambassadors – though the idea of a revolution driven by the aesthetic of The Velvet Underground's *White Light/ White Heat* (1968) does carry a certain neo-Lippardian appeal.

## Horror and the Cold War: Stephen King

The world's best-selling author Stephen King (1947– ) is also a frequent and a candid interviewee who, rather than seeing contradictions in American containment of misrule, stands by the single ideology and links it to his own writing in the horror genre, as in this interview of 1983:

[H]orror fiction is really as Republican as a banker in a three-piece suit. The story is always the same in terms of its development. There's an incursion into taboo lands, there's a place where you shouldn't go, but you do, the same way that your mother would tell you that the freak tent is a place you shouldn't go, but you do. And the same thing happens inside: you look at the guy with three eyes, or you look at the fat lady, or you look at the skeleton man or Mr. Electrical or whoever it happens to be. And when you come out, well, you say, 'Hey, I'm not so bad. I'm all right. A lot better than I thought.' It has that effect of reconfirming values, of reconfirming self-image and our good feelings about ourselves.[10]

Far from subverting the *status quo*, horror in King's hands becomes a way of 'reconfirming values', of approaching the alien only to crush it so as to reinforce the power of the known and the domestic. In this way the Fall – into evil, the strange, the other – is reversed, and the Eden of small-town America reinstated as the smoke clears. Of course there has to be a sense of threat for the Reconfirmation Crew to be called in, and King's sensibility, as expressed in both the novels and the interviews, is for all its folksiness and determinedly hale Yankee-isms, exceedingly bleak. He repeatedly describes his life in terms of the Fall – 'I'm a fallen-away Methodist' (25) – given to tumbling for years at a time into abysses of alcohol and drugs, kept just about on track by marriage and family.

In fact, children are frequently the adventurers and agents of redemption in the novels, and King has rationalized his aim to shock as a means of enabling the parent-reader to cope with the nightmare of one of the kids coming to harm: 'If you write a novel where the bogeyman gets somebody else's children, maybe they'll never get your own children' (14). For a writer of his baby-boom generation to compare his literary world to the 'freak tent' of Mr Electrical and the skeleton man suggests more of a panacea for the writer rather than the reader. After all, those tents were folded up and entered history some time ago. The cultural background on which King draws is that of the horror movie, the *Classics Illustrated* adaptations of *Frankenstein* et al., the fanzines such as Forrest J. Ackerman's *Famous Monsters of Filmland* and the rather more literary *Castle of Frankenstein*, together with the gruesome EC comics such as *Tales from the Crypt* that ran from 1950 to 1955. It is crucial to King's development as a writer that his sources were always already second-hand. King is almost certainly too young to have bought EC comics as they appeared, and so their absorption into his work (notably the short stories, the novellas gathered in *Four Past Midnight*

(1990), and among the movies, the underrated *Sleepwalkers*) has about it an immediate nostalgia.

That nostalgia is for the years just prior to Vietnam, and is a nostalgia for certain anxieties as well as for pre-Sixties certitudes. King worked for Goldwater in 1964, voted for Nixon in 1968, and agreed with General Westmoreland's interpretation of foreign policy, 'Let's bomb 'em into the Stone Age' (140), a position modified as his hair grew longer at the University of Maine, by which time he had also failed his Army medical. King tells an anecdote that pinpoints his own anxieties in relation to the paranoia of the national psyche. On a Saturday afternoon in October 1957, when the author had just turned ten, he went to see *Earth vs. the Flying Saucers* ('a horror flick masquerading as science fiction') at the local flea-pit in Stratford, Connecticut. The film's plot-line is standard Cold War fare: earth has been invaded by aliens from a dying planet. Eden is burning:

> [J]ust when it was reaching the good part, with Washington in flames and the final, cataclysmic interstellar battle about to be joined – the screen suddenly went dead. Well, kids started to clap and hoot, thinking the projectionist had made a mistake or the reel had broken, but then, all of a sudden, the theater lights went on full strength ... then the theater manager came striding down the center aisle, looking pale, and he mounted the stage and said, in a trembling voice, 'I want to tell you that the Russians have put a space satellite into orbit around Earth. They call it Sputnik. ...' There was a long, hushed pause as this crowd of fifties kids in cuffed jeans, with crewcuts or ducktails or ponytails, struggled to absorb all that; and then, suddenly, one voice, near tears but also charged with terrible anger, shrilled through the stunned silence: 'Oh, go show the movie, you liar!'. ... I still find it impossible to convey, even to my own kids, how terribly frightened and alone and depressed I felt at that moment. (61–2)

King, clearly, is not 'alone' but ubiquitous in the anecdotal scene, being simultaneously the creative intelligence behind the film (at least in prospect), the voice that interrupts normal service to bring shocking news, and above all the 'one voice, near tears but charged with terrible anger', that refuses to accept the reality of a breach in America's exceptionalist ideology, and that turns in distress to a sidelong peep at the truth through the dream-work and contained misrule of popular entertainment. The voice of the novels would itself be charged with a terrible anger, though prone to tears of sentimental allegiance at the breaking and remaking of the Union through blood sacrifice of one kind or another.

## King's Gothic models

King used to be labelled a bad writer, and is now generally reviewed as a good one, but while *Carrie* (1974) is undoubtedly a clumsier affair than *Hearts in Atlantis* (1999) thirty-six books later, this critical upswing is less a sign that his writing has changed than an acknowledgement of how long he has stayed at his post. A writer limited in many areas (prolixity excepted), he is particularly prone to cliché at the most basic levels of character and incident, but, being also a self-aware and a hypnotic teller of tales, King knows that in cliché lies his secret power of reassurance. Teaching *Dracula* and Thornton Wilder's *Our Town* to high-school students while writing *'Salem's Lot* (1975), he produced a fusion of the two. In interview he concedes the 'derivative' nature of his work, admitting that his first novel *Carrie* leans for support on a B-movie, *The Brain from Planet Arous*, while *The Shining* (1977) drew on Shirley Jackson's genre classic *The Haunting of Hill House* (73). His ponderous, though immensely popular, extravaganza *The Stand* (1978) apparently owes much to George Stewart's *Earth Abides* as well as to *The Purple Cloud*, purple prose by M. P. Shiel. To these open admissions by King might be added the fatigued reworking of an episode from *Lord of the Rings* at the end of what is otherwise one of King's most effective and original novels, *It* (1986), the echoes of any and every Cold War invasion film in *The Tommyknockers* (1987), and the resemblance of *The Dark Half* (1989) not only to *Frankenstein* and *Dr Jekyll and Mr Hyde* but to a number of EC efforts, most notably the one in which the hero limps back from a watery grave to revenge himself on the wife and boyfriend who killed him, but phones first and whispers endearingly, 'I'm coming: I'd be there sooner but little bits of me keep falling off along the way' (58). (That cartoon, along with King's most visceral shocker *Pet Sematary* (1983) are indebted additionally to W. W. Jacobs's fine story 'The Monkey's Paw'.)

On the face of it, this might appear to be a sad catalogue of imitation characteristic of a hollow culture. The literary equivalent of a Big Mac and fries (his own comparison), King's novels can be classified with Prozac and TV as means by which to block out and demonize threat. They are the voice of a vast but fearful segment of the nation, and King, allergic to the self-inflation of New York and Los Angeles, has spoken in interviews of his beloved Maine as the true America. While his fiction never rises above these limitations, a criticism that seeks always a transcendence of the popular and the customary is itself strictly self-limiting. Stephen King is a lightning-rod for American anxieties, and that ever-present fear of danger with roots in the Civil War, in Puritan watchfulness, in the Cold War, in every step of the historical journey. Moreover, as the sections of this book on Hawthorne's use of the Gothic and Whitman's immersion in the *Zeitgeist* were intended to show, the idea of great literature being produced at a remove is untrue to America, and perhaps untrue altogether. King's open admission of the derivative nature of his work is grounded in an accurate understanding of the persistence of Romanticism. 'In *The Shining*, instead of a gothic castle you have a gothic hotel, and instead of chains rattling in the basement, the elevator goes up and down – which is another kind of rattling chain' (178–9).

# Horror and the persistence of Romanticism

At the high-spec end of literary production in the English language – for example in poetry – no development in the last 200 years has driven such a wedge between its own projects and inherited taste as Wordsworth's and Coleridge's *Lyrical Ballads* (1798). The monumental structures of Tennyson and Browning, the lyrics of the gas-lit 1890s, the High Modernism of T. S. Eliot, the diversely historical projects of Pound and Auden, and the avant-garde that drew on Williams and came to maturity in the second half of the twentieth century, all develop while never moving beyond the expressivism, the exploratory treatment of selfhood, the phenomenology of landscape, the tussle between symbol and allegory, and the echoes of revolution initiated by the first-generation writers. It is not only Stephen King whose work is 'derivative' in this more honourable and extended sense of writing as operative within a persistence of Romanticism. Yet *Lyrical Ballads* is itself unthinkable outside a conception of what constitutes the popular and the actual. This includes reworkings of folk and other ballad materials, and most certainly includes Gothic horror as part of a cyclical project of defamiliarization and reconfirmation linked ancestrally to Stephen King's invitation to the taboo zone, the freak tent, followed by the return to the daylight world.

A tour of P. T. Barnum's Museum used to conclude with a sign, 'This Way to the Egress'. Rather than encountering some fabulous bird, the less literate members of the paying crowd would be surprised to find themselves out in the street. Notwithstanding – indeed, including –

the manipulations of commercial entertainment, this ticketed journey replicates the structure of the Romantic meditation poem, exemplified by Coleridge's 'Frost at Midnight', where the speaker is drawn into an inner exploration, a voyage into dream and memory and the uncanny, to be returned at last to a world that is the same and not the same, a world changed by the fact of having crossed into the strange, breaking the membrane of homeostatic normality. This romantic structure is what a Stephen King novel does, at the macro-level, and what it offers at the micro-level of narrative episode: the journeys in and out of the changing painting in *Rose Madder* (1995), in and out of the white nights of one of King's most engaging books, *Insomnia* (1994), in and out of the old dark house where *It* lives.[11]

# *It*

*It* is more than 1,000 pages long. The main plot-line is easily sketched: a group of children are menaced by a nightmare shape-changer that lives in the storm-drain, the shuttered house, the sewer and the corners of the mind. They grow up and move away from Derry, Maine, but are called back as adults to deal with and defeat It, a journey that simultaneously involves confrontation with sundry child-hood traumas, adolescent rites of passage and the warping effects of the past. In dealing with a group of characters, it side-steps a recurrent failing of King's novels: his dedication of narrative to the travails of one embattled individual, which becomes claustrophobic in works of such length. In other respects *It* is typical, its most effective moments often side-glimpses at the America of fractured hopes and unreliable economics, small-town life trapped in late autumn, the beauty parlor closed, the band-shell stained with attempts to find escape, silence broken by the whistle of the freight train. Here Bev Rogan takes the archetypal Stephen King journey into the dark:

> These memories (or memories of memories: that was really closer to what they were) were like islands that were not really islands at all but only knobs of a single coral spine which happened to poke up above the waterline, not separate at all but one piece. Yet whenever she tried to dive deep and see the rest, a maddening image intervened: the grackles which came back each spring to New England, crowding the telephone lines, trees and rooftops, jostling for places and filling the thawing late-March air with their raucous gossip. This image came to her again and again, foreign and disturbing, like a heavy radio beam that blankets the signal you really want to pick up. She realized with a sudden shock that

she was standing outside of the Kleen-Kloze Washateria, where she and Stan Uris and Ben and Eddie had taken the rags that day in late June – rags stained with blood which only they could see. The windows were now soaped opaque and there was a hand-lettered FOR SALE BY OWNER sign taped to the door. Peering between the swashes of soap, she could see an empty room with lighter squares on the dirty yellow walls where the washers had stood. *I'm going home*, she thought dismally, but walked on anyway.[12]

Nothing here is out of the ordinary, and yet everything communicates, or blocks understanding like the Hitchcockian grackles, on a double level, where 'home' and the 'foreign and disturbing' can be one and the same. The windows of life are 'soaped opaque', but to finger letters through which to peer inside is to risk a glimpse of the real beneath the real, where death is at home, waiting patiently. (Home is where the horror is, in American fiction from Poe through to 'The Yellow Wallpaper', Edith Wharton's *Ethan Frome* and the work of Stephen King.)

Returning to 127 Lower Main Street, Bev hesitates before ringing the bell: 'She looked at the mailboxes. Third floor STARK-WEATHER. Second floor, BURKE. First floor – her breath caught – MARSH' (559). The meteorologically apt 'Stark-weather' recalls Charlie Starkweather, the teenage serial killer who murdered eleven people across the Midwest in 1958, the year after King's visit to the cinema was interrupted by Sputnik, and about whose activities the boy who would be King kept a scrap-book. 'Burke' may of course allude not to the future, but to Edinburgh night-life of a past medical era, and if 'Marsh' (Bev's father's real surname) suggests quicksand, those associations are only heightened when the door is opened by Mrs Kersh, whose name Bev has misread. Once again, what is home and what is foreign and disturbing have been conflated, or superimposed in a miasmatic double exposure. The harmless old lady in faded silks, who knew the father, asks Bev in for a cup of tea. Her accent is tinged with her Swedish origins, the floor is stripped to its original wood, a cedar chest 'breathed its gentle aroma' (562). Stitched on a quilt, women draw water, while men build haystacks. 'A picture of Jesus hung on one wall, a picture of John F. Kennedy on another' (563). What ensues is entirely forseeable in outline, unexpected in detail. To argue that such episodes are clichéd would be to miss the point, for it is only through the quietly excruciating rise in tension – I am selecting from an episode covering twelve pages – that King, who excels at this kind of performance, can use the forseeable to such powerful effect.

At first the slight imperfections Bev notices are simply those we all begin to notice in each other after a first encounter. 'Her teeth were very bad – strong-looking, but bad all the same' (564). As Bev realizes belatedly that the name did read 'Marsh' rather than Kersh, everything goes to hell:

> Her fingers were claws. She grinned at Beverly. 'Have something to eat, dear.' Her voice had risen half an octave, but the octave was cracked in this register, and her voice was the sound of a crypt door swinging mindlessly on hinges clogged with black earth .... Her breath was the smell of long-dead things burst wide open by the gases of their own decay .... 'Oh, he loved his joke, my fadder! This is a joke miss, if you enjoy them: my fadder bore me rather than my mutter. He shat me from his asshole! Hee! Hee! Hee!'
> 'I ought to go,' Beverly heard herself say in that same high wounded voice – the voice of a small girl who has been viciously embarrassed at her first party. There was no strength in her legs. She was dimly aware that it was not tea in her cup but shit. (565)

As the entire house turns to rotting food, John Kennedy fires 'a stinky wink' from the wall, the witch turns into the father, dead and making pornographic overtures, succeeded by other diverting transformations, including a cannibal clown waving a severed leg. His balloons read 'IT CAME FROM OUTER SPACE', in reality a Cold War movie title, and his mad shuck-and-jive on the porch steps is not without wit: 'The only survivor of a dying planet, I have come to rob all the women ... rape all the men ... and learn to do the Peppermint Twist!' (567). Escaping from this version of Hansel and Gretel into the outer world only to skirt death under the wheels of a baker's van, Bev echoes John Keats: '*Was I really in there, or did I dream it all?*' (568), and concludes that 'It' will not be happy with a draw. 'THAT'S WIGHT, WABBIT', a yellow balloon announces in letters of electric blue. 'As she watched, it went bouncing lightly up the street, urged by the pleasant late-spring breeze' (568).

Stephen King tells *It* like it is, at least according to the depressive, liverish view that life is a cup of shit and then you die. Again, from an interview, on reading horror: 'it's a rehearsal for death. It's a way to get ready. People say there's nothing sure but death and taxes. But that's not really true. There's really only death, you know' (Underwood and Miller, 23). To essay literary originality would then be a fool's errand, when the conditions out of which writing and reading emerge are viewed so starkly as unchangeable facts of life. Only a cliché, an authorless quotation such as the Hansel and Gretel fable, can speak truth. King's early life was ruined by a cliché when his father walked out to get a pack of cigarettes (a beer, in more recent interviews) and never came back. The author's rage at this abandonment has not abated, to judge both by interviews and scenes such as Bev's 'homecoming', where Father is the devil, makes advances to his daughter, or drops a stinky wink in the guise of John F. Kennedy, another compromised patriarch.

## The novelist and the consumer

None of this comprises a come-hither look on King's part, begging Freudian or psycho-biographical interpretation. King works on the assumption that his daily stint at the word-processor off-loads a darkness which might otherwise swallow him, a strategy for writing that moves the reader's role to the fore. The readers are often young, and fans. Occasionally a demented one turns up in his kitchen. Understandably keen to avoid contact that might swamp him (his website is plastered with refusals to consider unsolicited manuscripts), King in another sense goes out of his way to enrol the fan in his projects. Earning $40 million in a good year, King is currently writing 'The Plant', released on to the web for downloading by fans on the honesty principle: as long as those downloading send him a dollar, he will keep writing chapters, but if the trickle of dollars dries up, so will the story.[13] The backwoods folksiness of all this suggests once more a nostalgia, this time for a capitalist Eden of fair dealing and firm handshakes, which only vast wealth and the impersonality of the Internet make it possible for King to indulge. King's nostalgia, his unoriginality and confinement by cliché coexist with writerly skills of suspense, social representation and a grotesque wit. The first do not undermine the second, but offer reassurance to the reader as essentially Republican and parochial values are reconfirmed after the threat of the monstrous has been lifted. More interestingly, the element of *déja-vu* allows the fan to play the book like an instrument, one which has been constructed to allow only prefixed scales with no false notes. This relocation of the reader at the centre of things recalls King's own beginnings as a fan of EC comics and magazines such as *Famous Monsters of Filmland*, a collector.

The importance of the personal collection in post-war American culture will be explored more fully in relation to Harry Smith's *Anthology of American Folk Music*. Despite his immense success, Stephen King is an anachronistic figure, though in a sense that does no disservice to him, at all. He is one of the last writers who came up by the route of selling short stories to magazines. Those magazines are gone, and King's experiments with electronic publication are a way of at least trying to keep pace with the mass marketing of the techno-logical that has reconfigured American society in the twentieth and twenty-first centuries as based on the complementary tropes of super-sedence and replication. In his book *From the American System to Mass Production 1800–1932*, David Hounshell argues that the bi-cycle was the first object to be replicated *ad infinitum* by way of advanced manufacturing techniques that was not strictly speaking a tool. Following on from the Colt revolver and the sewing-machine, the bicycle helped move a variable element of recreation to the centre of the arena of manufacture, sale and use. This ambiguous zone between work and pleasure would be the site of American advances in replicant culture from the passenger car to the personal computer. The passenger car, the movies and the telephone identify a first generation of the twentieth century, succeeded by the television, family car and suburban home with lawn at mid-century. The computer, which thoroughly ambiguates the boundaries of work, pleasure, information and purchase, constitutes the triumph of repli-cation-with-supersedence, combining elements of previous informa-tion conduits including TV, phone, hi-fi and the postal service. Despite Stephen King's protestations that Maine is the real America, the real America is to be located in the sameness, from sea to shining sea, of the currently triumphant devices and the spatial arrangements they require in order to be switched on.

## American ideology

Such an analysis of the pre-conditions for literature informs the recent work of Philip Fisher, one of the most trenchant critics in American Studies to have emerged from the New Historicist swing away from text-based post-structuralism and into cultural studies. Fisher is able to illuminate that curious sameness that coexists with the blatant differences of climate, geography, style and region in American soci-ety, and that strikes Europeans in particular as spooky on a first visit.

> Lacking a single *Volk*, a coherent geography and climate, or a strong common culture of reference, the unity that solved the two great diver-sities – that of geography and that of population – was a unity that had about it a quality of abstraction or rigidity. It was a uniformity rather than a unity. What would have been called, a few years ago, American

conformity, or even American blandness or thinness of character, was a solution to a diversity so unmanageable that only by the creation of an almost mechanically applied pattern could it be composed or settled. This easy, light-fitting American personality Walt Whitman celebrated as 'the loose drift of character, the inkling through random types'.[14]

This situation, considered as a scene or a drama, contrasts noticeably with Baudelaire's Paris, the London of Dickens or Dostoevski's St Petersburg, where could be seen a 'paradoxical, close connection between a brittle, memorable uniqueness of character and the city crowd' (72). American space is non-European, uncrowded, and produces as a first stage in the self-characterization of American life an unpicking of the prior *vericulum* of origin, especially in language. The 'subtraction of differences' from diverse immigrant groups is an essential first stage in the induction process which a potentially unmanageable diversity might threaten, otherwise. The hyphenated American identity referred to earlier in this study, Cuban-American, Armenian-American, is unequally weighted in favour of the new, as the vestiges of the old tend to disappear within a generation or so. That the American language is historically a form of English is of secondary importance to its actual, experienced end-use as a language by adoption. To the extent that a residual 'Englishness' has any importance, it operates as a reminder of what America is no longer umbilically connected to, in terms of politics.

Fisher's representation can of course be challenged on a variety of fronts. It privileges examples of social recurrence over the glaring differences between the cultures as well as the terrain of, say, Massachusetts and Idaho. Its emphasis on lateral spread may be said to collude with, rather than critique ideology, since it fails to get to grips with vertical divisions of class. Moreover, a text such as Baudelaire's 'Les Sept Vieillards' could be read as a premonitory rebuttal of Fisher's assumptions about European urban society. Nevertheless, the analysis is acute, and has repercussions for an end-user such as Stephen King. If language is conceded to be a functional bridge between adjacent users who need to avoid misunderstanding and alienation at all costs, stylistic originality begins to look traitorous. The internationalism of the American modernists and the varied defections of James, Eliot and Pound are salient here, as is Carlos Williams's self-immersion in the American parochial. King's language is un-Modernist, save for the odd gobbet of pastiche stream-of-consciousness. It is often vastly bland. Yet its livelier passages are sulphurous, bubbling, riotous, excremental, hardly emblematic of the abstraction and rigidity which Fisher diagnoses and which seem much more connected tonally to the blankness of the Vietnam War

Memorial, which exactly confirms his thesis. If King's writing confirms Fisher's thesis, it would be in the vehemence and excess of the doomed feints through which abstraction is attacked – by regionalism, by Gothic assaults on the customary, and by an emphasis on non-abstract local detail.

Less effectively, there is an emphasis on the embattled individual, so extreme as to disable *Bag of Bones* (1998) and ruin *The Girl Who Loved Tom Gordon* (1999). The latter is a lost-in-the-woods fable of a girl who finds herself through her struggle in the wild. It is contemporary with *The Blair Witch Project*, a worthless horror film entirely lacking in horror but made literally sickening by the lurches of a hand-held camera, and marketable by virtue of a clever Internet-based publicity exercise. The college students who get lost in the woods searching for the Blair Witch confirm Fisher's thesis throughout, by their youthspeak clichés, and also in the film's one effective moment when, trudging forever in search of escape from the trailing green and snapping branches characteristic of Maryland off the highway, they discover that they have walked around in a circle back to their starting-point. By contrast, *The Girl Who Loved Tom Gordon* is a nostalgic exercise in frontier mythology, residual Natty Bumpoism with a touch of *Walden*, the self-communing American's rite of passage a purification ritual to which mosquitoes and mud slides are the props. King's more effective works – *It, Hearts in Atlantis, Insomnia, Rose Madder, The Dark Half, Four Past Midnight, Dreamcatcher* – are those that blaspheme against the sameness and uncover the *Invasion of the Body Snatchers* mindlessness in American subscription to ideology. King's writing in its most vital stretches is a power surge upsetting the Republican conservatism to which it eventually reverts, those stretches being as a rule the most horrid or depressed episodes, which in fact occupy very little space in the context of one of his mammoth fireside chats. Fisher writes of a moment of estrangement within the sameness that begins to index the point at which King also applies the surgeon's knife, and at which a writer such as William Burroughs (discussed in chapter 6) is so much more adept a sawbones:

> Everywhere across the varied geography and climate the suburbs are comfortably the same, equipped with the same schools and parks for children; the same shopping centers with the same stores selling Levi's, Tide and power lawn-mowers; the same array of churches and car dealers; the same fraternal organizations and specialized doctors. The reduplication of the same housing types with the identical appliances, the familiar street names with the same automobiles on those streets, anchors a modern social space that has identity from point to point. Because of this identity American social space invites a mobility that

becomes nearly cost free. Ultimately, wherever one moves will be enough the same to feel very quickly 'like home'. It is an interesting American invention, both semantic and literal, to live not 'at home' but in a place that feels 'like home'. (75)

Like home, but never really home, *unheimlich* but liveable space, without while within the heartland of America. This is the pressure point to which *It* as well as more powerful works such as *The Naked Lunch* address themselves.

Even this anti-social posture is one that can achieve celebrity. Following his return to America in 1974 after a period of anonymity in London, Burroughs became a star of the indie rock circuit, luring college audiences with his inimitable voice, recording CDs solo or with hip-hop and new-wave juniors. King is a mainstream star. Both careers, the one avant-garde, the other mainstream, follow a pattern set down in the aftermath of the Civil War. A paper triumph for democracy, the emancipation of the slaves and the cessation of hostilities set the scene for the rise of industry and undemocratic forms of forced equality, aimed at ensuring the universal availability of the material signifiers of a successful basic induction. *E pluribus unum*: America began to become the society of the one and the many, the rich and the poor, the star and the public, in a culture of performance wherein ante-bellum anarchy became marketed as style, the economy clamping down on the actual assertion of individual difference, while the confidence man led the way to the movies and the rock stadium. Philip Fisher judges the space inhabited by speaker and audience as undemocratic *an sich*, even where the aim of the speech (as with Martin Luther King) is the goal of a more inclusive and democratic America. Stephen King's position is built on the suspicion that democracy is Babel or infernal clamour, and an ambivalent urge to bottle and let it run riot. His writing is oppositional, in its darkest and most explosive episodes, but only as the Black Mass is oppositional, stressing by blasphemous inversion the original doxa from which it has strayed. Like all writers of popular American literature, King projects alternative histories. Where he departs from the norm is in the ruthless demolition of those histories prior to the inevitable return of normative culture.

## Philip K. Dick: alternative history

The most memorable alternative history in modern American fiction is Philip K. Dick's *The Man in the High Castle* (1962), a novel whose main narrative is set in an occupied United States following the victory of Germany and Japan in the Second World War. In a sense all of the work by Dick (1928–82) is alternative history, combining the speculation fundamental to the science fiction genre since the days of Jules Verne and H. G. Wells with an evolving record of the Californian *Zeitgeist* in the changes from the nadir of the Cold War to the exhilaration and vertigo of the 1960s. *A Scanner Darkly* (1977) documents so accurately the overlapping worlds of drugs, petty crime and paranoia in the years of Haight Ashbury and the Furry Freak Brothers that it hardly qualifies as science fiction at all. By contrast, in *Counter-Clock World* (1967), an ingenious fantasy in which time runs backwards, the dead awake and adults face death in infancy; and in late, preacherly works such as *Radio Free Albemuth* (1985) social realism is abandoned for metaphysics, stretching the limits of popular genre but from another angle. Dick had tried initially for success in the literary mainstream, and some of his realist fiction, published posthumously, while not without talent, appears straitened by comparison with the pyrotechnics of *High Castle*, *The Game-Players of Titan* (1963) and *The Three Stigmata of Palmer Eldritch* (1965), novels in which the rapidity of the transitions across alternative worlds as jostling realities evaporate in hallucination requires the springboard of genre, but only in order to surpass science fiction, in much the same way as it was required by Alain Robbe-Grillet's *Les Gommes* (1953) in order to break the rules of the detective story.

As with Edgar Allan Poe, the French were more quick to applaud the skill of Dick's heuristic kaleidoscopes, not that this prevented the paranoid Californian from informing the FBI when two Parisian Marxists from the *Tel Quel* zone turned up in May 1974 hoping for an interview. Dick was damaged by the culture he also helped create. Many of those who threw the I Ching in the 1960s and 1970s to dither over its hexagrammatic enigmas came across it in *The Man in the High Castle*, which has the distinction of being the first American novel in which *The Book of Changes* is mentioned and features as a plot device, generating a history alternative to the first alternative history, this time one whereby the Allies emerged victorious from the Second World War. Dick had shared a house in Berkeley with the poets Robert Duncan and Jack Spicer, and his adaptation of the imagery of Jean Cocteau's *Orphée*, in which the writer travels through mirrors to meet Death and hears enigmatic poetry transmitted through the car radio, parallels Duncan's use of the same materials to structure his *Passages* and Spicer's metaphysical riddling and addiction to *trompe-l'oeil* Surrealism. But where Spicer was brought to an early death by alcohol, blaming the 1960s pop culture for wrecking the literary bar scene apart from which he had no social role as a poet, Dick passed through the psychotropic mirror with alacrity, his heroic absorption of amphetamines in particular contributing to the visions that broke into consciousness with increasing regularity, as well as feeding his prolificity – six novels in a twelve-month period in 1963–4, including some of his best work. Looking back over his career, Dick would protest in 1981 that 'I am a fictionalizing philosopher, not a novelist; my novel & story-writing ability is employed as a means to formulate my perception. The core of my writing is not art but *truth*.'[15] However, where contemporaries such as William Burroughs and J. G. Ballard were able to gain some leverage on the literary world from their brief containment as genre writers of science fiction, Dick wrote books that were too Venusian for mainstream respectability but too *outré* for the boys of all ages in pebble glasses who take Heinlein and Asimov seriously. Where Stephen King placates the fan by the reassuring sameness of his conformity to genre, Dick uses genre as the nearest working portal to frenzied speculation.

In one way his protest is justified, in that the two key themes of his work – what is real, and what it is to be human – are the foundations of philosophical enquiry. A voracious reader along syncretically Californian fault lines, Dick by 1955 had ingested Hume, attending to the argument that causality cannot be verified; in other words, that B follows A, does not prove that A caused B. Other classic unpickings of the *vericulum* included Bishop Berkeley's emphasis on the creation of allegedly objective reality by sensory impressions, and Kant's distinction between noumena and phenomena, particularly in its impact on the individual's experience of space and time. (Dick rejected Einstein's General Theory of Relativity and wrote a letter to the Soviet Academy of Sciences encouraging their efforts at discrediting it. He later learned that the letter had been intercepted by the CIA, a discovery that no doubt fuelled his conspiracy theories (96).) According to Dick's biographer, he took from Jung the theory of projection, whereby what is seen takes colour from the psyche of the seer, and a tenet of the Romantic poetry initiated by Wordsworth and continued variously in the work of Spicer and Duncan.

To these tendencies were added an interest, again typical of the times, in Vedic and Buddhist conceptions of *maya*, the doctrine whereby 'true reality is veiled from unenlightened human consciousness', and we see only what we fear or desire (96). These oriental traditions of thought were popularized in books on Zen and the Tao by Alan Watts. The view that reality may stand independently of what we conceive it to be had, however, been formulated in a different kind of vocabulary by William James, a favourite of Dick's from an early

stage. In one way wildly eclectic, Dick's thinking was typical of the
sixties in its Amerasian emphases. What undercuts his claim to be
treated as a philosopher and what made him incorrigibly an artist is
his lack of interest in exploring these questions outside a dramatization of the *experience* of them by an individual caught in the choices,
conflicts and actions of a narrative.

*Time Out of Joint* (1959), the strongest of Dick's novels prior
to *High Castle*, is a case in point. Its wry sketches of Martini and
Capri pants suburban mores yoke the valuable aspects of Dick's
realist writing to a narrative not dissimilar to an extended episode
of *The Twilight Zone*. Ragle Gumm (*Règles/Gommes?*) is a local
celebrity by virtue of his untarnished record as winner in a daily
newspaper game. It turns out that the game is being used in the future
of 1998 as a defence system by Earth against Luna missiles. The
military have built a fake 1958 town recalling the continuities
of Ragle's childhood, to keep him socially sedated while making use
of his unique talents, unsought skills that make him a sibling of the
'precogs' and 'psis' in the more frenetic books of the following
decade. As Lawrence Sutin notes in his biography of Dick, while the
plot of *Time Out of Joint* is ingenious and carefully crafted, its neat
ending 'in no way explains the happenings that give the novel its
uniquely cerebral surreality' (95). The genesis of the book lay in
Dick's reaching in his San Francisco bathroom for a light cord that
didn't exist, the light being operated from a wall switch, a cerebral
misfire he interpreted as a glimpse of an alternative world or history,
and which he makes Ragle undergo in chapter 2 as the first prompting
to ask *'Where have I been that I don't remember?'*[16] These fugues
deepen and lengthen:

> The child ahead of him received its candy bar and raced off. Ragle
> laid down his fifty-cent piece on the counter.
> 'Got any beer?' he said. His voice sounded funny. Thin and remote.
> The counter man in white apron and cap stared at him, stared and did
> not move. Nothing happened. No sound, anywhere. Kids, cars, the
> wind; it all shut off.
> The fifty-cent piece fell away, down through the wood, sinking. It
> vanished.
> I'm dying, Ragle thought. Or something ...
> The soft drink stand fell into bits. Molecules. He saw the molecules,
> colourless, without qualities, that made it up. Then he saw through,
> into the space beyond it, he saw the hill behind, the trees and sky. He
> saw the soft-drink stand go out of existence, along with the counter
> man, the cash register, the big dispenser of orange drink, the taps for
> Coke and root beer, the ice-chests of bottles, the hot dog broiler, the

jars of mustard, the shelves of cones, the row of heavy round metal lids
under which were the different ice creams.
   In its place was a slip of paper. He reached out his hand and took
hold of the slip of paper. On it was printing, block letters.

SOFT-DRINK STAND                    (40)

The curious distinction of passages such as this resides in their
working effortlessly on literary levels that would have proved inimical
to another writer. A nightmare version of Saussure's theorizing of the
sign, this proto-structuralist vignette also recalls those episodes of
psychosis experienced by schizophrenics and anticipates the 'trips'
on LSD that would feature in the next decade's self-medication,
while remaining generically a piece of science fiction of the kind
dramatized for television by Rod Serling's *The Twilight Zone*. Neither
a top-down criticism that conceives works of art to be autotelic and
removed from workaday culture nor a bottom-up populist history
that wants culture to symptomatize grievance will be able to catch the
whole spectrum of connotation in an aesthetic such as Philip K. Dick's.
Appropriately the 'K' stood for 'Kindred'. Once again we see here an
American art-form in which vertical categories of high and low lose
their meaning.
   A critical perspective derived from Modernism that confers value
on writers in part through their stylistic innovations and originality
will disqualify Dick *ab initio*. Expert at the construction of narratives,
he is, in terms of style, no Proust. But then his approach had to be
stripped of any such ambition in order to perform its functions
cleanly. Dick lived, internally and socially, in a world of invention,
and to him the language of the novel had to resemble nylon, a flexible
and versatile means to certain specific, modern ends. Clearly the
writing also emerges from a love-hate relationship with the objects
that characterize America: the alarm clocks, broilers, hair-dryers, the
ice-chests and jars of mustard that are the same from coast to coast.
Science fiction allows Dick to both satirize and relish the universal
replication of these objects which, made to talk like the flying cabs in
*Now Wait for Last Year* (1966), become his most appealing incidental
characters. In fact, what speaks most eloquently in Dick's world are
its objects rather than its people, for he shares the weaknesses as well
as the strengths of science fiction. Yet again, Leslie Fiedler's accusation of an inability to handle intimate relationships and female
characters is proved true, but yet again, other projects are in play
that the canonical works devoted to those topics did not handle.
And one of the great pleasures of Dick's work, as with an effective

genre piece such as *The Space Merchants* (1964) by Anderson and Kornbluth, is predictive satire that anticipates accurately technological and other developments beyond the time of writing, and does so in a way that mocks the ideology of the present.

In one of the short stories, 'The Electric Ant', the protagonist wakes in hospital to discover that, while he lacks a right hand, he feels no pain. Jolted by the news that he is in fact an organic robot, he begins to query the workings of his own insides, conjecturing that since he has been programmed to experience reality in a certain way, a snip here or a tweak there might cause reality to rewrite itself. At the conclusion of the tale his experiments on his own internal tapes have implications for other characters who thought themselves real, and the dénouement leads Dick on to his favourite terrain of collective hallucination. Once more the neatness with which the Chinese boxes and Russian dolls can be nested fails to account for the most engaging aspects of the writing, less this time a bequest from Surrealism than an extrapolation from everyday, market-driven life, as when the robot looks at the bones in his new hand and asks if it is under guarantee: 'Ninety days, parts and labor,' one of the technicians said. 'Unless subjected to unusual or intentional abuse'.[17] The premonitions of the present in this tale of 1968 are uncannily exact, as when the robot, baffled by the maze of circuitry around his heart mechanism, decides to consult what would come to be known after the author's death as the hotline to his Internet service provider:

> I need help, he said to himself. Let's see ... what's the fone code for the class BBB computer we hire at the office?
>
> He picked up the fone, dialed the computer at its permanent location in Boise, Idaho.
>
> 'Use of this computer is prorated at a five frogs per minute basis,' a mechanical voice from the fone said. 'Please hold your mastercreditchargeplate before the screen.'
>
> He did so.
>
> 'At the sound of the buzzer you will be connected with the computer,' the voice continued. 'Please query it as rapidly as possible. ...'
>
> 'Scan me visually,' he instructed the computer. 'And tell me where I will find the programming mechanism which controls my thoughts and behavior.' He waited. (294)

The pathos of the anxious object is not merely a mirror reversal of our human fears that the sameness of our affections and behaviour makes us the mechanical slaves of ideology or biology. American society is the first to be constituted, at least following its internal war, on a principle of self-destruction. The whole purpose of an American advance is the supersedence of accepted practice and current devices. Dick knew the true meaning of modern freedom: it is what your hair-dryer thinks in the moments before its retiral behind glass in the Museum of American History.

# 5

# Going Fishing

## Harry Smith, the Anthology of American Folk Music, and the Fan

### Culture and the fan

An analysis of American culture such as that urged by Philip Fisher and confirmed by the fiction of Philip K. Dick sets what is valuable and valueless, collectable and disposable, in ratios that are as questionable as they have been instrumental in the advance of America to its current position as world-leader. Perhaps the recycling of styles as fashionable, outmoded and acceptably retro within the space of a decade or two, or the proximity between such icons of the banal as Andy Warhol's tins of soup and Campbell's 'originals' indexes an acceleration of what was latent in American industrialism from its first consolidation as supplier of the latest car, phone or gadget. Within such an accelerated culture of disposability the product (about which there will hang an immediate aura of the phantom, presaging its supersedence) and the producer (detached by the priorities of investment and profit from an identification with the commodity as a real object) come to possess an increasingly virtual reality. In this situation the package, rather than the content, becomes the essence of transaction, most famously in the case of the 1916 Coca-Cola bottle. From this time also the consumer would move to centre-stage in the production process, and begin to multiply into types amongst which the fan – the consumer as completist and devotee – would become increasingly crucial to market success in the post-1945 years that saw a growth in teenagers with disposable income. A further hybrid of the fan, and one central to the current development of consumption focused on the Internet, is the buff, a figure combining in an unstable blend the qualities of Fisher's expert, inducting a mass audience into the latest technology, and the consumer, whose work and leisure operate in a constructively ambiguous blur. As DJs with computer skills replace musicians on-stage, and fashionable art becomes predominantly conceptual rather than expressive, these changes in consumption and production have had important cultural repercussions. This chapter is in part about Harry Smith, a fan who was able to become an artist through the coupling of old music and new technology.

Smith's *Anthology of American Folk Music*, released first in 1952, then in 1997, constitutes *inter alia* an archive of music and lyric from the nineteenth and twentieth centuries; a diachronic slice of the rural culture of the South, 1927–32; and a template for a cultural form, rock, that came into being just after its appearance on vinyl and that arguably waned to exhaustion around the time of its re-release on compact disc.[1] At once a salvaging of cultural detritus, of lost names on crackling 78s, and a template for the artistry of sampling and collage in an electronic age, the *Anthology* is a pivotal American creation. Indeed, America can experience itself only through the creation of such a hybrid form. Harry Smith was at once the adversary and the paradigm of the culture in which he operated, scorning its materialism but, in turning aside, turning himself into an alembic of influence and energies that would eventually permeate that culture as it strove to evolve.

## Harry Smith and the things he gathered

Harry Smith (1923–91) made films, painted pictures, collected music and objects. A recent book about Smith concludes with 'A Partial List of Things He Gathered', which over his lifetime included vast collections of Ukrainian painted eggs, dolls, string games and 20,000 gramophone records.[2] Smith also collected a reputation and wove stories about himself. Some of the most unlikely ones are true. His parents were Theosophists, and his mother taught on an Indian reservation, where, by the age of fifteen, Smith was making wire recordings of Lummi songs and rituals, gathering artefacts and compiling a dictionary of dialects. His father taught him to draw the symbols of the Kabbala, which led in time both to the intricate designs

in his paintings, most of which survive only in photographic repro-
duction after Smith lost or destroyed them, and to his lifelong involvement with magic and the Ordo Templi Orientis of which the English
magus Aleister Crowley had been head. (Smith was eventually made a
bishop of the Order.) He liked to say that on his twelfth birthday his
father had presented him with a complete blacksmith's forge, and the
injunction to turn lead into gold. While this does not carry the ring of
truth, his background did spark an interest in the mechanical realization of metaphysics that would give his work a huge, albeit indirect,
influence. The light shows that accompanied rock concerts from the
mid-1960s onwards, together with certain aspects of contemporary
dance culture, derived from his experiments with oil and water on
projected slides, and from the films such as *Heaven and Earth Magic*
that comprise Smith's main auteurist achievement. However, the most
influential thing he gathered would turn out to be his assembly of an
anthology of recordings that itself incorporates his visual and literary
energies.

Harry Smith studied and intermittently practised alchemy. Alchemy
is blind-alley science, the doomed attempt to master reality by the
transformation of its base elements into something higher. A photo-
graph taken in 1985 by Allen Ginsberg finds Smith in the inauspicious
confines of New York's Breslin Hotel, following his temporary ejec-
tion from the Chelsea, the legendary tolerance of whose management
was stretched as much by the alchemist's self-transformations through
drugs and drink as by his chronic lack of funds. Prematurely ancient,
dwarfed by enormous horn-rimmed spectacles, he is shown in the lens
of his poet benefactor reduced by dyspepsia to 'transforming milk
into milk' (106). The photo of the young hipster reprinted on the back
of the third volume of the *Anthology of American Folk Music* could
not be more different: enigmatic shades, beard, the epitome of Fifties
cool, except that the hand pointing at the camera seems to warn as it
beckons, identifying the chosen ones but signalling that they will not
leave the same persons they were on entering. In the world of the
*Anthology*, as opposed to the Breslin, alchemy worked.

## The *Anthology*: memory and Modernism

The *Anthology* comes in a box decorated with an imposing design, a
drawing attributed correctly by Smith to Theodore DeBry and taken
from Robert Fludd's four-volume *History of the Macrocosm and the
Microcosm*, published in Germany between 1617 and 1619. In the

drawing we see the hand of God tuning, on what appears to be a single-string dulcimer, the Celestial Monochord: that is, drawing up into celestial harmony the four base elements of earth, water, fire and air, a symbolism perpetuated by the colours chosen for the sleeves of the albums inside the box. (Earth/brown is missing, as Smith was never satisfied with the notes he had written for this quarter of the music. He had, however, selected the tracks, and a careful reconstruction has been issued recently, happily completing the project.[3]) On opening the box, the listener finds a variety of materials, some added for the reissue. These include an essay by Greil Marcus on Smith and 'the old, weird America', which also forms a chapter of the latter's landmark study of Smith and his influence on Bob Dylan and the 1960s, *Invisible Republic* (1997).[4] More arrestingly, the listener who is at this stage, as throughout, a reader will find Harry Smith's original handbook to the eighty-four recordings in the *Anthology*. This is a scholarly document that lists dates of recording, alternative versions, origins where known, catalogue numbers and so on. The anthology is an iceberg-tip selection from Smith's personal collection, chunks of which broke away and drifted into the New York Public Library. What strikes the eye, however, is an anti-scholarly, presentational Surrealism that informs only to cast a spell of doubt over the outlines of fact. A kappellmeister taps his score, while a hand points to the legend 'All Please Sound' beneath the American eagle; he will reappear on the back cover with a giant trumpet balanced on his finger leading skywards in a blast of notes to an Apollonian lutanist in a circle of majors and minors. Pictures of musical instruments jostle reprints of the sleeves of 'race' records, as music aimed at an African-American audience was labelled, as well as quotations from Fludd and Aleister Crowley. The lyric of each track is summarized by the anthologist, sometimes helpfully, given the moschiferous condition of 1920s recordings and the twists of regional enunciation, but more often idiosyncratically.

Smith's retrieval of the lost was to be read as news, and his summaries eschew the daily for banner headlines that cross history: 'MEDIEVAL WOMAN DEFEATS DEVIL DESPITE HUSBAND'S PRAYERS' is his summary of Bill and Belle Reed's 'Old Lady and the Devil', which, like many tracks, is a Child ballad transmuted by Appalachian and blues traditions. Elsewhere a lazy farmer's boy is in deep trouble ('YOUNG AGRICULTURIST NEGLECTS SEED – LOSES BOTH CROP AND FIANCÉE'), though times are equally hard in town ('TECHNOLOGICAL UNEMPLOYMENT HITS SHOE INDUSTRY'); the bandit Cole Younger goes down ('BANK ROBBER VOICES REGRET FOR ASSOCIATION WITH JAMES

BOYS IN NORTHFIELD FIASCO'), but so does the Titanic; President Garfield's assassin speaks from the scaffold, but four songs later it is someone else's turn to suffer the 'White House Blues' ('MCKINLEY SWEARS, MOURNS, DIES. ROOSEVELT GETS WHITE HOUSE AND SILVER CUP'). Echoes of Joyce's methods in *Ulysses* are intentional. The sublime insinuations of Mississippi John Hurt's 'Frankie' (played at such a lick that Segovia, an early listener, refused to believe that only one guitar was used) are paraphrased obliquely by Smith as 'ALBERT DIES PREFERRING ALICE FRY, BUT JUDGE FINDS FRANKIE CHARMING AT LATTER'S TRIAL', while altogether elsewhere a parrot sings his refusal to alight on a murderess's knee, a boll-weevil avoids destruction by answering questions correctly like Oedipus in reverse, and froggie goes a-courting ('ZOOLOGIC MISCEGENY ACHIEVED IN MOUSE FROG NUPTUALS [*sic*], RELATIVES APPROVE'). Each track is connected by one link to the next. Sometimes the relationship is obvious, as the stabbing of 'Henry Lee' that opens the collection is succeeded by ritual child murder in 'Fatal Flower Garden', originally a Somerset folk-song and now sung to the melismatic keening of Hawaiian guitars. Sometimes, however, the links are conjectural or occult, as Smith attempted to organize rural music of the Southern States in the later 1920s along Fluddian and magical lines.

Memory is the key. The anthology is, like *Ulysses* and *The Cantos*, an epic of memory. As an ethnomusicologist, Smith had some affinities with Béla Bartók, whose forays into the indigenous rural music of Hungary and Romania would also result in a new fusion, equally primitivist-modernist. Fittingly, it was the composer's son Peter who transferred Smith's discs to tape for the *Anthology*. Like that of the Modernists, Smith's work questions the relationship between established history, buried histories and the creative role of consciousness. Where is America? Is it located in the minutiae of rural life or the accidentals of music, combined in the rise and fall of Casey Jones's fateful whistle? Or is the old, real America a matter of *region*, the last bastion against the loose, democratic Union hymned by Whitman that would impose its grid of highways, malls and Taco Bell from coast to coast? The *Anthology* presents a multi-faceted picture of the South, and is willing to try, but reluctant to settle for, any single explanation of the relationship between economics, oppression and artistic work. Smith chose tracks 'because they were odd' (Igliori, 126), 'exotic' in relation to both the music of high culture and the received idea of the 1920s as summed up by the Charleston and the Black Bottom. That elusive oddity questions the neatness of both an analysis that would root art exclusively in ethnic identity and subjugation and one that would airily dismiss history as mere material for the individual talent.

Discrepancy between voicing and presupposition recurs as an issue throughout: the Reverend Sister Mary Nelson sounds, frankly, like a man; the wonderful 'Spanish Merchant's Daughter' is credited to Hattie and Ernest Stoneman, but the mounting cry of 'No sir! No sir! No sir!' sounds to many like a male falsetto. Early listeners could not believe that Mississippi John Hurt was black. The choice of performers such as Hurt, Richard 'Rabbit' Brown, Henry Thomas and Prince Albert Hunt was strategic. The first three were 'songsters' moving easily from rags to ballads or blues. Brown was one of the first exponents of the twelve-bar blues, and he and Thomas (born at the end of the Civil War) go back to the time before the blues had established its hegemony in African-American music. Meanwhile Prince Albert Hunt, whose intriguing career was terminated at gunpoint by a jealous husband, gives evidence that a diversification of cultures in Texas and Louisiana could certainly entail the ready absorption of Magyar accent variations by fiddle-and-banjo dance music. Just as the narratives and styles of juxtaposed recordings shoulder each other out of the way, so models of influence based on monolithic lines of ethnicity or region become audibly and legibly simplistic.

The temptation for the scholar, particularly one of Harry Smith's eclectic and compendious tendencies, would be to say that America is all of this, in sum – all the recordings, all the sources, all that the archaeologist-collector can find and piece together so as to give a sense of how the past felt to those for whom it was the present. Here again memory is the key, and the anthology is, to use the title of an important essay by Robert Cantwell which has done much to shape my own understanding of the project, 'Smith's Memory Theater':

> Smith seems to have called upon the hermetic epistemology that fascinated the learned minds of Elizabethan England in the decades before Bacon and Descartes refined it into the scientific method. Robert Fludd had developed out of the old art of memory pertinent to the study of eloquence a so-called memory theater ... whose aim was to present the entire cosmos of knowledge in the form of alchemical, astrological and cabalistic symbols arranged in particular sequences on the terraces of a small circular amphitheater; a scholar could enter the theater to study, discovering in drawers or cabinets beneath each emblem those manuscripts summarizing the information represented by the emblem. (Cantwell, 204–5)

This description of Fludd's mnemonic library recalls the desktop of a personal computer, and Smith in interview used the phrase (as

Cantwell notes, esoteric in 1968) 'program the mind' (205). By study-
ing and using the emblems of the memory theatre or the PC, the adept
can access by systematic recall information larger than what can be
retained by the single consciousness. Writ large, such a practice points
ambiguously to a final and universal comprehension that would spell
the end of history, and an Edenic and unmediated apprehension of,
well, everything.

This is quite a lot to expect from six compact discs and two leaflets
in a box. That the *Anthology* does not disappoint expectation but
rather encourages deeper questioning, just as its own contesting
models of understanding are allowed to shatter in sequence, is a
testament to Smith's abilities as a dialectician of materials housed in
the cause of suggestion. To put it another way, the *Anthology* is a
Modernist collage – perhaps the last such, as the decade of the 1920s
that produced the great and varied collages by Pound, Joyce and the
Surrealists is the decade not of Smith's activity but of the artists'
whose work he reconfigures. Of course the music he chooses is
(generally) terrific, but in purely musical terms there are alternative
collections deriving from the *Anthology* that do the job as well. The
four-volume *Times Ain't Like They Used to Be* on the Yazoo label has
an arguably better track by Blind Willie Johnson, Skip James's suicid-
ally depressive 'I'm So Glad', Rabbit Brown's 'Sinking of the Titanic'
with its unforgettable gargling of 'Nearer My God to Thee', a blues
by Henry Thomas out of the 1890s that would draw tears from a
stone.[5] One of the functions of the *Anthology* is precisely to send the
listener out armed with the knowledge and the appetite that will open
other doors. At the very least, Smith's work demonstrates that the
second half of the 1920s discharged in a tremendous outburst of
artistic energy the accretions of centuries of words and music as
they had been shared in a thriving oral culture just before careers
were ruined by the Depression, followed by the loss of precious
shellac to recycling for wartime purposes. The discs that Smith collected by placing advertisements and cruising thrift shops were vanishing just at the moment of his approach.

Necessarily, there is also something of the vanishing trick about
Smith's collage, something inherently fey and of the circus tent. The
ludicrous paraphrases, the giant black numbers for the tracks, the
cartoons and quotations from Aleister Crowley (whose genius was for
publicity, whatever his darker talents) are intended to recall not only
the memory theatre of Robert Fludd but also the medicine show and
museum of oddities. One contributor to *American Magus: Harry
Smith* calls him the 'Barnum and Bailey' of magic (Igliori, 37). The
emblems, drawers and cabinets of the memory show ought to recall

the 'escritoire' of Melville's *The Confidence-Man*, with its sign of 'NO TRUST' and its black songster who must swallow irony to keep hold of the coin between his teeth. The model of the Elizabethan memory theatre is an important one, but its ultimate rejection in Smith's dialectics is what gives the *Anthology* its uniqueness and its critical edge.

There is something of the *Verfremdungseffekt* even in Smith's enthusiastic annotation. Smith elevated the role of critic to that of artist in his anthology, but was prescient in taking two further steps. First, this is the critic-artist, the creator, as *fan*, rather than as conservative curator in the Eliotic tradition enjoying its ascendancy at the time. The discs are the first historical example of something that would become popular as a gift and provide solace on long journeys at a later date: the personal compilation tape. Secondly, the process of listening to and reading the project opens up questions which, crucially, it is left to the reader/listener to arbitrate. The work does not seek to control its materials, but to collage them in the most provocative and questioning ways for the audience to turn over, and so half-create, and so take out into a world that can never now be quite the same again. The work fits an economy where the consumer has moved to centre-stage, but restores an element of creativity to consumption by handing over such complex historical materials. Smith was quite clear that his work was a counter-cultural and political statement: 'I felt social changes would result from it' (134).

## Radicalism and regional identities

At mid-century in the age just preceding the triumph of the credit card, Smith's pact with the listener marries elements of the bootleg economy and the radical left. Peter Bartók worked from Smith's own records rather than master tapes which would clearly have had to be paid for, had they been available; the first release perched on the border of legality and piracy. In another sense the reverse is true, in that anthologization was made possible by the new microgroove technology that released the music from its captivity in 78 rpm format, elevating it to the status of classical music and the community of hi-fidelity buffs. 'Hence the Folkways Anthology in effect legitimized its material, investing it with the cultural authority both of its advanced technology and its rarefied sociopolitical connections. What had been, to the people who originally recorded it, essentially the music of the poor, the isolated, and the uneducated, the Anthology reframed as a kind of avant-garde art' (Cantwell, 190). Robert Cant-well's implication of innocence exploited is open to question, at least in the case of certain artists. His 1996 study of the Folk Revival and its association with the Civil Rights movement is entitled *When We Were Good*, and, for all its usefulness, reminds us that when we were good, we could be awfully prissy. The discs were issued on the Folkways label, now controlled by the Smithsonian, but then run by Moses Asch, whom Cantwell presents persuasively as a Fludd for 1950s America and 'a kind of ethnographer ... proposing a complete acoustic record of the human lifeworld' (190). Alongside mountain ballads, Woody Guthrie, cowboy songs, the speaking voices of Sig-mund Freud and Martin Luther King, Asch recorded 'infant cries, technological sounds from office equipment and locomotives, bird calls, and the sound of the rain forest' (191). This sounds very like Smith's unfinished project *Materials for the Study of the Religion and Culture of the Lower East Side*, which included bird-song, talk and children's skipping rhymes. And so Asch too was a fan turned artist, hooked on echo, innovation, correspondence, the local becoming the universal.

As already noted, the *Anthology* activates various models by which its materials can be interpreted, only to subject them to unceasing dialectical pressure. These include the understanding of music in its minutiae, as the expression of region, and as part of a totalization whose ancestry lies in an Edenic and pre-scientific holism. A further route to constructing a sense for the whole is that of literary allegory. The pieces are sequenced in generic groups, with the first two albums labelled by Smith 'Ballads', the second set 'Social Music', subdivided into dance and church music, followed by the final Volume of 'Songs'. The two albums of 'Songs' are the climax of the project; they are where the going gets weird (Didier Hébert, Dock Boggs, Clarence Ashley), where bravura performances jostle for attention (Lemon Jefferson, Hurt, Lunsford), and where the ordering of materials pro-duces an allegorical narrative. The narrative moves from the isolated experience of danger and desire, on to prison, work songs, death and finally to competing and contradictory versions of Paradise. It is in this area that the *Anthology* outperforms other collections of music in the complexity of what it can offer, and it is noticeable that in this extra dimension music becomes the means to the construction of a work that is essentially literary. A new national epic, dealing with models of enslavement and freedom, the *Anthology* is also one man's performance, using his own record collection as material. The final tracks are alternative exits from the memory theatre, any one of which may turn out to be an egress, in Barnum's sense. They have to be read actively and critically as versions of America, and not simply appreciated by passive listening.

## Allegory, prison and Paradise: work songs, dissidence and the minstrel tradition

Tracks 71–84 begin with five prison songs, succeeded in a straightforwardly allegorical gesture by Lemon Jefferson's plaintive 'See That My Grave is Kept Clean', a version of which would appear several years later on Bob Dylan's first album, together with two other songs from Smith's box. The next cut, 'C'est si triste sans lui', mourns someone's passing in the almost atonal surges of Cajun music from so obscure a source that Smith has no annotation to offer, a historical lacuna that turns the patois of the lyric in a self-referential direction. There follow two songs by Uncle Dave Macon, one of the oldest performers represented. Many of his songs contain vignettes of social and political life in the South. The first, 'Way Down the Old Plank Road', is about working on a Georgia chain-gang, though the signals sent out by the words and music are intriguingly at variance, as Uncle Dave's ecstatic playing, singing ('KILL YOURSELF!') and dancing (unless it's someone whacking the floor with a chain) make forced labour sound like a Dionysiac rave. By contrast, track 79, 'Buddy Won't You Roll Down the Line', a superb recording for 1928, offers a clear-eyed account of the Coal Creek Rebellion which took place in East Tennessee in the 1890s, when mining companies hired convict labour as an instrument to break the miners' union. This plan backfired when, in an armed rebellion, the miners freed the convicts, though their leaders went to gaol. We are back in a zone like Dock Boggs's Virginia, where guns go off like firecrackers and 'people were afraid'. Such rebellions were still common at the time of Macon's and Boggs's recordings, and have been played down in modern accounts. For example, in 1920, West Virginia's Logan County was effectively a state within a state, with striking miners, company assassins and detectives shooting each other (and the mayor) in the streets. By August of the following year, between ten and twenty thousand men were firing at each other in a civil war around Blair Mountain, which, as Greil Marcus notes laconically, exceeded the number mobilized by George Washington in the battle that changed the course of the American Revolution (Marcus, 57).

The theme of political dissidence is picked up by Mississippi John Hurt in 'Spike Driver Blues'. This is a 'John Henry' song, one of many in a genre centred on the steel-driving prowess of a mythical black man. Cantwell builds on the work of Alan Lomax, whose early field recordings were instrumental in the retrieval of the lost musics, to argue that 'John Henry' songs are the primal scene of folk-song, one where 'sexual potency, physical beauty, strength, endurance, and grace, the search for authenticity, the recovery of democracy, and the industrial age itself make clandestine meeting in an actual and symbolic underworld where America's images of itself are forged' (Cantwell, 76–7). Cantwell's and Lomax's reverence for the 'orgasmic' thunderbolt of the driver with his hammer sounds like a guilty inferiority complex, vulnerable to ridicule as many white posturings on the left–folk axis were. More persuasive is Cantwell's spotting of the 'secretion of power' in the image of John Henry. The hammer that rivets the industrial machine is also the 'kingpin' of the folk-song that sets a man against it, but the power is buried, a man in a mine, an image related by Cantwell not only to 'the social unconscious' but to black minstrel, and indeed black-face, traditions.

It appears that the ruling elite of seventeenth-century Virginia, mindful of their own place in the English hierarchy, were prompted by cultural nostalgia and the exigencies of social control to compel their African slaves to play the role of English serfs – in David Fischer's words, 'to dress like English farm workers, to play English folk games, to speak an English country dialect, and to observe the ordinary rituals of English life in a charade that Virginia planters organized with great care' (23). The minstrel-serf would mutate over time into the black-face minstrels who were ousted from the television screen of my childhood less by outraged sensibility than by the arrival of pop singers who were, ironically, their latest mutation. For an English youth like Mick Jagger to sing black rhythm and blues from the stage of the London Palladium with his trademark loucheness and ragamuffin shuffle was to continue the fey artifice of a minstrel tradition that runs from the Virginia plantations to videos of rappers or Michael Jackson. The implications of this for the transmission of folk-song from Scottish or Somerset origins to Texas or the Appalachians undo any po-faced account of folk tradition as rooted in authenticity and its synonyms. Cantwell remains in thrall to such sentimentality even as his own best insights blow its cover.

Harry Smith's choice and arrangement of tracks evidence a historical imagination that, in attending to the nuances and secreted powers of the past, could predict with accuracy. Significantly, he concentrates on voice and guitar, so the keyboard is barely represented in his *Anthology*, despite its centrality to both church music and the bar-room. In returning to the 1920s, he conjures by these means the image of the singer of 'Mystery Train' and 'Hound Dog' a little (1952) before the coming of Elvis. A price is paid, for Smith's focus on the recordings of the pre-war tradition is as male-dominated as the rock and roll tradition would be. Anyone wanting to hear Big Mama Thornton's original 'Hound Dog' or the lesbian blues of Ma Rainey and Bessie Smith ('I went out last night with a crowd of my friends. / They must have been women 'cause I don't like no men'), the octave range of Ethel Waters, or the work of white blues singers such as Mildred Bailey will unfortunately have to look elsewhere.[6]

In other respects, and to return to Mississippi John Hurt, historical resonance and range are exactly what the *Anthology* stands for. 'Spike Driver Blues' is a document rich in suggestion, as when Hurt's inimitable, caressing whisper carries to the inner ear the line 'This is the hammer that killed John Henry, but it won't kill me'. The repetition intrinsic to the blues form and which signifies despair in more clichéd efforts becomes in this case an explosive political promise: '*no, it won't kill me.*' On that note, history shoots from the anthology through the two-dimensional cut-out Presley to become the conflagration of the Watts riots. This music anticipates the era of Civil Rights and assassinations, the speeches given and the bullet taken by Martin Luther King. Decades not yet lived seem implicit in the next track also, as the Memphis Jug Band's 'KC Moan' subdues their usual jollity to the atmosphere of a funeral parlour. Three alternative egresses follow.

J. P. Nestor recorded four songs in Tennessee in late middle age, of which track 82, 'Train on the Island' (with Norman Edmonds on fiddle), is one. That excursion appears to have been enough, for, despite invitations to record, Nestor never left Virginia again. 'Train on the Island' is the kind of discovery which Bartók understood fully. The level of skill in play is so high that any notion of folk-music, let alone *Volk* music, as beguiling by its untutored innocence is knocked out of court. Yet the texture of the music moves to such a level of complex implication – for example, in its subdivision of the semitone – that the folk-musics of other lands and times, including most definitely Asia and North Africa, are evoked. Notes tumble over each other in a bravura display of telepathic fingering, an early and unsurpassed example of the kind of approach that would be brought to popularity in later years by Flatt and Scruggs, and which remains the template for bluegrass. In a deeper sense the heart of the music beats in infinitesimal silences generated by a slight lag between Edmonds's soaring cadences and Nestor's frailing. It is as if things could move so fast that, as in certain technological contexts, a paradoxical stillness ensued in which clock time stops and things float. This is reinforced by the train theme, to which various sorts of animate and inanimate coupling are clearly germane, as the hortatory intimacies of the ballad tradition – 'go tell my true love' – are wedded to ambiguity – 'I can't roll the wheel'. Cantwell's musicological explanation of ambiguities in the lyric stems from his identification of the melody as a descendant of an Irish reel, 'Lady on the Island', traditionally coupled with a work song, 'Callahan's Reel', the ensuing lyrical ambiguity a function of mingling elements from two different pieces. Whatever set it in motion, 'Train on the Island' is a musical Paradise of speed and unfettered agility, its overlapping ecstasies of sound, sex and flight into the hyperborean Galax of a Virginia aptly named, and nevermore to leave.

The penultimate way out of the anthology is Ken Maynard's 'The Lone Star Trail'. Maynard was the first singing cowboy in the movies and starred in more than 300. He worked as a real cowboy, a rodeo and circus performer, and a stunts man touring with the Kit Carson show. 'The Lone Star Trail' came from the film *The Wagon Master* of 1929, but the song itself dates back to the old days of cattle drives. 'Oh, I love the rolling prairie that's far from trail and strife. / Find a bunch of longhorns, I'll journey all my life.' To Cantwell the song is simply awful, ersatz, and Maynard's stumbling into the exalted company of the *Anthology* shows him up as 'the classic bumpkin, utterly out of place' (230). No bumpkins on Folkways then. By these lights, Smith's decision to include the track must therefore be an egregious error of taste or, more likely, given its crucial position in the set, a deliberate impertinence that reminds us of white America's willingness to airbrush out exactly the kind of pain and unabridged oppression that the preceding songs document. While this is at least plausible (and Smith's box wants to be open to exactly these sorts of questions), it overstates the case, exposing the fault lines in the authenticity cult of the Folk Revival. Maynard's vocalizations are hardly more restricted, more 'white', than those of Frank Hutchison singing the impeccably canonical 'Stackalee'.

Most likely the interest to Smith of a figure such as the singing cowboy was not that he drowned the authentic in the ersatz, but that he incarnated a period in which the one turned rapidly into the other, willy-nilly. The cattle drives began in the aftermath of the Civil War, and were gone in a generation. As Philip Fisher writes, in America's modern economy 'the forms of life move and the claims of regional or stable identity weaken in the face of the obvious survival value of change and mobility' (172). One American version of Paradise is the recycling for cultural nostalgia of what was in active use a moment ago; the authentic and the inauthentic are joined at the hip, and often cover for each other when the going gets rough out on the trail. The results can be intentionally or unintentionally camp, which in Susan Sontag's famous definition entails the setting of inverted commas around what was previously simply there. Ken Maynard is more camp than camp-fire, and sounds as if he's singing in inverted commas: 'But I can "twist a lassoo" with the greatest, "killin'" ease / Or rope and ride "a bronco" most anywhere I please.' But camp, in certain other contexts the signature of sexual orientation, can also spell something utterly different, as here: the unmeant, hapless broaching of a critical perspective by the acceleration and whim of ideology. By 1914, Kit Carson was 'Kit Carson'.

Greil Marcus is more taken than Robert Cantwell with 'The Lone Star Trail', reading between the lines of its blues-rinsed yodel and affable commercialism a figure of freedom. 'The shape of the land, its vast expanse, its indifference to who you are or what you want, looms up as this solitary figure says his piece: I am the first cowboy and the last. Here no one sees me, myself least of all, I am happy, I am free' (Marcus, 111). Marcus is a seductive interpreter of America, and perhaps the most important these days. An enlivening historian of popular culture, he convinces through the kind of close reading for which Literature departments no longer have much time. What appeals in his picturing of Maynard is its capture not only of a sentimental and an anti-sentimental image of the cowboy – gone from working man to movie and myth in the space of Maynard's lifetime ('I am the first cowboy and the last') – but also of the bleak freedom of existentialism and its lonely choices that were cooling the air at the time of espresso and black polo-necks, while Smith fashioned his contesting narratives of America.

But these are time-bound questions, whereas the final track, Henry Thomas's 'Fishing Blues', conjures Paradise from timeless sound. I hope I am using the word 'timeless' in a precise and not simply a clichéd sense, just as I believe that when Greil Marcus describes this performance as 'the freest song imaginable', his words are loaded and carefully chosen (111). It is a simple thing, more of a rag than a blues. The lyric is about going down to the river, hooking a catfish and frying it in a skillet. However, the reader/listener is led to open doors that lead in widely different directions, both by Thomas's artless art and by Smith's positioning of it. 'Here's a little something I would like to relate / Any fish bite if you got good bait.' Fishing images in the blues tradition are often sexual, and the performance is highly effective in retaining those possibilities, lightly, alongside its simple idyll of escape. Innocence and experience are not antithetical here, in a primal American text. Huck Finn comes to mind.

Thomas was a songster, virtually contemporary with the shipboard minstrel of *The Confidence-Man*. He learned some of his material in the 1890s. And just as Thomas's musical memory reaches so far into the past, so some songs have an untroubled prescience, for example, 'Bull Doze Blues', which one of the best rhythm-and-blues bands of the 1960s, Canned Heat, would rework only slightly as 'Goin' Up the Country'. It is telling that they rewrote the lyrics to incorporate references to the turbulence and riots of America in 1968, but were able to retain Thomas's melody without seeming to offer a piece of nostalgia. They also duplicated note for note, on a flute, the solo Thomas plays on his quill – pan-pipes he cut himself from canebreak.

It is above all the pipes that give 'Fishing Blues' its distinctive charm. Of course, a busking itinerant African-American singing about catching his own food and playing the quills is manna for the folk cult, and the sound of those pipes sends Cantwell's prose into outer space: 'It is the sound of something breaking free, something above the world, Andean, forged in that limbic region where natural forms, animated by human forces, return to throng a human consciousness evacuated by its own projections' (Cantwell, 235). Indeed, the quills sound ethereal yet real, as fresh and yet as old as going fishing. You could hear some arrangement of that handful of notes played tomorrow in Cuzco or Washington DC. Equally, one might have stood idly practising those pipes while another scratched the earliest surviving instance of writing, on the wall of a sapphire mine in what is now Iran. All of Thomas's playing has that timeless charm. All of Smith's assemblages have an anthropological perspective. The two in tandem, in the *perpetuum mobile* of the *Anthology*, create a collaborative form proposing journeys whose limits are, even now, not in sight.

## American space

In his study *The Anxious Object*, Harold Rosenberg observes in passing that modern artists have been driven to choose between an art of deep or of layered space.[7] To an art of deep space belong all questions and certainties of metaphysics, religion and the extremes of consciousness. Any hierarchical ordering of perceptual data has the potential to lead to an art of deep space, in whatever medium. The tradition of Northern European landscape painting that depicts the inner by recourse to representations of the outer world, epitomized by Friedrich or Turner, is clearly a move into deep space that has repercussions for the history of painting up to the present day. For example, the work in the 1940s and beyond by the Abstract Expressionists centred in New York – Jackson Pollock and Mark Rothko *inter alia* – absorbs the bequest of the landscape tradition, and pushes it to new extremes of inwardness. That body of work can be viewed as both the assertion of subjective, inner space over the Cold War demands of the social centre and an ironic confirmation of a newfound world-dominance happy to fund culture while investing in the more literal explorations of deep space pioneered by its technocracy. Being abstract, this expressionism could depict nothing so controversial as an issue. So it was that the art of Jackson Pollock could be seen, without contradiction, as both the psychodrama of an outlaw Romanticism and the latest adornment of bourgeois culture (used, as it was and with the artist's consent, by County Homes Inc. of Tarrytown, New York, to help sell their executive villas). The artists painted, the galleries sold, the museums housed, and the State Department funded the triumph of the avant-garde. This is the house that Jackson Pollock built, and there are some very deep spaces here.

However, to return to Harold Rosenberg's key terms, the more crucial and pugilistic advances in painting, literature and music tended in the twentieth century to be made in the service of an art of layered, rather than deep, space. This is noticeable in the European art that influenced (and in certain ways prompted) American art in the wake of the Armory Show. A layered space art would be typified by the innovations of Mondrian, Léger and Picasso in his Cubist phase. Here paint is configured in shapes and flats which, be they referential, semi- or non-representational, are freed from metaphysical ambition and press their claims on our attention by virtue of their *intensity*, rather than their place in some order. Such an emphasis on instantaneous effect suggests the adaptation of the late Romantic cult of the moment to the tempo of a society for which change is becoming a *modus operandi*. Meanwhile, in poetry, the work of William Carlos Williams presents a layered-space manifesto as influential in its sphere as Picasso's and Braque's Cubism. Crucial early poems such as 'The Great Figure', which would in time help shape the practice of Frank O'Hara, Robert Creeley and other poets cited in chapter 7, press the case for a materialist poetic in which any metaphysical extension to the visible surface, or the experienced moment, is happily and polemically denied. So the line 'I saw the figure 5' is weighted equally at both ends, the first-person singular claiming no privileges over the numeral in Williams's layered-space world.[8]

Williams's bequest would be perhaps the most widely spread in modern American poetry, wider than that of Pound or Stevens; yet the fierceness of his disavowal of deep symbolism for the layered everyday is so extreme as to make him a frontier loner in the history of his nation's poetry, even today. And ideas of the nation are bound up with his poetics. When asked where the language of his poems came from, Williams famously replied that it came out of the mouths of Polish mothers, an allusion, truthful no doubt but polemical, to the immigrant inflections he heard as a doctor in general practice in New Jersey. The retort is not just anti-*The Waste Land*, as is all Williams's mature poetry, but a measured refusal to get involved with the deep spaces, of origin, of hinterland, of Poland, that induction into American citizenship must denature to complete its work. Out of Polish, Ukrainian, Mexican mouths comes material for the American poem; democratic, Whitmanesque, a loose assemblage: layered. It is still generally true that in an English social gathering or an English poem, the elements invited know where they stand, know their place. In any American gathering people mill, vaguely but amiably, somehow at a loss, but still more free to come and go. It has to be a layered space to work. In the deeps would lie danger and flight, difference and the past; ancestral voices prophesying war.

No doubt my amplification of a passing remark by Harold Rosenberg into the animating principle of a nation and its literature is as susceptible to deconstruction as any other use of a binary opposition. And even if the terms are acceptable, it is actually the case that poets, perhaps to be distinguished from the painters in this area, have shown the influence of both kinds of mind-set, rather than an extreme commitment to either a deep- or a layered-space view. T. S. Eliot, for example, in one sense the high priest of deep space, shows even in his late work a recourse to collage and to the fragment as the poetic unit, which qualifies subtly his determination to find cycles, full circles and wholeness. The same might be said of Robert Duncan, and in a different way again of W. H. Auden. Conversion to the rituals of the Episcopal Church brought no deeper spaces to the sharps and flats of Auden's talky, worldly poems. The only deep space, to Auden, might have been the whole that all the Audens, churchy, gay, English Marxist-Freudian, American liberal-professorial, might have made when hypothetically conjoined; but any possibility of conjunction is made fantastic by a rigorous commitment to knowledge as dialectical. The poem to Auden is what makes the next poem possible, and not another stone in the ziggurat of prior achievements, as one senses that Yeats thought, despite the seeming allegiance to layered-space experiment in his later rhetorics and calculated impatience with age.

Depths and layering, the cosmic and the close at hand, flip in and out of each other. In some ways this is not an American phenomenon, but a way of reading phenomena that stems from the ideas developed by Novalis and sundry Schlegels in the later 1790s; one that, beginning from a base in Germany, has influenced countless ideas and institutions, from art for art's sake to permanent revolution, conservative and socialist models of the State: in short, modernity. The Romantic generation that grew up reading Schiller or knowing Goethe was bent on a revolution of the spirit to surpass the bloodier revolt in France, where a deep-space State symbolism of divine and regal stratification had been levelled to fragments. Just as the Gothic begins here, so Novalis's rather bluesy title *Urtöne meiner Empfindung* ('Urtones of My Feeling') begets a Romantic individualism which, like the German interest in *Naturphilosophie*, would pass to the English Lake Poets via Coleridge, and hence to Emerson. Keatsian synaesthesia, Baudelaire's *correspondances*, Wagner's opera, Symbolism, environmentalism, both the fragmentation into -isms and the urge to bring them into interdisciplinary conversation in a moment such as structuralism or an idea like the modern university, all begin here, in what Friedrich Schlegel called the *Symphilosophieren*, the symphonic thinking, of the Jena Circle. The English poets were, from the outset, of a more doubting cast of mind than the popular image of Wordsworth as an ecstatic nature-lover suggests. When to this were added the weight of tradition and the apparent perils of radical upheaval, the English avant-garde began its retreat into quietism. Emerson, by contrast, lived on the cusp of settled achievement and infinite possibility following a successful revolution, an Eden that could claim material place, an effectively unlimited stretch of the earth, as the grounds, literal and intellectual, of its newly won freedoms. In the advanced study of these developments in universities, we see today a nicely balanced mutual blindness. America concedes its emergence from Europe in what is ultimately a gesture of dismissal rather than affiliation, an understandable reflex action which risks denying the debts the nation's governing tropes and ideas owe to European Romanticism and to Jena in particular. Meanwhile, to British scholars of British Romanticism, 'America' is either a poem by Blake or a place to give a paper, but rarely acknowledged to be the *real* outcome of the bygone literary and philosophical debates in which they claim expertise.

England saw its French neighbours in revolt, saw its Empire grow to dominate the world, and saw the fall of both, stained. American revolt reinforced the trope of a New World in one sense bruised irrevocably but in another consolidated by the experience of the Civil War. These variations in Romantic nationalism and its aftermath lead to a difference in the likely ratios of deep to layered space within the self-understanding of the British and the American. Britain is characterized by irritable and contesting layered spaces – of nations within the nation, of class antagonism, of capitalist development – that collide and find compromise inside mythic images of deep space, emblematized by the Royal Family, that have proved surprisingly durable. They have lasted because, if Britain truly modernized and got rid of them, it would be small, naked, simplified: a more urbanized Norway. This is not thought desirable, for reasons that are as tenacious as they are perhaps irrational. America loves deep-space symbolism, from Cape Canaveral to the Washington Monument, canyons photographed by Ansel Adams, the American Dream – dreams are the deepest, most duplicitous spaces imaginable – above all the flag, and the mysticism of Union won from struggle. Secretly, America is about venerating the deep while allowing the layered to win every time. The dream breaks on waking. A region, pre-eminently the South, can image itself as a deep space, but such presumption merely draws attention to its failure as a pseudo-State. The States are layered spaces.

## 'Don't move! The eggs will explode!'

At no point in this sketch of concepts have Harry Smith and his *Anthology of American Folk Music* been left behind. Rather, the reverse: the occult secrets of Smith's box of tricks collapse into transience and improvisation, much as the unblown eggs he would paint, gaseous and fragile, soon reached their expiry. 'Don't move! The eggs will explode!' was a frequent warning to the innocent visitor (Igliori, 153). Smith observed more evenly in an interview, with the blend of Dada and anthropology that characterized his activities, that 'a rotten egg is about the most transient medium, it is about the most difficult thing to paint on' (140). A layered space, then; a shell, the decoration of a passing moment. The *Anthology* is a succession of such aural and literary moments, yet questions of deep space recur in its perpetual motion. As Greil Marcus notes, our first reaction is a question: Who *are* these people? Who is singing? The past that was lost offers itself to partial reconstruction, but, more importantly, the voices become a counter-cultural band, a prompt to Smith's 'social changes' and the understanding that if things could have been so different then as to sound so other now, then the future could be different again, and the present not what it seems.

## Fishing for hidden meanings: Rabbit Brown, Bascom Lamar Lunsford and the lyric

This Möbius strip runs through every track at the micro-level. 'Old times ain't now nothing like they used to be. / And I'm telling you all the truth, you can take it from me.' Beginning its song, Rabbit Brown's voice sounds ancient, the echo chamber of his guitar confirming the rounded and aphoristic quality of the lyric. This is 'James Alley Blues', in the real history of New Orleans Jane's Alley, also known as the Battleground, a place where the police did not venture. Brown sings from the depths, the deep well where the excluded are invited to drown themselves. Yet the guitar style is in no fixed sense regional, and its bass runs and flamenco strumming testify to a mix of ethnic and cultural influences, as does Brown's voice, its changes throughout the song a self-aware piece of acting. He's seen better days, but he's 'putting up with these', the roguish world-weariness a blatant put-on, influenced vocally by the stage, rich with artifice and nothing like the insistent negritude, the fierce adherence to gospel tones and prophecy to be heard in, say, Blind Willie Johnson. ('Scary! Lion!', was my two-year-old son's correct reaction on first hearing Johnson growl 'His Blood Will Make me Whole'.) The penultimate and final verses of Brown's 'James Alley Blues' canvass as wide and as nuanced a spectrum of tones as could be slipped into the available time. Brow-beaten aggression is succeeded by plaintive affection, protested fidelity, possessiveness, lust and a murderous disregard. The last verse follows a curve from love to misogyny, while never straying from dark humour and a certain psychological acuity regarding the confinement and abrasion to be negotiated in any relationship:

> Sometime I think that you too sweet to die.
> Sometime I think that you too sweet to die.
> And another time I think, *you ought to be buried alive.*

The layerings of tone are in one sense swallowed in the deep space of the grave and that vicious last line, and yet in this shifting performance burial is just another noun-token in the give and take of the relationship, like the sugar and salt given and taken in an earlier verse. The flamenco strum of the opening chords would be reworked by the group Love in their classic 'Alone Again Or' (1967), while the salt and sugar would find their way into Bob Dylan's 'Down in the Flood', a track from the *Basement Tapes*, never released officially in their entirety, but which are effectively Dylan's rewriting of the *Anthology*, songs from which have found their way into recordings by him covering a span of forty years. Smith's project is literally interminable, the music reworking material so old that it never had a starting-point.

Inasmuch as there was a point of origin, it was in the British ballad tradition of materials gathered earlier by Child. One of the paradoxes of Smith's achievement is that, in helping to trigger the American Beat movement and its diffusion into Civil Rights politics and hippie disaffection, he retrieved a body of work which more than any artefact since the seventeenth century reminds its audience of the umbilical ties between American and British literature. Tracing such lines of descent allows deep to become layered space in a Möbius strip, the hum of the circum-Atlantic, as news and myth interrupt each other's claims. Sometimes the most baffling texts, their literary bones eburnated and rearranged by the winds of time, are the most sharply effective.

What *is* Bascom Lamar Lunsford's 'I Wish I Was a Mole in the Ground' about? If it were knowable, it would not be so powerfully what it is, another aspect of primitivist-modernism: 'If I was a mole in the ground, I'd root that mountain down.' Mountain metaphors are undone by metonyms, deep spaces by layered, the whole – the whole what? the whole thing, is all one can say – brought to ruin by the burrowing vengeful mole. It is as if Paul de Man's diagnosis of allegory undoing symbolism in the rhetoric of Romanticism were retold as a farmyard ditty. Fragments of different songs and rhymes seem to have found themselves cohabiting over time, like skeletons separated by generations finally embracing in the same burial-ground. Some of the limbs are recognizably American, as bangs curl around and their owner asks sweetly for a nine-dollar shawl, but the 'o'er's and 'tis'es and the syntactical structure seem much older and from another place. In the strange middle reaches of the song, who can say what's at stake and in play, as the voice wishes he was 'a lizard' in the spring. Priapic, suavely serpentine, without meaning: the possibilities flatten, balloon, alternate without rest. Lunsford's voicing is at one with these mysteries. Generally given to the clearest enunciation, here he lets his vowels slide crazily, an element of weirdly unctuous laughter in the voice setting an umlaut on each vowel like a lizard on a stone. Where is 'the Bend'? – 'I've been in the Bend, with the rough and rowdy men, / 'Tis baby where you been so long' – this is particularly teasing, when 'been' and 'Bend' are given almost identical pronunciation. Rewritten slightly, the following lines would find their way into Bob Dylan's 'Stuck Inside of Mobile with the Memphis Blues Again', but whereas *Blonde on Blonde* epitomizes Sixties cool,

Lunsford is anything but: 'O, I don't like a railroad man. / If I was a railroad man, they'll kill you when he can [*sic*] / And drink up your blood like wine.' In what incident, myth or mishearing did this travesty of Communion have roots? Is time the only mole that can root these mountains down?

There is no end to these trails of enquiry. When the sign on the door reads 'Gone Fishing', that is the ultimate layered space, the flat card telling us that nothing is going to happen except an absence. Yet this is also a deep space, a withdrawal of the person to a private adventure, from which he may return like a child or an Ancient Mariner, with a tale to tell. Such duplicity begets a career for Bascom Lamar Lunsford, whose 'Memory Collection' of several hundred performances lies waiting in the Library of Congress, a canon in itself, yet one of the least-known *oeuvres* by an American great. His renditions are all, to put it mildly, double. I never heard a singing voice that could inhabit so deeply, while standing so far outside to watch, the developing outline of a song. Though his loping banjo playing is strategically effective, this is a reading of poetry raised to the power of music.

He lived many lives inside and outwith the many Americas: postgraduate student, teacher, lawyer, ballad collector, fruit-tree salesman, court solicitor, secretary of the Marion board of trade, founder of America's first folk festival, political campaign manager for Congressman Zeb Weaver, a federal agent in New York. A biography would cast light on Carolina and Kentucky life in those times. It would surely uncover the connections that took him to the White House, to play for the President and Mrs Roosevelt and King George VI, in 1939. Lunsford was obviously a great host, and was often called on to be so, a powerful man of obscure involvements as well as origins:

> His cozy white home on South Turkey Creek has long been a gathering spot for musicians, singers, dancers and even State Department-squired guests to this country ... the latter many times stiffly-correct (at first) delegations from behind the Iron Curtain.... The Europeans may have come across an ocean, but folk dancing is folk dancing the world over. But one request, to add his name to a group of folksingers opposing US policies in Viet Nam, riled him good. Lunsford says folk music often has patriotic themes and he went on to criticize those who would use it for political motives, particularly in opposition to their country.[9]

We have only begun to uncover what lies beneath the scratched surfaces of Harry Smith's 78s.

# 6

# Modernism and the Subversive Imagination

## Trashing tradition

Writing in 1921, T. S. Eliot argued that poetry 'must be *difficult*', producing the 'various and complex results' of a complex civilization playing on the modern sensibility.[1] However, to Pound in his Imagist phase or to Gertrude Stein in her insistence on repetition-with-variation as textual motor, clarity of line was to be valued over Victorian vagueness. (Comparable alternations can be found in the histories of twentieth-century music and art.) Allied to these first two sets of binary oppositions is a persisting debate over the contents, value and meaning of the rubbish heap. When William Carlos Williams chose to forage on the wrong side of the tracks for his Americanist poetic, aesthetic and ethical imperatives combined to lead him to picture '[t]he old man who goes about gathering doglime' whose tread is more majestic than that of 'the Episcopal minister' (Williams 42). While the Eliot of *The Waste Land* is hardly sniffing the same air, both writers are up to their necks in a Modernist attention to debris, the unacceptable, the broken, the rejected. This tradition is as much as anything the base for modern American writing, evolving decades later into such texts of provocation as Allen Ginsberg's *Howl* and its partner in disgust, William Burroughs's *The Naked Lunch*.

In their dissidence and individualism as emerging writers, all these figures repeat the American pattern of Revolutionary parricide. The Modernist impulse is to repeat Huck Finn's urge to light out for the territory, even where the spaces to be negotiated are urban, conceptual or technologically determined. However, they show an unexpected affinity in exactly those areas where the discoveries and advances of their work unpick individualism, disclosing in anti-Marxist America a sense of the individual as the product of the system, which in key respects runs parallel to Marxist analysis. African-American writing, such as the poetry of Amiri Baraka and Stephen Jonas, also examined in this chapter, begins from an acute apprehension of the effects of the system on identity, grounded in the history of slavery and segregation. In Baraka's case this leads, in one phase of his career, to a commitment to revolutionary Marxism. This is temporary and untypical. More characteristically, American unravellings of the individualist *vericulum* lead to a contained misrule. The textual anarchy and carnival-esque effects of Ginsberg and Burroughs, the jazz poetry of Baraka and Jonas, push dissidence to a limit, America's perimeter fence, and stop there. No matter that Ginsberg has a metaphysics of universalism that allows him to meditate until the fence feels unreal; no matter that Burroughs would jump the fence for years at a time to live in Tangier or Paris or Mexico. They never truly leave America, and Whitman and Emerson remain Ginsberg's spirit guides, just as Burroughs's repudiation of government brings him closer to backwoods survival-ism and the NRA than it does to a real *non serviam*, the real ideo-logical alternatives ingrained until recently in European and other experience. T. S. Eliot was arguably as radical in the implications of his work, while remaining the most conservative in terms of his self-construction as an author and arbiter of culture. It is precisely a self-awareness regarding the constructed nature of identity that gives Modernism its negativist, critical intensity – even as its practitioners were driven to political commitments that contradict their own best insights.

Ezra Pound (1885–1972) is the classic case. When you travel back in time, you can see, but you cannot be seen. In other words, you have memory. Meanwhile, in the flat public records called history, you can be seen, but have no power. It was Pound's distinction to attempt to 'gather from the air a live tradition' (to adopt the formula of Canto LXXXI) in which selfhood and history could at last confirm each other.[2] The phenomenological poles of self and not-self would be replaced by a medium, poetry, where each is articulated through the other. Such ambition and scope had not been seen in poetry since the Romantics, of whom Pound the critic was not a great reader, but to whose work Pound the poet remained indebted, by way of their aesthete inheritors. *The Cantos*, the unfinished epic of poetic collage on which Pound worked from 1915 to 1969, retains a modernized Pre-Raphaelitism as the preferred stylistic route to those numinous moments that signal the nearest thing to a credo in Pound's word-hoard. Lines such as 'the coral face under wave-tinge' in Canto II, or 'Eyes floating, in dry dark air' in Canto VII, evoke the world of Swinburne and Dante Gabriel Rossetti just at those moments where Pound's poetry rises to its own highest peaks of visionary intensity. Nor is this kind of effect confined to the early Cantos, as a wistful and much-quoted fragment from the Pisan section makes clear: 'To build the city of Dioce whose terraces are the colours of stars' (451). Here the things and forms of the world are neither subjective nor objective, but rather moments of reciprocal harmony, instances of phenomeno-logical equilibrium, a modernization of Pater's cult of the instant. The visionary emphases are backward-looking, find more in the past than the present, and led Pound the activist towards a tapinocephalic politics. In another sense, it is precisely the emphasis on the instant, there since the snapshots of Imagism, that generates Pound's bequests. The fragmentation that spelt a botch to him became the starting-point for a younger generation of writers, some of whom, Allen Ginsberg or Charles Olson, visited him during his enforced sequestration in St Elizabeths Hospital, Washington. 'I cannot make it cohere' is the verdict of the late Canto CXVI, but Pound, depressed in old age, was photographed at the Spoleto poetry festival of 1965 surrounded by younger admirers who were to prolong his reputation precisely through their attention to the discontinuity, intermittent opacity and, to adopt a choice phrase of Ed Sanders's, 'the melodic blizzards of data-fragments' that criss-cross his work.[3]

Variously associated with the Beat, Black Mountain and New York schools, the younger poets such as Robert Duncan, Robert Creeley, Frank O'Hara and Ed Dorn would come to prominence in Donald Allen's anthology *The New American Poetry 1945–60*. Along with Pound, their shared influence is William Carlos Williams (1883–1963). A student at the University of Pennsylvania alongside Pound, Williams resolutely refused to Europeanize himself after an initial exposure to Parisian bohemianism. But then it is at least arguable, *pace* Lawrence, that Paris was straining to reach a neo-Rimbaudian *dérèglement* that the Americans already knew from the inside. 'The pure products of America', wrote Williams, 'go crazy,' and among these rootless products he cited the 'devil-may-care men who have taken / to railroading / out of sheer lust of adventure – ', anticipating in 1923 the later photographs of Jack Kerouac, dusty from burning up the miles with arch-hipster Neal Cassady, or perched on Ginsberg's New York fire-escape, a brakeman's manual jammed in the pocket of his jeans (Williams, 217). A restless egalitarianism is what Williams sees in America and delivers to younger poets. It took him a while to get started, and the early work pastiches Keats. It is only with the poems of 1914 that we begin to see the half-poised, half-fractured lines that characterized Williams's aesthetic. An insistent, at times insolent demand that the reader thrust his nose into the conventionally unexaminable, or bend her ear to catch the strain of the unmusical, gives early Williams the energy of heresy which in time would make him the appropriate author of a preface to Ginsberg's *Howl*. In the poem could be found a social and materialist equality which the public world would deny or suppress. 'No one / will believe this / of vast import to the nation' is Williams's stereophonic verdict on both the poor man's shack and his own improvised poem (65). The egalitarian-ism is rigorous, and not just a selective attack on glaring social inequal-ity. Williams's poetry ponders the desirability of an equal attention to all things.

In this easy conjoining of the local and the universal Williams no doubt transmuted habits of thought instilled by his Unitarian upbring-ing. More importantly, his willingness to be led by whatever or whomsoever comes into view, the attention to curvaceous young trees and young women being remarkably similar, is politically a continuation of the Whitman line. (Ultimately it could be taken back to the impatient and conflationary rhetoric of Puritanism, scru-tinized in chapter 1.) Philip Fisher argues that Whitman 'was the only artist that America has ever had who understood the profound thrill of democratic uniformity' (Fisher, 57). Surely Williams runs him a close second: poems such as 'Young Sycamore', 'Spring Strains' and 'The Great Figure' offer moments of perception that are unique, but only as an individual blade of grass is unique. The title of Whitman's *magnum opus* signified not only a democratic interest in common ground, but an aesthetic and political welcome to the 'indefinitely repeatable unit' (ibid.). A hard sell, shrilly Adamic, runs deep in Whitman's and Williams's American grain. The profound thrill of democratic uniformity is at once America's Eden and its dangerous fruit. Once tasted and accepted, that uniformity changes the percep-tions, producing both America's *unheimlich* sameness and the individ-ual's baffled sense of being somehow outside, no longer contentedly inside the Garden. Hearing American singing; not quite being there, not wholly; for if we all were, what would be the point of poetry? 'And what I assume you shall assume, / For every atom belonging to me as good belongs to you' (Whitman, 188). This is a democratic promise, but it is also a provocation (suppose I don't care for your assumptions, don't want to share your atoms?), and its rhetoric sutures over trauma, just as the embrace of the word 'United' inhibits the wriggling differences of individual 'States', and indeed the individuals within them. There will always be times, reading the American sentimentalists from Whitman to Maya Angelou, when, not wanting to be hugged today, thank you very much, one puts the book down and steps outside to breathe a different air, perhaps preferring *Les Fleurs du Mal* to *Leaves of Grass*. Just so, Williams begins 'A Unison':

> The grass is very green, my friend,
> and tousled, like the head of –
> your grandson, yes? And the mountain,
> the mountain we climbed
> twenty years since for the last
> time (I write this thinking
> of you) is saw-horned as then
> upon the sky's edge – an old barn
> is peaked there also . . . [4]

I know grass is green. You don't need to tell me, and I refuse to be amazed. I don't have a grandson, and I hate country walks. Most of all, I don't want to be addressed as if your ancient friend and I were interchangeable; that's exactly the Whitman touch. And here comes yet another sentimentalized American barn. Now I understand why James Purdy chose a barn as the ideal site for a crucifixion in *Narrow Rooms* (1978), one of his more acidic novels.

# The meanings of Modernism

Williams never abandoned his vocation as a doctor, and there is a sense in which his two occupations were absolutely characteristic of Modernist emphases. Louise Bogan wrote in 1928, 'Our time just loves poems about the internal organs of the body, the mechanisms of sex, abortion, fecal processes, etc. It's like looking inside the hood of an automobile, or watching the shafts and gears and sprockets in a factory' (Rasula, 60). These two realms, the interior/organic and the exterior/mechanical, recur by turns independently, at odds and in synergy, through the inter-war years. An emphasis on clarity of outline is shared to a significant degree by the Imagist poems of Pound, the paintings and prose of Wyndham Lewis, and certain of the rhetorics mobilized by Williams in his attention to suppressed conditions. Europe and America are at one here: the direct conclusion of Rilke's 'Archaischer Torso Apollos', 'Du mußt dein Leben ändern',[5] the visceral metaphors of Lorca and the mobilization by the young Auden of a vocabulary of sickness and cure are among the extensions to this anatomizing tendency.

It is as well to recall that although the word 'Modernist' appears in the title of a 1927 survey of poetry assembled by Robert Graves and Laura Riding, its use by writers between the wars is scant and casual. 'Modernism' is used only once by Wyndham Lewis in *Men without Art* (1934), even though that study (well worth reviving) deals with the work of Eliot, Joyce, Woolf, Stein and Hemingway. 'Modernism' is a retrospective creation of the university literature department, gaining in currency from the 1960s. Hugh Kenner's *The Pound Era* (1971) probably shows the high-water mark of Modernism more than anything written by Pound himself. Peter Viereck (a Pulitzer winner of 1949) asked forty years later whether modern poetry was 'a tale told by an Eliot, full of Pound and fury, signifying Williams' (Rasula, 113), but this amusing scenario is one experienced by the present-day student with a deadline rather than by the readers or writers who were stopped in their tracks by *The Waste Land*. Indeed, as Jed Rasula shows in one of the most lively books on modern American poetry to appear for some years (*The American Poetry Wax Museum* (1996)), Eliot's investiture by the New Critics as simultaneous leader of two poetic traditions, the British and the American, is only the most pivotal example of a relationship between poetry, the university and the influential prize committee that merits an iconoclastic scrutiny it rarely receives, not least because the best-placed scrutineers are frequently also the beneficiaries.

While it is assumed, for example, that Allen Ginsberg's citations of Blake, Whitman and Christopher Smart helped *Howl* on to the university syllabus, reassuring tweed-jacketed squares that the beast had a pedigree, it is more subtly the case that, by giving contemporary voice to past poets' concerns, Ginsberg, in Rasula's words, 'actually advanced their fame along with his own' (142). The argument is not that the Beats were anything but inept at, or uninterested in, wooing the academy. Nor is it my argument that Eliot's poetry was not prizeworthy. But the first unwritten law of canon formation is that its activities never actually cease, despite the position of cultural equipoise implied by the famous publishing house or the course bibliography. The recent tendency towards a canon based on inclusiveness, diversification and apology, in the names of ethnicity and gender, begs for analysis. Here Rasula's jabs may supply an inoculation against the worst symptoms of cultural torpor:

> [W]ith the present conundrum of a revised canon ... it is *essential* that minorities be included, yet their minoritarian features must not be

essentialised in any way. In the newly configured revolving-door multi-cultural canon a procedure that always was arbitrary is now more openly disclosed as such. Which is to say, we now see the shameless opportunism of a curriculum designed to reflect political correctness; whereas, formerly, the connivance of a sanitary cordon of white men fielding a canon of taste could masquerade as Literature, or Poetry, 'the voice that is great within us' where the deictic term (*us*) was conveniently ambiguous and thus seemingly open to all. (279–80)

These swings of the pendulum are ultimately set going by a tension between the principles of competition and uniformity in American society, including academe. The anthology has a crucial role to play here, because its formal ambiguity implies a momentary stilling of the pendulum. The anthology is much bigger than the average book, is inclusive, contains all you need; and yet it remains a partial selection, necessarily slanted, a competition with winners and excluded losers. This ambiguity holds as true for the vast Norton anthologies as for Donald Allen's *New American Poetry* or, for that matter, Keith Tuma's *Oxford Book of Twentieth-Century British and Irish Poetry* (2001), a compendious and refreshing account. There are tremendous vested interests with a London base that maintain a long-established rapport between established poetry presses, the books chosen for review in the broadsheets, what the BBC says and what students are given to read. Woe betide the man, even a good man from Ohio, who edits an anthology whose conclusion is that time spent reading Seamus Heaney might have been better spent reading J. H. Prynne. London polices British culture by subtle and unsubtle filtration. The cultural tensions of the United States are less tied to internal empire and specific places, New York and Los Angeles being *de facto* capitals in certain respects, rather than Washington. There the tussles over which different voices best do the *polis* have revolved around race and privilege, those hierarchies and exclusions that, notwithstanding the thrill of democratic uniformity, continue to affect the politics of the sign.

## The politics of the scion

The current emphasis on hyphenation in American identity politics – gay-American, Cuban-American – examples of being within yet without America – are in part an attempt at redress in a society still dominated by WASP surnames in many instances. And in the literary world, it did not hurt T. S. Eliot's carefully constructed self-image as arbiter of culture to have the surname he did, with its reminders of the

Massachusetts pulpit, New England clarities of mind and light, the street names off Brattle. Moving from the politics of the sign to the politics of the scion, it would not, at first sight, appear to have hurt a later Faber poet, Robert Lowell (1917–77) to carry a similar pedigree. A grandfather had been head of the fashionable St Mark's School. James Russell Lowell, poet and ambassador to the Court of St James, was a great-grand-uncle. Elizabeth Bishop wrote in a letter to Lowell, 'In some ways you are the luckiest poet I know! Most poets could name their forebears ... but what would be the significance? Nothing at all ... Whereas all you have to do is put down the names!' (Rasula, 255). Lowell's poetry deteriorated rapidly after *Life Studies* (1959), collapsing not so much into free verse, for the profoundly un-free Lowell was propped up and strait-jacketed at every turn, as into chopped prose. If there is more to a book such as *History* (1973) – 'this open book ... my open coffin' – it certainly wasn't history, which requires a real attention to the world outside the self.[6] But to the scion Lowell, his story *was* history. Norman Mailer, a fellow-writer who shared Lowell's honourable detestation of the Vietnam War, put it charitably: 'Lowell gave off at times the unwilling haunted saintliness of a man who was repaying the moral debts of ten generations of ancestors.'[7] Thus an agonizing over the fallen condition of America and the agonies of repeated nervous breakdown would allow a magnification of internal trial that defined Lowell's later thinking and curdled his poetry. Exposure to Beat writing in the later 1950s, with its Whitmanian brio and jazz-like experiment, pushed Lowell into the worst of all stylistic worlds, as explicit confessionalism and dissatisfaction with traditional form were forced to cohabit with the unshakeably patrician.

The confessionalism has worn particularly badly, as it brings private hurt and public document into such questionable proximity. Lowell, in short, wants you to feel his pain, but would rather play with it himself ('I wanted to handle and draw strength from my scar' (Rasula, 250)), a career move that may have helped wheel him into the day-room of international success on the pillows of an America convalescent after the McCarthy hearings. Lowell's crowd were the control freaks of a moment of transition in America's cultural aristocracy: well-heeled, cracked, alcoholic. The past tasted of ashes, but lunging into sixties counter-culture generated only divorces and mess. There is also perhaps a history of pressure here, to do with having to shout to be heard, the public reduced to a wailing wall in a cultural context where poetry was constantly rewarded but never mattered. Lowell may have had an audience in a strictly literal sense, but no real interchange.

This is the reverse of O'Hara's or Olson's worlds, micro-communities of reader/writers at Black Mountain College or the Lower East Side. Lowell's influence helped carry the calculated despair of Berryman, Roethke and others through a fashionable phase to a late apotheosis in England, and the sufferings of Ted Hughes, wrought to a crescendo in the massive commercial success of *Birthday Letters* (1998). Hughes's best-seller is a rattling good read, frequently crude and repetitive, but remarkable for the openness of its admission that what matters in establishment poetry now is its resemblance to other genres, in this case a medley curiously reminiscent of 'Women's Magazines' in its juxtaposition of celebrity confession, agony aunt problems, and pages devoted to astrology and cookery. In the era of Lowell and Hughes, parody-modernist rather than postmodern, the press that had published Eliot, Pound and Auden began a genteel decline. Admittedly, it has Paul Muldoon and Mark Ford. However, it is hard to imagine that the current regime at Queen Square would countenance publication of a book as radical as Auden's *The Orators* (1931) – or, for that matter, *The Waste Land* (1922).

# The Waste Land

The latter was of course brought to its final form by Pound's excisions, with intriguing implications for the nature of collaboration in poetry, given that the text is more radical than a poem completed by either man working alone would have been. (Breton and Eluard's *L'Immaculée Conception* (1930) is a parallel case.) In a very special sense, *The Waste Land* is a load of garbage: over its less than twenty pages Eliot tips 'this stony rubbish', 'a heap of broken images', the dug-up earth around a corpse, rats, bones, false teeth, out-of-date furnishings, an aborted foetus, empty bottles, cigarette ends, 'other testimony of summer nights', stockings and camisoles, tins, drifting logs, 'falling towers', more bones, mud, rocks, fragments, ruin, a desert, one broken Coriolanus and the whole of Western and Eastern culture, not to mention the murk disturbed by the shoal of red herrings that constitutes the Notes, as integral to Eliot/Pound's collage as its verse.[8] Eliot's tongue-in-cheek insistence that the poem was just a piece of rhythmical grumbling evades, through an apparent modesty about the poet's skill, the issue of the poem's fundamental and wonderfully immodest self-centredness. The rapidity of the poem's transitions, which still leaves subsequent generations of fast workers looking like amateurs in the cutting-room, and Eliot's unsurpassed powers of ventriloquy, draw attention away from the fact that it is still he – however allegedly 'impersonal' the Modernist posture, however surgically recontoured by *il miglior fabbro* – who is pulling the strings and doing the voices.

Eliot's 1919 essay 'Tradition and the Individual Talent' is a characteristic triumph of manner, prose addressed to a point on the ceiling, its emphases recalling a raised eyebrow and the tips of long fingers forming a bridge. The second section ends with a resonant yet evasive formula:

> Poetry is not a turning loose of emotion, but an escape from emotion; it is not the expression of personality, but an escape from personality. But, of course, only those who have personality and emotions know what it means to want to escape from these things. (*Essays*, 21)

As with his weaker descendant Lowell, pain and the desire for escape stoically resisted are linked by Eliot to an elite ('only those who have...') in a Modernist reformulation of the tradition of aestheticism brokered by Keats in the 'Ode on Melancholy': 'Though seen of none save him whose strenuous tongue / Can burst Joy's grape against his palate fine'.[9] The writers invoked so feverishly by the melancholic Eliot (Keats, Webster, Baudelaire, Dante and the rest) are, in the long run, not guides through a cultural desert external to the poet and pushed into aridity by the First World War or other external cause. Rather, they form a hall of mirrors, showing Eliot a Jacobean or a Symbolist reflection, distorted but his own. Madam Sosostris is not the poem's only 'famous clairvoyante', for the constant literary allusions are all moments of consultation in a darkness of spirit where the veiled figure will always be Eliot, though, as poetry is, at least on the surface 'an escape from personality', that figure will only rarely be *revealed* as a version of the self. 'You! hypocrite lecteur! – mon semblable, – mon frère!' It is characteristic of the poem's brilliant duplicity, and appropriate to the collaborative aspect, that its most wrenched and personal moment should be voiced in a quotation from another poet that tips the whole issue into the reader's lap (64–5). The poet has 'not a "personality" to express, but a particular medium, which is only a medium and not a personality, in which impressions and experiences combine in peculiar and unexpected ways' (*Essays*, 20). That medium does not rejoin the self and history, as in Pound's major work, but neither does it ask the reader to touch the stigmata of pain and believe, as in Lowell. (And it certainly does not invite the reader to look for keys in the bedroom of the poet's first marriage, *à la Birthday Letters*, though some have tried.) Duplex, it generates readerly involvement in the sculpting of a personality, but one imbued with a modern understanding, certainly more modern than that of Lowell or Hughes, of the ways in which the personal is made up of quotation, echo, the past, the culture, the others – the system.

# Kinds of blues: Langston Hughes, Amiri Baraka, Stephen Jonas

Notwithstanding the achievements of writers from Frederick Douglass through to Toni Morrison, African-American literature remains overshadowed even in its diversity and power by the world of black music, which perfused and often redirected the twentieth-century media, even as it was co-opted and subjected to dilution. Oppression on ethnic lines is a massive wrong, simply and entirely. Depicted in literature, the silhouette of that wrong will tend inevitably to the simplicity of either realism or allegory. Musicians, by contrast, project a non-referential medium, but have at their fingertips all the resources of drama, argument and interchange, together with the freedom to move at will into explicit theme and out into the abstraction and pleasures of rhythm, sound and number. To make music can be to voice the conditions of oppression, but in the aesthetic dimension of that articulation can be heard a liberation from oppression, however transient. Lectured as a student at Juilliard on the blues as an expression of the share-cropper's misery, Miles Davis pointed out with an understandable acidity that his father was a dentist.

Davis's middle classness was an issue even for his admirers, notwithstanding the street credibility and the bad behaviour. Writing after the musician's death, Imamu Amiri Baraka (1934– ) makes a range of points about class and the articulation of the whole being in cultural practice that have resonance beyond that immediate context. Rejecting as a simplification the accusation that Davis was anti-white, Baraka notes that, from early days, Davis played 'in "mixed company". In the early Bop context ... many of the groups playing the "new music" were socially, aesthetically and psychologically "open",' a situation removed from the segregated conditions imposed in the society outside the gig.[10] The more 'open' situation of Davis's recordings for Prestige following his beginnings as sideman for Charlie Parker has affinities with Baraka's being published as a poet (as LeRoi Jones) alongside Ed Dorn and Frank O'Hara, though the musician's control of his working context could be contrasted with Baraka/Jones's more tenuous position as the sole black poet anthologized by Don Allen in *The New American Poetry.* Baraka's comments on Miles Davis recall the affinity in expressivism between jazz and the new poetry, as both sought a redefinition of America:

> [ W ]ired to the whole mad spectrum of Americana (as in the flight with Bird), his personal antics reflect a self-conscious desire to be 'outside', even while, in some ways, being an insider (except he *was* Black) – something like the rebellion of the American middle class. (ibid.)

The uncomfortable inverted commas and Baraka's shifting location of the musician from insider to outsider set both Davis and the poet without America, of it and yet not (for they *are* black) and yet most of it when rebelling, when most tuned in to 'the whole mad spectrum'. This doubleness characterizes the interior of the music as well as Davis's sartorial flamboyance, so that it is the linchpin chord progressions of the best-selling *Kind of Blue* that enable both the spontaneity of the blues and a contemplative self-awareness. I have already suggested that this doubleness is more readily engaged by music than by writing, and the mix of Zen-like simplicity and lush romanticism in *Kind of Blue* remains wordless, so is not, like Harry Smith's *recherche du temps perdu*, made literary by what is done with it. Like Langston Hughes (1902–1967) before him, Baraka desires a jazz aesthetic that would be both warm and analytical, be insider and outsider to the weary blues, a project stretched to bursting point in the later writer's abandonment of One-Nation politics for Marxist Leninism.

Baraka began his poetic career with a quasi-existentialist individualism shared with white bohemians: 'Let my poems be a graph / of me', as a poem in *The Dead Lecturer* (1964) has it.[11] Other pieces recall the Whitman influence on Frank O'Hara; 'It's so diffuse / being alive' recalls the famous line from 'In Memory of My Feelings': 'Grace to be born and live as variously as possible'.[12] Yet the title of the Baraka piece from which the quotation is drawn, 'Look for You Yesterday, Here You Come Today', reworks the title of a blues by Jimmy Rushing recorded by the pre-war Count Basie band, the echo a reminder that certain lives enjoy more diffuse opportunities than others. The ironies and permutations of being an insider/outsider retrace a Whitmanian heritage of being out of the game and in it, while documenting a pressure over exclusion on ethnic lines that Whitman never knew from inside. The two conjoin in the opacity with lucidity of the title of Baraka's selected poems, *Transbluesency* (1995). The term was coined by Duke Ellington ('a blue fog you can almost see through'), and these ambiguities of the jazz aesthetic are partnered by ambiguities of freedom and timekeeping in jazz itself

(Baraka, p. xi). Just as Pound and Eliot did not actually break the pentameter, but rather loosened the rhythm of the poetic line as far as it could go without losing contact entirely with traditional measure, so BeBop allowed the maximum freedom for improvisation to rapid-fire players such as Charlie Parker and Bud Powell without ever leaving the chordal structure and return to the main theme of the popular tunes they reconstructed, such as Ray Noble's 'Cherokee', given a Bop superstructure by Parker as 'KoKo'. (It might further be argued that the linear and non-chordal properties of the saxophone, an instrument of layered space, were more suited to the kinds of improvisation originating with Parker and extrapolated by Ornette Coleman than the piano, whose chordal verticality produces deep space sounds.)

The most effective poems by Baraka are those that explore such ironies of freedom and containment by the use of double meaning, while his least effective pieces are those that attempt to resolve ambiguity by a simple affirmation in the Langston Hughes tradition. The closing lines of Baraka's ten-page tirade 'Reggae or Not!' are not among his best:

> Only Socialism
> will save the Black Nation
> Only Socialism will save
> America
> Only Socialism will save
> the world!
>
> (185)

This kind of declamation works better in performance, and Baraka's intoning of his venomous 'Black Dada Nihilismus' ('Rape the white girls. Rape / their fathers. Cut the mothers' throats' (*et cetera, ad libitum*) over the boiling and brooding of the New York Art Quartet retains a certain period fragrance.[13] On the page declamation goes flat, as most of Langston Hughes's poetry went flat, once its time was gone. Pieces like 'Po' Boy Blues' (1926) were important for their incorporation of a blues aesthetic, but their lines limp by comparison with recordings by John Hurt, Willie McTell or any other effective musician of that period and form:

> I fell in love with
> A gal I thought was kind.
> Fell in love with
> A gal I thought was kind.
> She made me lose my money
> An' almost lose my mind.

Weary, weary,
Weary early in de morn.
Weary, weary,
Early, early in de morn.
I's so weary
I wish I'd never been born.[14]

It can be argued that to subject a verbal blues such as this to analysis deriving from the New Criticism is to miss the point, and that the affirmative gestures of recognition such a work offers and receives constitute its cultural value. But poems have an inside, operating not simply as a trigger to automatic reaction, and complexities of the linguistic interior should surely not be barred to black or any other practitioners. As Langston Hughes noted in 'The Negro Artist and the Racial Mountain', '[C]ertainly there is, for the American Negro artist who can escape the restrictions the more advanced among his own group would put upon him, a great field of unused material ready for his art' (1269). This would be borne out by later writers such as Baraka, whose early poem 'The Bridge' explores ambiguities set up by jazz musicians' uses of words with other meanings – 'bridge', 'head', 'changes', 'strung out'. 'Symphony Sid' (a reference to a radio MC from the Bop era) celebrates ambiguity in the depersonalization that can paradoxically spell intimacy, in a sexual context:

>                 The scale
>     is music, black shadow
>     from highest wild
>     fingers placing evening
>     beneath our
>     tongues.
>         A man, a woman
>     shaking the night apart.
>                 (Baraka, 36)

With its placing of a jazz sacrament beneath the tongue, recalling also the traditional synonymity of jazz and sex, the poem looks sideways to 'A Poem for Vipers' by John Wieners, most underrated of the white Black Mountaineers, whose *The Hotel Wentley Poems* (1958) finds echoes in Baraka titles such as 'A Poem for Democrats' and 'A Poem for Neutrals'. Even less acknowledged than Wieners is Stephen Jonas, a poet taking off from many of the innovations of both these writers to produce perhaps the most effective working through of the jazz aesthetic, and a poet whose racial, sexual and political identity have ensured his exclusion from even the most inclusive of revolving door canons.

## The *Dominations* of Stephen Jonas

Stephen Jonas (1921–70) was baptised Rufus Jones, in Atlanta, his chosen surname the name used by Jesus when referring to the prophet Jonah (Matthew 12 and 16, Luke 11). Swallowed by a whale, Jonah took a circuitous route to Nineveh, a reluctant prophet. Stephen, by contrast, does not appear until the Acts of the Apostles, where he stands as the epitome of martyrdom and willing prophecy. If I may be forgiven the pun, Stephen got stoned for his pains, and at Jonas's autopsy following a heart attack his body was found to be 'filled with drugs in general'.[15] Matthew 12 is also concerned with demonic possession, and Jonas, prey to conflicting voices on and off the page, died unheard by a larger audience than the community of fellow-poets. He had served in the US Air Force from 1942 to 1944, when he was given a medical discharge following a nervous breakdown. As a damaged veteran, he had been of use, but was now only an embarrassment. As a homosexual and a multiple drug-user, he was of no use whatsoever. Consigned to the shadows, he could only regain the centre by one totalizing act of imaginative reappropriation, which is his poetry. That work is full of appropriately desperate measures, including imagery of alchemy and dark magic, pseudo-solutions to intractable reality and a repertoire item shared to some extent with Robert Duncan, Jack Spicer, Robin Blaser and other members of a 'Boston School' of poets for whom Jonas would host and tape what he called 'Magic Evenings'. However, just as his exquisite sense of rhythm and lineation derived from Pound (along with jazz and the Elizabethan poets) so, alas, did his politics:

> to write poetry yr 'facts' be hangd   to write poetry you need
>    emotional upheaval to write poetry you need *Lightning over the*
>    *Treasury*
> more you need Lincoln's end of first term farewell address' concern
>    for the future safety of The Republic ...
> and fer yr 'facts' you can go to it might as well be hell ...
>             Wall St, where Gen'ral Washington was
> sworn in so the star of david cld fly over the White House[16]

'[E]motional upheaval' is one way of putting it. Though friction between the black and the Jewish communities in the USA has regrettably become common in recent years, it was much less a feature of the period when Jonas's writing flourished, which coincided with the Civil Rights movement. One might guess, though it would be only a guess, that a self-hatred stemming as much from his sexual orientation as his race caused Jonas to hallucinate agents of oppression in what he mistakenly took to be the outside world. People romanticize and forget the paranoia of the 1960s. Even more incredibly, there is an anti-black strain in his writing, an internalization of ideology allied by mirror reversal to his minoritarian status as a writer in multiple senses on the edge.

The scabrous stuff, repudiated in interview, permeates the sequence known alternately as *Orgasms* and *Dominations*, never published in its entirety, but sampled along with some more lyrical pieces in *Transmutations* (1965). The other full-length collection to be published in Jonas's lifetime is *Exercises for Ear* (1968), which, with its frontispiece parodying Golding's Ovid, introduces Jonas's skill at lyric poetry. One of the uncomfortable realities of that skill is his fashioning satirical successes as well as crazed disasters partly from the material of racial stereotyping:

> damn if I didn't out &
> met me up w/ a good
> nigger,
> t'other day
> ('N they's harder to come-by
> then hen's teeth,
> now'a-days
> -what w/ their demonstrations
> & what have you's):
>
> shuffled his feet;
> rolld them eyes:
>
> 'yassur,
> thangs show ain't what dey
> use'ta be'[17]

This, the penultimate Exercise, ought to exercise the nerves of a reader who must surely spend a first encounter cringing in expectation of its turning into exactly the kind of neo-Poundian and self-lacerating gibe that it actually isn't. To add further margins to Jonas's exile from acceptance, the book was published by the English poet Andrew Crozier's Ferry Press, one of the more intrepid 1960s small-press outlets, to be sure, but operating at a distance from America and from any African-American context that might have supported Jonas.

Jonas's *Exercises*, with their stylish conceits and nervous punning, a mixture of elegance, dirty jokes, intellectual precision and paranoia, resonate with a reading of English verse from Campion to the Jacobeans, injected into the American idiom:

> ah would that
> > life were the long-
> est side Getz
> > ever cut & Death
> an ex-
> > tended play
> > > (XCIV)

This is 'Elizabethan' in its mixture of *carpe diem* conclusion while dallying with, rather than seizing, the moment. Recent re-evaluations of Elizabethan writing claim to have burrowed beneath the surface of style to discover 'a searching, dangerous knowledge of political domination'.[18] It may be that the *Dominations* of Stephen Jonas, as well as his prosodic ear, hold him in echoic relation to that period.

Speaking of the ear, Stan Getz seems rather a 'cool' preference for one who insists he likes his jazz low-down and his blues 'mutha-huckin' dirty', to revive the terms of Exercise LXI. But then the streetwise rasp is as self-consciously deployed as any other tone by Jonas. Once a poet of origins restricted by race or class emancipates her- or himself linguistically, there comes a Fall: the death of the concept of a natural speech. To have done the *polis* in different voices, to paraphrase the first title of Eliot's *Waste Land*, was to experience the same Fall from a different cultural and ethnic angle. All language is there to be used, and all language is equally unnatural. So Jonas's low-down blues are skits, and vice versa:

> ... blues aint nuthin'
> > but which gender you
> makin' it w'th
> > > split
>
> & you want
> > *some*-body to
> please come hear
> > > & gimme sum'um
> > > > (LXV)

To record what he hears here, the poet had to stand outside and inside, outwith, a black American voice. Likewise, his take on Charlie 'Bird' Parker, always active in his lower-case use of the word, expresses both ethnic fraternity, estrangement and the Poundian Imagist inheritance:

> a hollow
>         victory
>
>         you celebrate
>         bird singing alone
>
>         in this cold
>                 (X)

Many of Jonas's best pieces are blue dejection odes. This was true of Bird, who could make hollowness the substance of his playing. Their shared skill in coldness portrays the city as a stylized inferno, as Waste Land, in a BeBop acceleration of Modernist tendencies. Reading these lines of Jonas, I think of Parker riding the New York subway or walking for hours, unable to sleep after performing:

> cars zip past   fart & growl
> at intersections   streets of
> anonymous alcoholics   innocent
>
> pickpockets   hot angels cruising
> the crucified streets   burning
>         outsized lampbulbs
>
> illuminating nothing   save it be
> the gutter   ghosts of freud
> the deadliness of you
>                 (LXVIII)

High and in a hurry, eyes peeled, Jonas plays shrilly here, his *Howl*-like howl on the sharp side of staying in tune. That too was Parker's usual mood, though to pull the weary blues to life he had to hang, as in the Massey Hall 'Hot House' or 'Buzzy', from the down-side of the note. Parker was tortured, but fitted and is canonized. I see Jonas, who did not fit, mentioned nowhere in the copious and hopeful literature on Jazz Poetry one might have assumed to be looking for exactly his fineness and dark poise.

## Ginsberg's lost America of love

It might be tempting to suggest that Allen Ginsberg strained for what Stephen Jonas was, though what Jonas was itself begs questions, splitting on examination into an insider/outsider status that dismisses any social belonging or natural language as fake, its being outwith America, at home if at all in the recurrent apparition of the crowd or ghosts of Freud, haunting the mind at its most musical and flighty. By contrast, Ginsberg's dissidence was one that played at every point on the American literary past, and on key images of prophecy and New World Paradise. Like Robert Duncan, an instinctive didact, a hip teacher, Ginsberg made it new by recalling the primary American tropes. His latest biographer, Graham Caveney, quotes an exchange from Henry James's *The Portrait of a Lady* to urge this point. As with many such exchanges in James, the dialogue sets at polite loggerheads a European and an American sense of self, leaving it to the reader, as well as the heroine, to decide whether that opposition is true, false, binary or only to be proved on the pulses of individual actions and affections:

> 'I don't care anything about his house,' said Isabel.
> 'That's very crude of you. When you've lived as long as I you'll see that every human being has his shell and that you must take the shell into account. By the shell I mean the whole envelope of circumstances. There's no such thing as an isolated man or woman; we're each of us made up of some cluster of appurtenances. What shall we call our 'self'? Where does it begin? where does it end? It overflows into everything that belongs to us – and then it flows back again. I know a large part of myself is in the clothes I choose to wear. I've a great respect for *things*! One's self – for other people – is one's expression of one's self; and one's house, one's furniture, one's garments, the books one reads, the company one keeps – these things are all expressive.'[19]

To the poet's biographer, Isabel's spirited reply is one that could have been inscribed on Ginsberg's tombstone. Her response is an openhearted statement of her Americanness, a declaration of independence from tradition, from all custom and constraint:

> 'I don't agree with you. I think just the other way. I don't know whether I succeed in expressing myself, but I know that nothing else expresses me. Nothing that belongs to me is any measure of me; everything's on the contrary a limit, a barrier, and a perfectly arbitrary one.

Certainly the clothes which, as you say, I choose to wear, don't express
me; and heaven forbid they should!'
'You dress very well,' Madame Merle lightly interposed.
'Possibly; but I don't care to be judged by that. My clothes may
express the dressmaker, but they don't express me. To begin with it's
not my own choice that I wear them; they're imposed upon me by
society.'
'Should you prefer to go without them?' Madame Merle inquired in
a tone which virtually terminated the discussion.

Just so, Ginsberg incarnated the dissident energies of his own time
while chafing at restriction in ways that run deep in the American
grain, back to Emerson's self-reliance and Whitman's open road;
'nothing else expresses me'. Unlike James's heroine, the poet did
'prefer to go without' the clothes imposed by a society that had put
him in a strait-jacket, stripping to the buff on-stage in response to a
heckler who asked if the real Allen Ginsberg would please stand
up. 'Naked' is a favourite word in the poems, as it is in the whole
Beat pantheon; *The Naked Lunch* was Kerouac's title for Burroughs's novel. Yet there was always a touch of Madame Merle in
Burroughs's viperish cleverness, and a sentimental, sports-watching
patriotism lay at the heart of Kerouac's boozy odyssey. Ginsberg was
the one whose self-expression risked everything on candour: a search
for the naked truth, political or personal, his most far-reaching bequest a habit of conflating the two. Thus a certain Puritan self-steeling
enters into even his most Dionysiac experiments. He would write
essays while smoking marijuana or experiencing the onset of LSD
hallucinations, but neither these substances nor any other factors do
anything to disturb the teacherly momentum of the prose. On the
poetic side, 'Please Master' (1968), Ginsberg's homo-erotic hymn to
the ecstasies of self-abasement, one of the last really arresting poems
that he wrote, and perhaps the poem many of the others really wanted
to be, is not an unfettered expression of pleasure.

All of this got him into trouble. *Howl* (1956), his first major and
also his best book, landed the poet and his publisher Lawrence
Ferlinghetti in court on obscenity charges. Confident of winning,
Ginsberg turned the court room into theatre. The book would in
time become a staple of American Literature courses, its manuscript
history and legal wrangles documented and solemnized in a scholarly
edition modelled on the transcripts of *The Waste Land*. More cour-
ageously, and with far less certainty about the outcome, Ginsberg was
prominent in the anti-war protests at the Democratic Convention in
Chicago in 1968, and was duly tear-gassed for his pains. Called to

testify in the subsequent show trials, the poet was surprised to find himself cross-examined on the sexual content of three poems selected by a homophobic official of the Justice Department, rather than over his support for the accused, one of whom, Bobby Seale, sat bound and gagged before the court on the order of the judge. Such was the temper of the times. Rattled by assassinations, civil disorder and the disinclination of young men to fight an unjust war in South-East Asia, it is the military-industrial complex that appears mad in retrospect, living up to its prescient imaging as 'Moloch the incomprehensible prison' in *Howl*; meanwhile, the poet in his Old Testament beard and hippie regalia appears the epitome of mild benignity.[20] Extrapolations of saintliness are even harder to avoid when the tally of Ginsberg's lifelong care for relatives, unstable friends and various gifted or shiftless hangers-on is added to his unflagging support for good causes. (At one point he was paying the salaries of most of the faculty at Naropa, now a respectable college with alumni and fund-raising events, having changed its name from the Jack Kerouac School of Disembodied Poetics.) Such selflessness was not made comfortable by deep pockets; Ginsberg enjoyed no sustained financial security until his sixties, when the sale of his papers and a Distinguished Professorship at Brooklyn College facilitated a move to a larger apartment on the Lower East Side.

The poet was also handy with a camera, and the two published books of photographs show him to have been a gifted portraitist, particularly of fellow-writers and artists, Burroughs and Harry Smith. Susan Sontag wrote on the democratic vistas available to the American lens: 'In the open fields of American experience, as cataloged with passion by Whitman and as sized up with a shrug by Warhol, everybody is a celebrity. No moment is more important than any other moment; no person is more interesting than any other person.'[21] Thus the aesthetic of the moment in the poet's snaps is related less to the metropolitan tradition of the *flâneur* than to the profound thrill of democratic uniformity articulated by Whitman and theorized by Philip Fisher as an American archetype. Differences in geography, climate, time zone, not to mention race, class and the social costs of private wealth are among the factors that at one level or another question the unity of the United States. American identity, built from the hopes and exploitation brought about by four waves of mass immigration, is hyphenated into Cuban-American, Jewish-American, Armenian-American, the root preceding the hyphen cherished all the more nostalgically for the fact that it is all but dissolved by the acid of induction, stripped within a generation of its attachment to another time and place. For the deep spaces of origin America substitutes a sign system of minimal affiliation and immediate recognition; as perhaps it must, in such a huge space, dominated by marketing and technology, where a fifth of the population moves in any given year.

In his search for the naked truth, and his choice of poetry rather than the novel, Ginsberg could evade by lyrical rhetoric and an essentially religious sensibility the pressures of American sameness. The poet became a Buddhist, and his long poem of the mid-sixties, 'Wichita Vortex Sutra', frames in a devotional genre things thought and glimpsed along the road, on a long Kansas journey by car:

> Now, speeding along the empty plain ...
>           I claim my birthright!
>                reborn forever as long as Man
>                     in Kansas or other universe – Joy
>           reborn after the vast sadness of War Gods!
> A lone man talking to myself, no house in the brown vastness to hear,
>           imaging the throng of Selves
>                that make this nation one body of Prophecy
>                     languaged by Declaration as
>                          Happiness!
> I call all Powers of imagination
>           to my side in this auto to make Prophecy
>
>                                         (Ginsberg, 406)

The trouble is that there is more of P. B. Shelley than there is of Kansas in Ginsberg's Wichita. Even as early as 1966, Ginsberg was in a number of senses on 'auto', his grabbing of the mantle of spokesman for the counter-culture taking him at speed from microphone to microphone, rally to rally, the actual details of experience hardly sifted, but rushed by an aesthetic of improvisation into the kind of airy rhetorical conceptualizations that characterize Whitman's weaker stretches, and that Lawrence had parodied so archly four decades before. So little is *seen* by Ginsberg, at least after *Howl*. Rather, it is all boosted at once to the Emersonian infinite, on automatic, pigeon-holing wings.

From quite early in his career, Ginsberg was a literary figure first, and a poet second. He was as tireless a literary agent as Pound in his London years, but, unlike Pound's, his poetry suffered as a result of packing the diary. The problem, to return to the exchange from *Portrait of a Lady*, is that Ginsberg may not have been whole-heartedly on the Isabel Archer side after all. 'When you've lived as long as I you'll see that every human being has his shell and that you must take the shell into account. By the shell I mean the whole envelope of circumstances.... What shall we call our "self"?' Ginsberg had an unusually public 'shell', the whole 'envelope of circumstances' wrapping him in the flag of a Whitmanian egotism. In 'America', from *Howl*, amid the litany of dissident acts ('I smoke marijuana every chance I get', etc.), we are told the following:

> It occurs to me that I am America.
> I am talking to myself again.
>
> (147)

Here beats the sentimental heart of the American avant-garde. America's radicals have never been truly opposed to the system, but crave only a sentimental journey back to Jefferson and first principles. Meanwhile, away from the spotlight, poets such as Frank O'Hara (who knew Ginsberg well) were building with more subtlety a corpus of work whose relationship to the period is ultimately as close, but which feels no particular obligation to reflect the big public issues overtly.

The poems from 1967 to around 1971, particularly the elegies for Neal Cassady, sound a deeper note. Otherwise, *Reality Sandwiches* (1963) is not as gripping as *Kaddish* (1958), *Mind Breaths* (1978) not as good as either, and late efforts such as *Cosmopolitan Greetings* (1994) manage only a faint echo. But *Howl and Other Poems* (1956) is one of the great poetry books of the twentieth century, great not merely for its iconoclasm and its revival of the Whitman line, but valuable sometimes for its mistakes, or the clashes and arguments between poems and sections of poems. Where the later books issued from a mind made up, Ginsberg's first significant book is a record of that mind attempting to make moral sense of itself, of the nature of friendship – a new theme for modern American poetry – of Cold War and of the nation. Subsequent books would wane partly through their compact with the times, the envelope of circumstance, as the energies and actualities of the struggles over Civil Rights and Vietnam were replaced by the mixture of warrior escapades and vague universalism that characterizes the ecology movement, by New Age vapidities and an identity politics which Ginsberg himself had helped usher in. He had been open about his sexuality from the outset; it is ironic that his bad behaviour, courage and magnanimity should have helped catalyse today's political correctness.

But if Ginsberg is ultimately a one-book writer, he is not, as some have portrayed him, a one-poem poet. As with a later and very different collection, John Ashbery's *Self-Portrait in a Convex Mirror* (1975), critical readings of *Howl* have allowed the title poem to stand as a synecdoche for the whole book, which in reality contains poems that move in contrary directions, working to question and even undermine the long title-poem. The first public reading of 'Howl', at the Six Gallery in San Francisco in the autumn of 1955, was the inaugural event of the New American Poetry. But the other poems have their own specific life. 'In the Baggage Room at Greyhound' is a rackety, troubled piece, unsure what it thinks, but an effective, if inadvertent, rebuke to the Wichita Vortex Sutras of Ginsberg's rapid decline. Here details of the humans passing through the Greyhound terminal are observed memorably and precisely, in a dual focus that tries to hold in balance the contingent, the fleeting thing seen, and a perspective that would make each perception symbolic:

> nor an indian dead with fright talking to a huge cop by the Coke machine,
> nor this trembling old lady with a cane taking the last trip of her life,
> nor the red-capped cynical porter collecting his quarters and smiling over the smashed baggage,
> nor me looking around at the horrible dream ...
> nor the grayish-green whale's stomach interior loft where we keep the baggage in hideous racks

> (153)

The litany of 'nors' in one sense repeats but in another undermines the insistent use of 'who' at the beginning of the long lines in 'Howl' itself (for example, 'who were expelled from the academies for crazy & publishing obscene odes on the windows of the skull'), a use linked by Ginsberg to the improvisatory lines of the breath-driven saxophone of Parker or Sonny Rollins, wandering into the ether only to return to a root-chord. There is also a tilting of the poetic axis towards the Whitmanic and Hebraic traditions of litany, and away from Hellenic and English models excepting Blake (who famously spoke to Ginsberg in a vision) and Christopher Smart (who seems to have kept mum). As with all Beat insistence on the scatological and the iconoclastic, there is an accompanying reading list, and the moves are all acutely literary. Much is in play when Ginsberg allows his camera eye to take in the 'red-capped cynical porter' and the other Americans in the bus station, so casually listed and yet so reminiscent of the types roaming the decks of the *Fidèle* in Melville's *The Confidence-Man*, or of course the *Pequod* in *Moby-Dick*. Ginsberg's poetic rebellion might have given Lionel Trilling dyspepsia, but it reclaims, and indeed perpetuates, the literature of the American Renaissance.

'Howl' itself is marvellous: witty, erudite, religious, obscene, auto-biographical, civically minded, screaming but also singing with joy, *sui generis* for all the allusions:

who dreamt and made incarnate gaps in Time & Space through images
juxtaposed, and trapped the archangel of the soul between 2 visual
images and joined the elemental verbs and set the noun and dash of
consciousness together jumping together with sensation of Pater
Omnipotens Aeterna Deus

to recreate the syntax and measure of poor human prose and stand
before you speechless and intelligent and shaking with shame,
rejected yet confessing out the soul to conform to the rhythm of
thought in his naked and endless head,

the madman bum and angel beat in Time, unknown, yet putting down
here what might be left to say in time come after death,

and rose reincarnate in the ghostly clothes of jazz in the goldhorn
shadow of the band and blew the suffering of America's naked
mind for love into an eli eli lamma lamma sabacthini saxophone
cry that shivered the cities down to the last radio. (130–1)

There is a faint odour of the Shelleyan crucible in the recipe for
juxtaposing images (as there is of Surrealism and its experimental
collaging of the disconnected), but there is also something of the
Shelleyan ability to allegorize the personal in a way that is self-centred
only in a literal sense, generous in that very act of 'confessing', turning
the self into a laboratory for the future, 'what might be left to say in
time to come'. The latest biography points out, however, that if
'Howl' is truly going to shiver the cities down to the last radio, it
will be a nocturnal shiver. Forty years after Judge Horn declared that
'Howl' was not obscene, but in its way 'a plea for holy living', any
daytime broadcast of the poem in the USA is forbidden by law.

Mid-fifties Ginsberg showed a startling range. 'America' is a very
different beast from 'Howl', a stand-up comic's monologue, more
reminiscent of Woody Allen's stage routines than Lenny Bruce, in
other respects a kind of rap, *avant la lettre*. Meanwhile, the hoarse,
vulnerable 'Sunflower Sutra' sits alongside poems that echo William
Carlos Williams's Imagist phase, while in 'Transcription of Organ
Music' we see a most curious balancing act in terms of poetic rhetoric,
that manages to be both a high-as-a-kite, Edenic hallucination and a
witty parody of exactly that *faux-naïf* genre, one that links Williams's
ecstatic snapshots of earlier decades to the stoned Beat-itude of the
post-war period:

> I remember when I first got laid, H. P. graciously took my cherry, I sat
> on the docks of Provincetown, age 23, joyful, elevated in hope with the
> Father, the door to the womb was open to admit me if I wished to enter.

> There are unused electricity plugs all over my house if I ever need them.
> The kitchen window is open, to admit air.

The telephone – sad to relate – sits on the floor – I haven't the money to get it connected. (141)

More delicately balanced is 'A Supermarket in California', an extrapolation of lines in García Lorca's 'Oda a Walt Whitman' into the confines of the Cold War suburbs and out into a dream that, characteristically, pictures a better future in terms of nostalgia for the past, 'the lost America of love'. It was a stunning début. There were so many routes Ginsberg opened or reopened for American poetry, so few he was able to follow in his own later work.

Instead, Ginsberg developed the knack, as did his friend Bob Dylan and Dylan's friend, the guitarist Jerry Garcia, of managing a seamless transition from young tyro to *paterfamilias*. As with Garcia, the beard had something to do with it. Artistic micro-communities and the commercialization of the hippie were realms brought by instinct to adjacency by Ginsberg and the Grateful Dead's Garcia, who both inhabited the conflation of radicalism and sentimentality that is peculiar to the United States. Garcia was a fine guitarist, the most fluent in the rock pantheon, but, as with Ginsberg, it was the Whitmanian image that took hold of his audience – to use a George W. Bushism – subliminably, and restored dissident youth to the embrace of the grandfather, the Founding Father, the American tradition of staying, to use a Dylan title, 'Forever Young' in a self-enfolding history.

# The Naked Lunch

Like *Howl*, William Burroughs's novel *The Naked Lunch* (1959) was banned on first publication, the trials of both linking them with Henry Miller's *Tropic of Cancer* and the unbanning by an Old Bailey judge of Lawrence's *Lady Chatterley's Lover*, to form the climate of the Anglo-American 1960s. Burroughs (1914–97) joined the Modernist American tradition of publication in Paris, mainly because a loophole in French law allowed an exemption from censorship laws for material not printed in the French language. This lacuna provided the unstable foundation for Maurice Girodias's Olympia Press, which, alongside its soft-porn bread-winners, oversaw the first release of Nabokov's *Lolita*, Beckett's *Molloy* and Donleavy's *The Ginger Man*, as well as three major novels by Burroughs. That a first Olympia edition of *The Naked Lunch* now commands thousands of dollars at auction is not only an index of its author's eminence as the most influential novelist of the post-1945 period, the small print run and the fragility of the paperback, but also a sign that this is a book that was read with intense seriousness and hence scuffed and battered, by a first readership of travelling intellectuals. No American writer of modern times made the transition from an underground reputation to success and influence so authoritatively as Burroughs, a late starter and, notwithstanding sixteen years of heroin addiction and sundry other dangers to health, one who lived long.

After his return to the USA in 1974 from roaming in South America, Europe and North Africa, Burroughs, blessed with a hypnotic voice, became a star of the reading circuit, netting $75,000 from 150 readings in the decade following his homecoming.[22] It was clear from the make-up of the audience at these events that he had unequalled access to the rock audience, in part through the influence attested by Lou Reed's Velvet Underground, Patti Smith, David Bowie and other practitioners bent on welding three-chord anthems out of a tradition of Baudelairean dandyism. He was, more than Kerouac, the writer read by those who didn't normally read. As more recent efforts, such as Irvine Welsh's *Trainspotting*, have recycled wholesale Burroughs's imagery, subject-matter, criminal *frisson*, satire, black humour and love of the *spiel*, his appeal to a more recent audience can be situated in the fall-out from a post-war optimism that Burroughs never shared. More intriguing as a point of entry would be a reconstruction of his appeal to the first readership at a time when Modernist path-breakers such as Eliot, Pound, Auden and Williams were arguably past their best, but still dominant.

The question is particularly pertinent given that Burroughs's novel is so militantly noxious in subject and tone. The novelist's Talking Asshole and the sundry blood-filled hypodermics, pornographic hangings and other forms of verbal discharge find their most likeable incarnation in Dr Benway, arguably the only character in the book, in the traditional sense: 'Of course I'd made a few "dummheits" here and there. Who hasn't? There was the time me and the anaesthetist drank up all the ether and the patient came up on us, and I was accused of cutting the cocaine with Saniflush' (*Naked Lunch*, 39). A Swiftian humour configuring death and the absurd gives Burroughs powers of sardony that, in milder versions admittedly, join an American tradition including Poe, Bierce, Lippard, and even the *Sut Lovingwood Papers*. But it is character in a non-traditional sense that dominates. Just as the novel rejects sequential plot, so sustained characterization is abandoned for a gallery of pseudo-characters: Lee (Burroughs's mother's maiden name), Willy the Disk, Bradley the Buyer and the rest of a cast, reduced frequently, like turns in a freak show, to a single function. (The Shoe Store Kid's sole purpose in life is 'shaking down fetishists in shoe stores' (14).) It may be argued, as it can ultimately be argued of any fiction, that the characters are authorial personae. If so, this brings Burroughs into surprising proximity to Eliot and the contours of authorship and the medium advanced in 'Tradition and the Individual Talent', a proximity only increased by other affinities in negativity partnering these two St Louis collagists.

T. S. Eliot once wrote to Herbert Read that some day he would like to write an essay about a man who wasn't anything, anywhere. In a sense he had already written the essay, for *The Waste Land* is a collage of failure and rejection by voices given a fleeting ventriloquial life. Both Eliot's poem and Burroughs's novel are world collages built from displaced hurt and streaked with tears of memory and regret. Both writers may be read as recording the vertigo deeded by Whitman and Emerson to American writers less sanguine than themselves about the freedom to reinvent the self; but whereas Eliot retreated into the sanctuary of ritual and conservatism, Burroughs gives Babel free speech. He mistrusted all authority, an anarchism at the root of his science fiction utopianism, his dislike of socialism and his enthusiastic membership of the NRA.

The latter was a particularly curious enthusiasm for one who had shot the mother of his child to death in Mexico City, drifting quietly away from a homicide investigation and back into the States after the palms of ballistics experts had been suitably greased, and the charges downgraded to one of *imprudencia criminale*. Displacing the image of the junkie, the shooting provided the defining image of Burroughs in the second half of his career, adopted as the motif of the better of the two biographies and by David Cronenberg in his film *Naked Lunch* (1991), less an adaptation than a hallucinated biopic. In the preface to *Queer*, an early novella, Burroughs writes of the shooting as the catalyst to his writing, a displaced reparation, confession and defence in terms whose configuration never entirely excludes an element of deliberation along with those of accident: 'I am forced to the appalling conclusion that I would never have become a writer but for Joan's death'.[23] Nicknamed *el hombre invisible* by Mexican boy-beggars, the novelist had reason to absent himself. Only those who have personality and emotions know what it means to want to escape those things. While this is not a key that unlocks the writing in any conclusive way, to ignore its role would be to accede to one of the more implausible shibboleths of the criticism prevailing in the academy during Burroughs's lifetime.

This is the first page of *The Naked Lunch*:

I can feel the heat closing in, feel them out there making their moves, setting up their devil doll stool pigeons, crooning over my spoon and dropper I throw away at Washington Square Station, vault a turnstile and two floors down the iron stairs, catch an uptown A train... Young, good looking, crew cut, Ivy League, advertising exec type fruit holds the door back for me. You know the type comes on with bartenders and cab drivers, talking about right hooks and the Dodgers, call the counterman in Nedick's by his first name. A real asshole. And right on time this narcotics dick in a white trench coat (imagine tailing somebody in a white trench coat – trying to pass as a fag I guess) hit the platform. I can hear the way he would say it holding my outfit in his left hand, right hand on his piece: 'I think you dropped something, fella.'

But the subway is moving.

'So long flatfoot!' I yell, giving the fruit his B production. I look into the fruit's eyes, take in the white teeth, the Florida tan, the two hundred dollar sharkskin suit, the button-down Brooks Brothers shirt and carrying *The News* as a prop. (12)

The page reworks an episode from the author's first novel, *Junkie* (1953), where, after various feints and manoeuvres, 'I vaulted the subway turnstile and shoved the cigarette package into the space at the side of a gum machine. I ran down one level and got a train up to the Square.'[24] The terse sentences and level tone recall Hammett and, more distantly, Hemingway. Delinquent in content, they are filial in style. The later novel complicates *noir* flattening of affect with the colours of hallucination, jamming together what is factual and what is metaphorical without pointers, so that 'devil doll stool pigeons' and 'spoon and dropper' sound equally literal. This is standard practice for the Surrealist tradition, and is used, as we have seen, in *Howl*; but it formed a radical departure for an American novelist, part of the armoury of technique suggesting that, while Burroughs has been imitated, he has not been superseded. The bile sprayed over the agent's white trench coat locates it as a prop from a 'B production' like Raymond Chandler's *The Big Sleep*, an excessive conformity to type, to code. Ironically, it is the agent who is made a literary signifier, where the narrator is *el hombre invisible*, there and then gone as the train starts to move. The signs that confer social authenticity are seen through by the junkie, a social ghost exercising all the ghost's privileges of haunting and provocation.

The most curious aspect of this spectral humour and destabilizing of identity is its formal proximity to Eliot's sense of disembodiment in the personality. The new American writing is always close to its forebears in a telescoped view of history that is as alien to Europe as the use of alienation is central, paradoxically, to the American literary tradition. The subversive, the popular, the underground and the commercially successful present their most American aspects in their surprisingly high levels of interchangeability. The emphasis on youth and dissidence in American writing after 1945, and the various choruses of disapproval, helped sell books and gave the authors a canonical plot on which to build. However, in life, the Beat generation still seemed to stand in the shadows of a Modernism that had really fought to make it new, in Pound's phrase, and that had retained both avant-garde and traditional credentials. Now it is time to read the first and second generations in the light of each other. The results are unexpected. The achievements of Ginsberg, Burroughs and others are durable, more self-consciously literary than seemed to be the case as they stood in court, and yet that very literariness entails a final surrender to the embrace of America. By contrast, Eliot in particular appears, despite his chosen persona as the guardian of tradition, a self-fashioning innovator whose very development of multiple personae enabled him to jump over the side of Captain Ahab's second hearse, whose wood could only have been American.

# 7

# 'Dedicated to America, whatever that is'

## Contemporary Literature and the Egress

### American places and the pursuit of happiness

In reviewing American literature from the time of the Puritans' errand into the wilderness to that of Toni Morrison, a reader is struck not only by the inseparability of writing from place, but by the inseparability of place from imagination, personal or collective. The literature of recent years continues to show an America invented, not discovered, its loci interwoven with an ongoing conceptualization that may tend towards a metaphysics of deep space or a focusing on daily minutiae, or both, as with the writings of Northern California examined in this chapter. To turn to the opposite coast and the city of New York, the Western world's cultural capital, is to encounter on the street or on the page a trip-hammer vitality, both ubiquitous and mysterious, seeming to belong at one moment to a population with a unique sense of the daily grind as theatre, at another to the canyons of glass and steel that define, in the words of one of its inhabitants, poet John Ashbery, 'the lovely, corrupt, wholesome place New York is' (O'Hara, p. x). Yet those mountains and canyons are man-made, aims and aspirations taking material shape, and understood as such by Henry James as much as by Ashbery or Frank O'Hara. The link between place, imagination and aspiration means that to depict place in the American arts is immediately to ask questions about allegiance, in times of danger as well as at moments of desire. Toni Morrison's

*Beloved* (1987) makes us read place as history, the function of literature being its gifts of character and detail to statistics of oppression
otherwise too massive to take in. Yet, even in *Beloved*, African-
Americans denied basic rights in the land of the free are drawn,
against their will, to the Edenic possibilities that are still latent in
the place of their oppression. Americans' darkest dystopias carry
hopes, often sentimental, of a return to the Garden or an egress to
the promised land. *Beloved* was a prominent novel of the 1980s, a
decade particularly hard to fix, even in terms of mood, and Morrison's
novel, like other important fictions of that time – Richard Ford's *The
Sportswriter* and the novels of Don DeLillo – crosses genres with an
uneasy watchfulness. To Ford's protagonist Frank Bascombe, also,
place, happiness and ideas of America are indivisible, though the
mysterious fugues that Frank calls his 'dreaminess' undermine any
firm tenure on the American dream.

## Northern California: landscapes and mindscapes

There are two ways to take in the Sierra Nevada. Approached from
the east, it offers to the eye the snowy and jagged wall of granite that
the Spaniards saw, and that is famously reproduced in the photographs of Ansel Adams. Seen from the west, its gradations wear a
metaphysical aura – or rather seem the realization of a metaphysic.
This is the view recorded by John Muir (1938–1914):

> Along the eastern margin rises the mighty Sierra, miles in height,
> reposing like a smooth, cumulous cloud in the sunny sky, and so
> gloriously colored, and so luminous, it seems to be not clothed with
> light, but wholly composed of it, like the wall of some celestial city. . . .
> When I first enjoyed this superb view, one glowing April day, from the
> summit of Pacheco Pass, the Central Valley but little trampled or
> plowed as yet, was one furred, rich sheet of golden compositae, and
> the luminous wall of the mountain shone in all its glory. Then it seemed
> to me the Sierra should be called not the Nevada, or Snowy Range, but
> the Range of Light.[1]

Muir's efforts would lead to the establishment of a National Parks
Service, and Muir Woods outside San Francisco perpetuate his name.
However, the precision of his observations cannot be divorced from a
rhapsodic tone. Indeed, it could be said that Muir's observations are
inseparable not from the mountains at which he was looking, but

from the Romantic vocabulary he brought with him on the journey. Once more America is invented rather than discovered, this time as walls of light. But the movement of thought recorded here is specific to California, very different for example from Emerson's mobilization of Romantic tropes while standing on a snowy common on the opposite coast, where 'In the tranquil landscape, and especially in the distant line of the horizon, man beholds somewhat as beautiful as his own nature' (Emerson, 10). Energized by landscape, Emerson's thought is boosted and transcends place to meet and celebrate itself. The Californian tendency is to have the landscape appear, then swiftly de-realize itself in a moment, suggesting by synecdoche the fantastic nature of all phenomenal reality, at which point the landscape appears again. It is phenomena, not the Emersonian eyeball, that become transparent. This now-you-(don't)-see-it treatment of nature is as characteristic of the Beats and West Coast 'Buddhists' of recent decades, such as Gary Snyder, as it was of Muir on the mountains.

By the time of Jack Kerouac's garrulous epic *Visions of Cody* (1951), 'Dedicated to America, whatever that is', those remnants of California that could be deemed 'but little trampled or plowed as yet' were shrinking fast, and this picturing of the South San Franciscan hills and the pylons on Highway 101 reaches for Buddhist forms of intellection in estrangement as much as celebration.[2] The continuities and differences *vis-à-vis* Muir are revealing, and can make their point only in extended quotation:

The great spindly tin-like crane towers of the trans-territorial electric power wires standing in serried gloom with pendant drop of head shapes (the upper insulation Tootsie Rolls strapped securely in place by the pull and tort of the wires – and not really Tootsie Rolls but pagodas of Japan hung in a gray mist of South San Francisco to save from shock the void, the empty California gray white air with its roll of fogclouds marching to the beat of Bethlehem Steel mill hammers). Far off the misty neons of subsidiary, little used diners for the airport, with fried clams, ice cream, waffles; either that or it's an empty factory shining in the night an advertisement of itself in the nowhere of industrial formations; a rusty weedy marsh here, not a real marsh, a slag of drain waters from rusty foundry cans and pisspots, but muddy like a swamp, inhabited by frogs and crickets that madly sing at dark fall, croak.

Trucks growling up the 101 overpass surmount the South City yards where Cody worked, lines of shining headlamps coming up off the faroff ditch marshes and headed for the city; the sense of rain and steam everywhere in the fragrant distance of oil, mist, steam of engines and pure Pacific brine with that special California white raw air.

All hail the Giant Rat beneath the Stockyard platforms! – hail the poor whiteface cows drowsing in their evening stockyard fattening meadow with its call of faroff trains and almost Iowa-like valley green softness, that will be hamburg tomorrow when the wheels of industry have churned them through to reality and death. (353)

Kerouac's work has joined the canon only to be read more nostalgically than it deserves, as a Tom Sawyer-like fishing expedition in counter-cultural waters that would deluge the USA around the time of the novelist's death. A certain Edenic remoteness about the bohemian as well as the suburban 1950s has drawn attention away from the shadows and depth that frequently complicate the lyricism of his prose. He could write both brilliantly and badly, often on the same page. Kerouac produced almost as many books as he spent years alive, and gambled recklessly on the Ginsbergian dictum 'first thought, best thought'. There are sloppy repetitions in the passage quoted, and the breathless reliance on a rising cadence – as if obstacles could be talked out of existence – is a clear reminder of the damage that can be done to writers habituated to amphetamine sulphate or the prose of Thomas Wolfe. But it is also a powerful vignette, as was realized immediately by Ginsberg, who in 1953 mailed it to Charles Henri Ford for inclusion in a New Directions anthology of prose poetry. The breathless cadences are poetic, not merely by virtue of their aspirant tone, but in an echo of Whitman that is political and strategic. The balance between detail and theme is finely judged, without compromising the improvisatory rush that characterizes Kerouac's best writing: Cody, The Subterraneans (1958), Big Sur (1962) and Desolation Angels (1965), as well as more maudlin efforts like Visions of Gerard (1958). The swagger of Kerouac's prose should not deflect attention from what are frequently canny and sometimes brilliant effects. As with Muir on the mountains, the power of the writing appears to be observational, while relying hugely on an attitude and a taxonomy in place before observation begins. The description of the crane towers as part Tootsie Rolls, part 'pagodas of Japan hung in a gray mist', captures exactly the half-oriental, half-toytown charm which many visitors find in San Francisco's alternation of bright colours and fog. But it is the tenets of Buddhism that are all the time structuring Kerouac's perceptions, as objects dissolve in 'the void', and the flesh of unknowing animals is shorn of fake pastoral for hamburgers, when 'the wheels of industry', in that terrific, final, falling cadence, 'have churned them through to reality and death'. The life of the passage's observed details is inseparable from the meta-reality of death and the void that is also 'that special California white raw air'. The 'empty factory shining in the night an advertisement of itself in the nowhere of industrial formations' turns a human nowhere into a now-here, at the cusp of Buddhist metaphysics and a very occidental critique of capitalist spoliation. Kerouac's restlessness to get on the road always carried an anxiety that the freeway may, after all, be nothing but a corridor between suburbs.

The uniting figure in Donald Allen's anthology, or at least the poet with the widest range of affiliations among his contemporaries, has ironically proved the most intractable to mainstream taste. John Wieners (1934 – ) had more than one poem by Frank O'Hara dedicated to him. Allen Ginsberg would in time be responsible for the publication of two large selections of the poet's work, while John Ashbery has contributed a poem to a collection of *hommages*, and Robert Creeley has written of Wieners's 'painful survival in words' as emblematic in a time of Cold War.[3] While Wieners has been identified for decades with Boston, his Beat-ification came with his first, slim volume, *The Hotel Wentley Poems* (1958), that took its title from the hotel in San Francisco where he began recording his odyssey into drug use, homosexual encounters and loss, obsession, and a politics of identity and the sign whose most full-blown episodes are to be found in *Behind the State Capitol or Cincinnati Pike* (1975), a deranged masterpiece, at one and the same time the capstone of Wieners's career and the book that would sink his reputation. In 1958 Wieners's writing was already powered by hallucination, fitful hotel glimmers that dissolve in walls of darkness, rather than Muir's light. The Californian void in which things lose their materiality becomes in Wieners's work a psychic geography, bodied forth in San Francisco place-names. Those names point to real places that can be visited, but have no meaning outwith a text that turns them into a conceptual field.

The Hotel Wentley still stands, the name gone, over a fast food outlet in Polk Gulch, which has probably changed less than any other San Francisco neighbourhood over the last forty years. More an unhappy than a dangerous area, it served and serves as a place to pick up rent boys. That Wieners was at home on the social and psychological margins is clear from the titles of these early poems: 'A poem for benzedrine', 'A poem for cocksuckers'. Here is 'A poem for vipers':

> I sit in Lees. At 11:40 PM with
> Jimmy the Pusher. He teaches me
> Ju Ju. Hot on the table before us
> shrimp foo yong, rice and mushroom
> chow yuke. Up the street under the wheels
> of a strange car is his stash – The ritual.

We make it. And have made it.
For months now together after midnight.
Soon I know the fuzz will
interrupt, will arrest Jimmy and
I shall be placed on probation. The poem
does not lie to us. We lie under
its law, alive in the glamour of this hour
able to enter into the sacred places
of his dark people, who carry secrets
glassed in their eyes and hide words
under the coats of their tongue.[4]

There is a curious doubleness in the poem, which is not reducible to
the gap between experience and representation, though it may find
its origin there. It is 11:40 pm exactly, in this particular place and
this particular company; yet the montage of pun and metaphor with
which the poem closes will show something different from a realist,
snapshot mode à la Carlos Williams. Many poems in the Wentley
sequence are structured by a pun. In the case of 'A poem for record
players' the pun turns on what is 'here' and what 'I hear and shall
never/give up again', the 'dull details' of heard music, human crying
and sparrows in the alley equalized as layered spaces by their flight into
the void of past time, but rematerializing and given significance by
recollection in writing (27). 'A poem for painters' puns on the line:
of age, experience, artistry, drugs. The use of puns in 'A poem for
vipers' is part of its general insistence on the inherently duplicitous
nature of even the most sharply itemized moment of experience, the
deeps beneath each layer. The simplest word in the world, 'it', stretches
promiscuously across sexual and criminal possibilities, picked up
by the later pun on 'lie' (line 12). The customary agents of law
and order are ousted by the new 'law' of the talismanic poem, inside
whose cordon sanitaire 'we' can spin the fictions, the lies, that link
the make-believe of poetry to other kinds of statement fabricated
in order to resist arrest. This brings to the fore the question of who
'we' are, and to what forces we give our allegiance in times of danger.
This is the political question asked by American literature from the
1940s on.

   In Wieners's poem the instant that was monochrome becomes
chromatic, as the Dashiell Hammett realism of the opening gives
way to the layered bohemian rhapsody of the poem's close. The
expansion of awareness might be thought to mimic the effects
of marijuana, 'viper' being an old synonym for a smoker, but in any
case the altered consciousness of the drug-user only renders the
true state of things more vivid. The implication of Wieners's work is

that all human endeavour is bent on escaping arrest, ultimately by mortality; but what paralyses is, in reality, disintegration. The central, Romantic irony on which *The Hotel Wentley Poems* are constructed is that to linger with experience makes it impossibly kaleidoscopic, yet imprisoning. The blankness of Kerouac's raw white California air, the impalpable splendour of Muir's mountains, are alive in, yet critiqued, by Wieners's melancholy lyricism.

The vocabulary of the closing lines reminds us that there was no established counter-culture in 1958 that could be clearly separated from the underworld, and from a gaol term for what is no longer a crime under Californian law. The worlds of poetry, drugs and magic are fused, as 'hide words /under the coats of their tongue' implies both the pun of the poem, the hipster's code of a secret society at odds with the straight world, the hiding of illegal items in a long coat, and the coating of the tongue the morning after. Wieners writes in tongues, and the poem is a 'sacred' rite of communion only half-travestied, and echoing the alchemical *Transmutations* of Stephen Jonas, to which Wieners would supply a preface. These poems revive the dark romanticism and urban wariness of Baudelaire ('J'ai pétri de la boue, et j'en ai fait de l'or') for a contemporary setting, suggesting the tradition of dandyism as the preferred rhetoric through which poets could construct a relationship, albeit by antithesis, to industrial society. The poem's insistence on hard actualities is not obfuscated by the closing lines, and rescues the 'Invitation au Voyage'-style exoticism from its recent domestication at the hands of Eliot and Wallace Stevens, setting minutiae and defamiliarization in a matrix that implicitly chides the author of Nanzia Nunzio, Professor Eucalyptus and Mrs Alfred Uruguay for a disconnected aestheticism.

The summer 1951 issue of the *Kenyon Review* carried an article by Paul Goodman on 'Advance-guard Writing, 1900–1950', which, citing hardly any names from the period, was more a meditation on the directions that a progressive American literature might take in the second half of the century. As with Wieners, the question asked concerns the forces to which Americans can give allegiance in a time of alienation; but whereas Wieners offered a poetry of experience in whose toils he was caught, Goodman saw the poet as capable of – indeed responsible for – taking a guiding social role. Different aspects of Goodman's thesis would be refracted in different ways by the poetry of the time. Frank O'Hara's biographer Brad Gooch suggests that the article had a bracing effect on O'Hara, confirming the intimate, name-dropping congeniality of his poetry as a viable alternative to Modernist monumentality. Other poets such as Robert Duncan would develop a teacherly or shamanistic role in their work, aligned to Goodman's vocabulary of sickness and cure:

> The essential present-day advance-guard is the physical reestablishment of community. This is to solve the crisis of alienation in the simple way: the persons are estranged from themselves, from one another, and from their artist; he takes the initiative precisely by putting his arms around them and drawing them together. In literary terms this means: to write for them about them personally... in a small community of acquaintances, where everybody knows everybody and understands what is at stake... [T]he artist makes this culture.[5]

The Germanic formulations from the lexicon of psychotherapy are both dated and predictive. A Poundian sense of the poet having *power* reaches fascinating variants in the work of O'Hara and Duncan, but has pretty much expired with the passing of that generation. However, Goodman's prolepsis reaches out to an identification of the writer with the disenfranchised group and with the politics of identity which would reach its maximum influence in the feminist movement, and find its nadir in the drift of contemporary criticism towards the rejection of evaluation as a meaningful activity. I turn to 'Often I Am Permitted to Return to a Meadow', perhaps the most famous poem by Robert Duncan (1919–88), which, while rejecting Goodman's stress on authorial originality, heeds his call to the poet as a healer of estrangement:

> as if it were a scene made-up by the mind,
> that is not mine, but is a made place,
>
> that is mine, it is so near to the heart,
> an eternal pasture folded in all thought
> so that there is a hall therein
>
> that is a made place, created by light
> wherefrom the shadows that are forms fall.
>
> Wherefrom fall all architectures I am
> I say are likenesses of the First Beloved
> whose flowers are flames lit to the Lady.
>
> She it is Queen Under the Hill
> whose hosts are a disturbance of words within words
> that is a field folded.
>
> It is only a dream of the grass blowing
> east against the source of the sun
> in an hour before the sun's going down
>
> whose secret we see in a children's game
> of ring a round of roses told.

> Often I am permitted to return to a meadow
> as if it were a given property of the mind
> that certain bounds hold against chaos,
>
> that is a place of first permission,
> everlasting omen of what is.[6]

The fatherly embrace idealized by Goodman is implied here not by a self-figuring on the artist's part, but by a model of language itself as teacherly and benignly enfolding. Like many poems by Duncan, it discharges a massive amount of syncretic and overlapping allusion, the lyric impulse sparked by a sense that the data have reached critical mass, and become knowledge. The final use of 'omen', at first sight a curious choice, rests on its derivation from the Latin *omentum*, 'a fold', exemplifying the poem's method of presenting knowledge as a field folded. Superimposed references to Irish myth, Neoplatonism, Roman Catholic Mariolatry and Corinthians form a ring, a round of reference points, a collective unconscious or shared dream-space, of which particular myths are merely local variants. The 'children's game' alludes of course to the Black Death, its roses, pocketful of posies and atishoo the sores, protective flower amulets and sneezes dating from the epidemics of bubonic plague. The allusion is comic and redemptive; after the final falling-down we all undergo sooner or later, our or someone's children will rise like the sun, and start the dance again. Individual identity is less important than the fact that we are all 'likenesses'.

In an important pun, Duncan's meadow is 'a given property of the mind', and not the private property of any one mind in particular. Place is not the province of geography, but a scene or field of concepts, expressible in spatial or architectural terms. The condition of the world from this San Franciscan perspective is forever paradisal, forever fallen, the Platonic allusions to light and shadow bolstered by the epistemology of the medieval Light Metaphysicians, particularly Robert Grosseteste, whose *De Luce* images the birth of the universe as a spreading candle flame or unrolling carpet of light in which our opaque and impure planet and natures are snagged. It is also, like the passages quoted from Muir and others, characteristic of Northern Californian writing in its emphasis on light at the expense of form. Phrases such as 'architectures I am' imply a turning of the now-you-(don't)-see-it mysticism of light inwards, to questions of identity. Duncan's work, both here at the mid-point of his career and to the last, in *Ground Work II: In the Dark* (1987), goes much further, as an intellectual quest, than the eclecticism and traditions of Northern California, yet never leaves them behind.

# New York! New York!

A reader steeped in Henry James may recognize in my italicized ejaculation a quotation not from Frank Sinatra, nor even from Frank O'Hara, but rather from the alternating running headers on the recto pages of James's *The American Scene*, a trove yielding not only titles that might feasibly have headed short stories ('The Escape into the Past', 'The Scale of the Infusion'), but also the actual title of a poem by John Ashbery, 'The Burden of the Park'. In beating around the bush stylistically, James's rhetorical parentheses and peregrinations catch something essential to New York, then and now, that a more direct observation might miss. More than any other Western city, New York is, to deploy an un-Jamesian phrase, in your face. Its canyons of steel drive deep into the consciousness a statement about money and will. And yet the purposes of its citizens, virtually all of them from elsewhere, are more bound to aspiration than those of any other comparable space; conceptual, in some measure. Ellis Island was the way into Paradise, a Manhattan peopled, in James's phrase, 'by migrations at once extremely recent, perfectly traceable and urgently required'.[7] Seemingly un-literary in its devotion to commerce, New York is built on the business of writing. By 1840, Manhattan was the nation's literary capital. Whitman the journalist wrote of himself as 'manhattanese', and his contacts included Poe, editor of the *Broadway Journal*. Melville, James, Wharton, Dreiser, Dos Passos, Mencken, Wolfe, Crane and so many others, down to John Ashbery, lived and live there. Many of the publishing houses of James's day continued through the twentieth century: Doubleday, E. P. Dutton, G. P. Putnam, Charles Scribner's Sons, Knopf. Leaning on the rails at Battery Park City, looking out across the water to the Statue of Liberty and the big clock on the Jersey shore, you lean on poetry for support, if only because lines by Whitman and O'Hara have been sculpted in the rails.

James's record of a visit in *The American Scene* suggests that the essentials have not changed:

> For that is how the place speaks, as great constructed and achieved harmonies mostly speak – as a temple builded, with clustering chapels and shrines, to an idea. The hundreds and hundreds of people in circulation, the innumerable huge-hatted ladies in especial, with their air of finding in the gilded and storied labyrinth the very firesides and pathways of home, became thus the serene faithful, whose rites one would no more have sceptically brushed than one would doff one's

disguise in a Mohammedan mosque.... Here was a world whose relation to its form and medium was practically imperturbable; here was a
conception of publicity *as* the vital medium organized with the vital
authority with which the American genius for organization, put on its
mettle, alone could organize it. (75)

The 'innumerable huge-hatted ladies' may have gone, like the marble
and balustrade of the Edwardian hotel. (They can both be found in
Terence Davies's recent version of Wharton's *The House of Mirth*,
filmed for the most part in Glasgow.) But the gilded and storied
labyrinth, where a guiding idea, the vital medium of publicity, and
the 'very firesides and pathways of home' lead in and out of each
other: has that really changed? James pictures himself gliding through
the labyrinth in the guise of the faithful, the better to observe without
intrusion. Yet he too is a worshipper, and his giddy sense that all this is
a house of cards as well as mirth, founded on risk and recklessness,
makes his faith in the religion of 'the American genius' no less complete. The writer most closely identified with contemporary New
York echoes James's thinking:

> Most reckless things are beautiful in some way and recklessness is what
> makes experimental art beautiful, just as religions are beautiful because
> of the strong possibility that they're founded on nothing.... I feel this
> also even in the work of great modern painters such as Jackson Pollock
> or Mark Rothko. Everyone accepts them now as being major artists,
> and yet, does their work amount to anything? There's a possibility that
> it doesn't, although I believe in it and want it to exist. But I think that
> part of the strength of their art, in fact, is this doubt as to whether art
> may be there at all.[8]

Thus, John Ashbery. The Museum of Modern Art, with Alfred Barr at
its helm and Frank O'Hara as one of its curators, would house the
experimental Pollocks and Rothkos, identifying them for all time with
New York City as the world's art capital, following the fall of Paris in
the Second World War. The specifics of the Museum's foundation, the
role that State Department funding played in bringing the vital medium
of publicity to the avant-garde, have been amply documented. What
I want to point up here is the natural evolution of New York as the
world's culture capital during the lifetime of Frank O'Hara (1926–66),
on foundations seen perfectly clearly by James at a time when Paris
and London still held sway. James's view of the gilded and storied
labyrinth struck him as 'unforgettable', as 'one of my few glimpses of
perfect human felicity', New York's uniqueness aimed, in a phrase that
was old even then, at 'the greatest happiness of the greatest number'

(*American Scene*, 75). As with the abstract canvasses of Pollock or Rothko, to build the labyrinth on the daring of an idea, risks a crash. As with *Autumn Rhythm*, so with Wall Street. The mysticism of now-you-(don't)-see-it is back, and on the opposite coast, this time not a question of light and landscape, but of the market, in artworks or other things. The gilded stories of capitalism and the avant-garde are as intertwined in America as the conservative and radical traditions, unpicked in chapter 1, are intertwined at the Puritan root. Really it is all one story.

To Frank O'Hara, New York was one monumental act of will, a leap of faith. One poem ostensibly about a movie star's ill health begins 'Lana Turner has collapsed!' and describes O'Hara himself as 'trotting along...in such a hurry', concluding 'O Lana Turner we love you get up' (O'Hara, 449). Cartoon-like in its opposition between vertical living and horizontal collapse, the poem has an underlying seriousness. One has a duty to stay upright and to aspire. Partying, 'trotting' and behaving disgracefully at parties are all life-affirming, but don't for heaven's sake *collapse* – or we'll all go, like dominoes. There is an omen in the *omentum* of the falling star. O'Hara is worried that everything might fold, in a different sense of the term from Duncan. It might all, the whole shebang – love, New York, poetry – be based on recklessness of the kind that his friend John Ashbery saw in experimental art. Only more recklessness, a redoubled gamble of the kind we saw in writers of the American Renaissance, can ensure success. And so, in 'Steps', it might be a lover or a city or a conflation of both that is adored:

> oh god it's wonderful
> to get out of bed
> and drink too much coffee
> and smoke too many cigarettes
> and love you so much
>
> (371)

O'Hara ambiguates the word 'you' much as James did the word 'it', when he wrote:

> It sat there, it walked and talked, and ate and drank, and listened and danced to music, and otherwise revelled and roamed, and bought and sold, and came and went there, all on its own splendid terms and with an encompassing material splendour, a wealth and variety of constituted picture and background, that might well feed it with the finest illusions about itself. (*American Scene*, 74)

And this of course is New York incarnated – though James's serpentine grammar leads the word 'it' back to 'promiscuity' in the previous two sentences: 'the whole immense promiscuity'.

On an afternoon in April 1960, informed by a doctor on Fifth Avenue that he had caught syphilis from his lover, O'Hara wrote a short poem on the way home ('Song', beginning 'I am stuck in traffic in a taxicab' (361)). Here he pictures disease as an accident that emerges from our traffic with each other to become suddenly real, and that must, though it can't, be willed not to exist. A week later he wrote 'An Airplane Whistle (After Heine)', its title alluding to something else his lover had given him, this time a whistle from a Cracker Jack box:

> The rose, the lily and the dove got withered
> in your sunlight or in the soot, maybe, of New York
> (361)

The mood of the two poems is much the same, though one speaks of disease climbing the trellis of the nerves, the second of a dark Manhattan. O'Hara frequently addresses the private, the time of day and New York, in one breath, as in 'A Step Away from Them', 'Walking' or 'Seven Nine Seven', which speak of the 'profile of a city / exploding against the old dull bed' (433). 'The Day Lady Died', O'Hara's elegy for Billie Holiday and his most frequently anthologized poem, is a packed diary of dates, train times, dinner engagements, names of friends for whom presents must be bought, and then the shock of a *New York Post* with Lady Day's face on it:

> and I am sweating a lot by now and thinking of
> leaning on the john door in the 5 SPOT
> while she whispered a song along the keyboard
> to Mal Waldron and everyone and I stopped breathing
> (325)

The Five Spot was a jazz club where Thelonious Monk and John Coltrane had recently completed a celebrated residency. These, the closing lines of the poem, are a black-and-white snapshot of desegregated, Fifties bohemia, and the image of New York such poems convey has come to epitomize its appeal over the succeeding half-century. Indeed, O'Hara, for so long a poet's poet, now looks at us from the inside of the canon, not the coterie. In this account I am looking at some of his darker moments, but even here it was Frank O'Hara's New

York that turned out to be what everybody wanted. He turned difficulties into style, whether as a poet, a gay man, or a museum curator. The brio, the cultural cross-referencing and airbrushed punctuation have become a part of the national poetic repertoire. August Kleinzahler does it pretty well, though you can always see where he's coming from.

And yet, to return to that snapshot of bohemia, the treasured memory of hearing Billie Holiday sing turns out to be the memory of a criminal misdemeanour. Hounded by the FBI over drugs and so forth, the singer was banned from singing in New York at this point. The crowd had actually turned up to the Five Spot to hear poet Kenneth Koch read alongside Mal Waldron, Lady Day's accompanist. 'It was very close to the end of her life, with her voice almost gone, just like a whisper', Koch recalled: 'The place was quite crowded. Frank was standing near the toilet door so he had a side view.'[9] And so James was right: 'it' is and was all about promiscuity, not necessarily in the sexual sense, but in New York's permission to blur categories and boundaries, to quick-change artistry, to sing when you're not supposed to, or make love with those you aren't supposed to. In O'Hara's case the transgression of borders meant curating the work of artists who were also personal friends, doing this without a proper training in art history, being homosexual pre-Stonewall, collaborating on collages; a walking miscellany, a hybrid poet-critic. The line from 'In Memory of My Feelings' that would be chiselled on his gravestone simply says it all-encompassingly, in the Whitman mode. No one was ever so at home in their time and place as Frank O'Hara, in a special sense the greatest of New York writers, for, more than any other writer, he makes that place and time appear the best that could be experienced.

As a black woman, Billie Holiday had never been free to come and go as she pleased, even before the FBI got on her case. Unable even to share a hotel with the white musicians backing her, she lived a world away from Frank O'Hara, photographed in tuxedo, shaking hands with Nelson Rockefeller. Grace not to get too much abuse, and to live as surreptitiously as possible. However, even handshakes can be loaded: I can recall leading a class on O'Hara at the Harlem campus of City College in the late 1980s, and watching it split down the middle on the race issue as that came up in 'The Day Lady Died' and 'Personal Poem'. In the latter, O'Hara writes of lunching with Amiri Baraka (then LeRoi Jones), who tells him about Miles Davis getting clubbed by a police-officer, ironically outside Birdland. O'Hara concludes the poem with a handshake:

I wonder if one person out of the 8,000,000 is
thinking of me as I shake hands with LeRoi
and buy a strap for my wristwatch and go
back to work happy at the thought possibly so
(336)

Some of the class felt that this was an artificial rhetorical move,
and therefore racist; others, that it was a self-consciously liberal
gesture, and therefore anti-racist; still others, that O'Hara was a
white liberal, and therefore inevitably racist. New York in the 1980s
was more divided than at present. A little dazed after class broke up,
I wandered minus my glasses into a campus café, and gravitated
towards a beautiful young African-American woman running a book-
stall, who seemed to be smiling at me. On closer inspection, her
pamphlets turned out to be Nation of Islam, Farrakhanite tracts
with titles like 'White Man, You're Finished!'.

The O'Hara who shakes hands with LeRoi Jones seems vulnerable,
to me, and not only because of his wanting to make the friendly,
physical gesture across the divide of race. He's vulnerable because he
isn't wearing his watch. This is no small thing to O'Hara, who, now
viewed as being ahead of his time, wrote poetry against the clock,
recording his life and times in diaristic detail. Killed in an accident at
forty, he ran out of time, his death seeming, as with many who die
young, a shock in the immediate aftermath, but somehow, with
hindsight, implicit in the work. Was to shake hands across race to
step momentarily out of time, or consciously to push the hands of the
political clock a little further forward?

# The 1980s

*Beloved*, the fifth novel by Toni Morrison (1931– ), won the Pulitzer
Prize. The fame it brought, consolidated by a Nobel Prize, is welcome
in its acknowledgement of a body of African-American fiction that
could engage the interest of a wide and mixed audience just as it
delved fiercely into black issues and history, an achievement on a scale
not seen since James Baldwin, and exceeding the wide appeal of his
work. The hands of the political clock had moved forward (though
the daily experience of African-Americans indicates a stop-start or
even backward tendency in Local Time).

The novel is set in the mid-nineteenth century in the ironically
named Sweet Home, Kentucky, at a time when slavery was coming

unstitched under abolitionist pressures. The emotional world of Sethe, the main female character, is one in which love, violence and death are interwoven in the loss of her baby daughter Beloved, killed by her mother in appalling circumstances, and returning from the grave to claim a retribution on territory as defined by myth and poetry as by exigencies of plot. Although the materials of history and the methods of social realism are all germane, the novel travels across genres. In a most curious and original way, *Beloved* caught the Gothic revival of the 1980s, and although Morrison's work is as far from Stephen King's as Kentucky is from Maine, the recourse by horror film to symbol and fantasy as a means of negotiating issues of violence and American identity is paralleled in her novel. A bigger wave was that of 1980s feminism, building on its 1970s radicalism to touch all areas of the social spectrum, and not yet waning into the journalistic froth of Camille Paglia and other post – that is to say, anti – feminist agents. Essentially a traditional novel in its fealty to plot and character, *Beloved* has touches of dreamy, dallying lesbianism in tune with the sisterhood courted by those times, and also appears to test-drive concepts of *écriture féminine* in its abandonment of conventional syntax late in the novel for white spaces and a kind of poetry. Given this alertness to such a broad spectrum of ways to represent and understand identity, it is surprising how dated the novel seems today.

Morrison can summon a formidable range of approaches in a brief space of prose, and is a dexterous manager of transitions. Hungry, lonely and on the run, Paul D knocks on the first back door he finds in the 'colored section' of Wilmington, Delaware:

> She fed him pork sausage, the worst thing in the world for a starving man, but neither he nor his stomach objected. Later, when he saw pale cotton sheets and two pillows in her bedroom, he had to wipe his eyes quickly, quickly so she would not see the thankful tears of a man's first time. Soil, grass, mud, shucking, leaves, hay, cobs, seashells – all that he'd slept on. White cotton sheets had never crossed his mind. He fell in with a groan and the woman helped him pretend he was making love to her and not her bed linen . . . . Eighteen months later, when he had been purchased by Northpoint Bank and Railroad Company, he was still thankful for that introduction to sheets.[10]

The novel is packed with these vignettes, sometimes, as with the example quoted, metonyms for the book's central themes, sometimes just passing worlds within worlds: 'In Ohio seasons are theatrical. Each one enters like a prima donna, convinced its performance is the reason the world has people in it' (116). Wit and the Gothic can feed each other: 'What was unusual (even for a girl who had lived all her life in a house peopled by the living activity of the dead) was that a white dress knelt down next to her mother and had its sleeve around her mother's waist' (29). In a novel so full of inventiveness it therefore comes as a jarring note, and one worth pausing over, when Morrison lapses into cliché: '"Let me tell you something. A man ain't a goddamn ax. Chopping, hacking, busting every goddamn minute of the day. Things get to him. Things he can't chop down because they're inside"' (69). '"Sethe", he says, "me and you, we got more yesterday than anybody. We need some kind of tomorrow"' (273). Perhaps these are clichés deployed from a sense of their being true to character, though on other occasions Morrison shows a delicacy in tracing the effects of class and education on behaviour that is almost worthy of Dickens: 'She couldn't read clock time very well, but she knew when the hands were closed in prayer at the top of the face she was through for the day' (189). The implication, then, is that the dead metaphors are an indulgence and one which, unexpectedly, can be identified by asking the question, once again, of what or to whom the American gives allegiance in times of danger.

Morrison has been a brave social critic, and not merely over issues of race. Her defence of President Clinton, as well as of the improved position of black Americans under the Clinton administrations, sounded a note of rationality at a point when European observers could not believe from the quantity of opprobrium hurtling around that the President had been dallying with a gullible intern and not a whole harem of Russian spies, a period when blood was not only scented but extracted hypodermically by opportunist Republicans of the worst sort (perilously close to the best sort, latterly), headed by 'special prosecutor' Kenneth Starr, a creature straight out of Old Salem. And while the public humiliation of one powerful white American is hardly commensurate with the daily, unrecorded humiliations visited on an entire ethnic group, Morrison's moral imagination speaks out over the noise of the pack. Such inclusiveness is the site of the novel's most and least original moments, as Morrison's characters are driven to concede attachment to America even as it harries and drives them to ground. The dream of an Edenic America, unleashed and sassy, is shared by 'the great heart' of Baby Suggs in 'the Clearing', a 'wide-open' primordial space hidden in the woods of Kentucky. It spells, for a brief moment, escape from racist ideology:

> Baby Suggs bowed her head and prayed silently.... Then she shouted, 'Let the children come!' and they ran from the trees toward her.
> 'Let your mothers hear you laugh,' she told them, and the woods rang. The adults looked on and could not help smiling.

Then 'Let the grown men come,' she shouted. They stepped out one by one from among the ringing trees.

'Let your wives and your children see you dance,' she told them, and groundlife shuddered under their feet.

Finally she called the women to her. 'Cry,' she told them. 'For the living and the dead. Just cry.' And without covering their eyes the women let loose. (87–8)

Call me churlish/male/Ishmael – whatever you like – I don't think this works. At all. Of course it only works for the characters briefly. Nevertheless, the episode in the clearing indexes Morrison's allegiance to that fundamental 'groundlife', the verdant sentiment of the American Dream. The contrast with Harriet Beecher Stowe's classic treatment of race is instructive. It might be said that Stowe used sentimentality remorselessly, as an implement of dialectic. But Stowe, unlike Morrison, feared the breakup of her nation, and wrote on the eve of the Civil War. Once again, place and aspiration are shown to be inseparable, but the clearing is no real place, but a symbolic space, a piece of wishful thinking. *Beloved* works best in its most harrowing and least poetic moments, located in sad truth.

After the fall of Saigon, the two-steps-forward-one-step-back of the civil rights movement and the absorption by commerce of hippie dissidence, some version of the American Dream became everyone's compensation for the failure of expectations on both Right and Left. The Dream, however, was troubled, the 1980s a period of uneasy success, when cliché figures such as the Wall Street broker returned in a more youthful form, the pin-stripe shirt and red suspenders clipping inverted commas of irony to the semiotics of achievement. In the White House an actor beginning to lose his memory symbolized a collective amnesia. Fearful of the deep space, the vertigo of recent change, American culture preferred to think of its literature, films and art as postmodern, playful and self-mocking in an age supposedly sceptical about grand narratives and good at pastiche. However, this scuttling for the shadows of retro stylization ran into a darkness that appears with hindsight to have been the true face of that decade. Serial killers popped up everywhere. The horror film enjoyed a serial revival with the *Nightmare on Elm Street*, *Halloween* and *Friday the Thirteenth* sequences. The *noir*/horror interface in fiction was handled best by James Ellroy, whose Los Angeles thrillers made canny use of genre to balance their hysterical pyrotechnics. More fashionable efforts like Bret Easton Ellis's *American Psycho* (published in 1991 after delays triggered by its content) could only fudge an uncertain juggling of satire and horror. Most successful of all was David Lynch's 1985 film *Blue Velvet*, a paradigm of the Eighties precisely through its deliberate blurring of that decade with the Fifties. In Lumberton, crooners and monster automobiles are the sounds of the suburbs, but men wear earrings. Lynch set his sights on the zone of discrepancy between small-town life in its social aspect and the desires and darkness of the individual, though the barrage unleashed swiftly exceeded the requirements of that familiar genre, culminating in one of the most alienated films to have crept passed the censors. Appearing in the same period as *Beloved*, *The Sportswriter* (1986) by Richard Ford (1944– ) addressed some of the same questions as Lynch, and reached some of the same battered and bleak conclusions, but through a prose medium as subtly bland as Lynch's cinema is (at least in the case of *Blue Velvet*) violent.

Frank Bascombe is a failed novelist who has become a sports writer, not through any special gift or enthusiasm. Rather, Frank is – or has to believe he is, this being one of the great novels of hoping for the best – 'as comfortable as an old towel in a locker room'.[11] Ford constantly has Frank give away more than he intended, though the precise constitution of that surplus or unconscious is not always easy to pin-point, and comes to stand by implication for a common condition of estrangement that wills things to be whole, and sociable, just as they crash into misunderstanding: 'The good-spirited, manly presence of naked whites and Negroes has always made me feel well-located, and I was never out of place asking a few easy-to-answer questions' (49). Frank, at thirty-nine 'midway around the track' (107), loves normality and small-town life midway between New York and Philadelphia. Haddam is 'simple, unambiguous, even factitious' (109), with a 'homespun air that reminds you of life pictured in catalogs (a view I rather like)' (55), its civilities and conformism keeping him from too painful a recognition of the *selva oscura*. Life through the eyes of Sears Roebuck has a particular appeal, as when Frank recognizes an old flame modelling in a catalog, 'though on page 88 *only* the eyes were visible behind a black silk balaclava worn by a woman modeling a pair of silk underwear from Formosa' (203). Frank finds this image redolent of terrorism and pornography reassuring, as he does his own urge to seek the model out and talk over old times. The wool nighties, cane fishing-rods, asbestos welding kits, virtuous screwdrivers and women in silk balaclavas and underwear standing by brick fireplaces are of a piece with 'ordinary good American faces...knowable, safe-and-sound' (202). So is the backslapping, fishing and sports talk of Frank's Divorced Men's Club, until the day one of the group confesses to a homosexual encounter and blows his brains out, sparking a train of events that will lead Frank to prowl the scene of the shooting at the invitation of the police, who unaccountably hand him a key to the abode of the deceased.

Thus are the *vericula* unpicked by oddities that will assume a greater prominence in a crude paraphrase such as this than in the perfectly judged medium of the novel, and its battered but cheerful cleaving to a normality 'founded on sincerity's rock' (116). Place, aspiration, allegiance are as one in Frank's Haddam, but his over-insistence on the rightness of his world implies its opposite. Frank would hate to admit to feeling outwith America, and hates Herb, an elderly sportsman whose mind has slipped a notch, allowing him to vocalize the unsayable: ' "I was just reading the other day that Americans always feel like the real life is somewhere else" ' (164). This is clearly so, despite Frank's protestations to himself. It states a fundamental American experience. In an incident barely mentioned, yet pivotal to the 'dreaminess' Frank feels but cannot describe fully, and which precipitated the breakdown of his marriage, burglars wiped his house clean of possessions, leaving behind Polaroids of bare rooms and the curiously Eliotean legend 'We are the stuffed men' spray-painted on the dining-room wall (21). This revenge of Modernism is perhaps not the only one in a book whose protagonist protests in every fibre of his being against the unbearable reality of a situation he strives and fails to reconstruct as safe, daily: 'New today. New tomorrow. Eternal renewal on a manageable scale' (154).

*The Sportswriter* lodged sufficiently in its author's as well as readers' consciousnesses to generate a sequel, *Independence Day* (1995). The successor is more sentimental, and fails to develop the earlier book's discovery (one Frank fails to see) that the dark side of American life is not merely close to its conventional surface, but complicitous with it. A more noisy and panoramic literature of that complicity, attentive to conspiracy theory, paranoia and information overload has been supplied first by Thomas Pynchon (1937– ) and then by Don DeLillo (1936– ). DeLillo began at the stylistic corner of Pynchon and Burroughs, but his most impressive work – *Running Dog*, *White Noise* and *Libra* – engages politics and history with a sophistication that Burroughs's vindictive anarchism never reached, while avoiding the fusion of monumentalism and whimsy that afflicts Pynchon's work. *Libra* (1988), which deals with the assassination of J. F. Kennedy and the opaque motivation of his probable killer, Lee Harvey Oswald, closes with an Author's Note on the subject of scale, ambiguity and information:

> In a case in which rumors, facts, suspicions, official subterfuge, conflicting sets of evidence and a dozen labyrinthine theories all mingle,

sometimes indistinguishably, it may seem to some that a work of fiction is one more gloom in a chronicle of unknowing.

But because the book makes no claim to literal truth, because it is only itself, apart and complete, readers may find refuge here – a way of thinking about the assassination without being constrained by half-facts or overwhelmed by possibilities, by the tide of speculation that widens with the years.[12]

This afterword, centred in the powers of the individual imagination and the traditional claims of the novel, draws a more hopeful conclusion than the novel itself, where alienation stems often not from a being outside but from always already being contained, produced and interpreted by a system one of whose surface effects is a feeling outwith America: 'He feels he is living at the center of an emptiness. He wants to sense a structure that includes him, a definition clear enough to specify where he belongs. But the system floats right through him, through everything, even the revolution. He is a zero in the system' (357). The frantic scrabbling to find an identity in some niche that 'the system' has always already costed and irradiated with its codes is treated with black humour and a certain redemptive comedy in *White Noise*'s negotiation of Hitler Studies and airborne toxic events. Both novels share a quasi-Marxian understanding of the production/deformation of identity by the system while seeing no Marxist, or other, alternative. Less successful after *Libra*, DeLillo's fiction by the time of the over-blown *Underworld* (1997) had slid over to the enemy's side. Burroughs noted famously that the paranoiac is simply the one in possession of all the facts; but, while DeLillo has been admired for his willingness to let the prose run to compendious extremes, *Underworld* is disabled by the very failure to encounter resistance. The book resembles a Sears Roebuck catalogue of everything that has happened in the last fifty years, not in the sports writer's sense, but in being equally interested in and unfazed by any manifestation of America; happy, ultimately. The unhappy novels of Burroughs and Richard Ford are more likely to endure precisely because of their vertigo, their lacunae, their picking at scabs in the promised land.

Thomas Pynchon's *Mason & Dixon* (1997) is a reimagination of that land, based on the activities of the two British surveyors who ran the boundary between Pennsylvania and Maryland known as the Mason-Dixon line. Written in a pastiche eighteenth-century English, the novel argues, as the present study argues, for the inseparability of America's founding and its contemporary ideals and failings:

Does Britannia, when she sleeps, dream? Is America her dream? – in which all that cannot pass in the metropolitan Wakefulness is allow'd Expression away in the restless Slumber of these Provinces, and on West-ward, wherever 'tis not yet mapp'd, nor written down, nor ever, by the majority of Mankind, seen, – serving as a very Rubbish-Tip for subjunctive hopes, for all that *may yet be true*, – Earthly Paradise, Fountain of Youth, Realms of Prester John, Christ's Kingdom, ever behind the sunset, safe till the next Territory to the West be seen and recorded, measur'd and tied in, back into the Net-Work of Points already known, that slowly triangulates its Way into the Continent, changing all from subjunctive to declarative, reducing Possibilities to Simplicities that serve the ends of Governments, – winning away from the realm of the Sacred, its Borderlands one by one, and assuming them unto the bare mortal World that is our home, and our Despair.[13]

There, in one remarkable sentence, is America, 'a very Rubbish-Tip for subjunctive hopes', roads not taken, all that the mind hears '*may yet be true*', even though the subjunctive is ploughed and trampled always into the declarative, the despair of malls and suburbs and the craven ends of government. The American Dream was Britannia's. Now Britannia is itself virtually a part of the 'Net-Work of Points already known', as is everywhere else, though the Dream is fitful and troubled, and even those at the heart of its simplicities feel themselves half-outside it.

Yet it would be false to end this book on this note, untrue to the energies of America's ongoing rewriting of itself. Steve Benson (1949–), a poet associated peripherally with the Language group, is a writer committed to risk. His early work – for example, *As Is* (1978) – takes off from O'Hara and the New York School into deadpan Dada, the movement from one line to the next a bolting-on of the unexpected:

> Since last night
> No bottle broke the floor
> No tea served instant fake coffee
> We did wrestle finally, on the rug
> Dancing to the neighbors below[14]

It is significant that Benson builds on the 'School' rather than the 'New York' influences of O'Hara and the St Mark's poetry scene. The specifics of place and time are less important than the way in which overall sign systems can be demystified, or reshuffled to surreal effect. This has been a general tendency in the American avant-garde post-1975, a point at which the productions of the Don Allen generation were collected (O'Hara, Spicer, Dorn, Creeley), some won prizes and were co-opted by the centre (Ashbery), and others slipped from view. The Language poets and other linguistically innovative writers have built on the achievements of that earlier generation in terms of style and method, but not in any attachment to places with the distinct impact of New York City, San Francisco or Black Mountain College. Yet, as I have tried to show, place in American writing is never separable from aspiration and imagination. The work of O'Hara's generation *has itself become* a place, for the writers who have followed.

Increasingly after his first book, Benson worked from the interface of improvisation and intense rehearsal, so that, for example, on a May evening in 1985 the audience at New York's Ear Inn was assailed by a spontaneous oral collage of passages from, among other sources, Thoreau's *Civil Disobedience*, Cabeza de Vaca's 1542 report to the king of Spain regarding his peregrinations from Florida to Mexico, Johnson's Life of Swift and *Peter Pan*. His book *Blindspots* (1981) comprised 'an unrehearsed, improvised oral poem I spoke as I determined it', along with monologues composed in relation to tape recordings audible to the poet but not the audience (a favourite Benson method).[15] It need hardly be added that Benson's work with pre-established materials has its humorous side, though the humour feeds into a larger-scale involvement in the abrasion and mutual criticism of discourses bolted on and sampled in this way. Another Language writer, Lyn Hejinian, wrote of Benson's poetry as arriving 'from within a full milieu', and this aspect of his (to put it mildly) conversational poetic is still of interest for its dramatic reversal of the traditional relationship between reader, writer and text.[16] The challenge of the work, its risk, is that milieu in a sense susceptible to structuralist analysis may not be the equal of a social 'milieu' of the kind that gave Frank O'Hara's poetry its life.

Conventionally, the act of writing a poem lays claim to certain experiences, the originality of the claim attested often by unusual images and expressive emphases that come to be housed in a reader's recognition of that poet's 'style', or 'voice'. Ultimately the poem privileges mind over its objects. Such a phenomenology had its heroic phase in the nineteenth century, surviving in a more self-questioning form along the strata of Modernism, and dwindling to a more or less polished conformism in the Creative Writing Program of today's academy. The Allen generation may be said to have balanced a revival of the egotistical sublime with a sustained interest in the materials of history and society, while never tampering with the defining individualism of style. A poem by O'Hara or Olson or Creeley could frequently be recognized from its visual layout on the page even before reading it. (It is significant that O'Hara's notes on exhibitions he curated, on file in the Museum of Modern Art, look just like his poems as shapes on the page.) In violent contrast, Steve Benson's work presents the poet's voices from the living and breathing intersection of codes and networks within which speaking subjects are constituted and perpetually reformed. The element of madcap humour in the work can be viewed as an exploded diagram of this social reality as it is inhabited by one speaker. The 'full milieu', the multiplicity of discourses whose conflict as well as conversation go to make up the single self, would become the nearest thing to a shared credo among the poets who had grouped beneath, and are now moving away from, the confining shelter of the Language umbrella. Benson's most engaging work is deformed by brief quotation in studies like mine, and the conventional implication that quotation produces a highlight or crucial nugget. With that in mind, I open his *Blue Book* at random, keeping it open with a hardback copy of DeLillo's *Libra* that obscures the top half of the page, find the following, and type:

nothing to report, no questions asked, if– And what would *that* be? There you are, you see? But okay, I wish you health. I'm angry at him, at you, at everybody, because the person I love most, or so I say, I won't be heard to think aloud when I'm around him, cause he's not interested, either to ask questions or to listen. Why? Why not? Why did I select him? He was, so patently,

for when you were going to ask me. Now lesson. I mean listen. A little lyrical sigh, or series of signs, would-be wise lines crumbling about each other's softens, going to see *The Clash*. Would you appreciate art? I have many negative connotations. I'm not afraid to name myself. You don't hear me. I'm afraid to name you. You don't exist, that's why. I think you're a fake, in recognizable form. Now (78)

The double column permits readings across as well as down. I'm angry at him, at wise lines crumbling. He's not to name myself; ask questions or I'm afraid to name you. I'm not afraid I'm around him. So patently fake in recognizable form, the poem – if such it be, for Language writers have not been afraid to go back to first questions by pushing to extremes – denies the originality of style and identity only to remind us of the facts of our case. The double column only pushes to a new extreme the fact that in a reading of anything there is a margin of varying size holding what we do not take in. Our selves, also, blur and change and are not confined by one recognizable form, even on self-inspection. His work never abandons truth claims and the here-and-now, but, in the implications and space his poetry bequeaths to the future, Steve Benson may be the most radical poet writing. Whether he or the other notable poets of his generation have located in their attention to the sign as powerful a motor to writing as earlier poets found in landscape or city is uncertain. I am arguing not that Language poetry is thinner than that of O'Hara's generation, but that in a curious sense it is fuller, so less liable to be shaped by particular experiences, places and aspirations into an individual voice, one of the bases of American literary achievement.

But now we have reached the egress. I confess to having thought long, but to having found no emphatic or startling way to end the tour. Looking for the right guides to part the curtain to the street, I thought once more of Melville, and of Frank O'Hara. But O'Hara is working late in a different museum, and the final pages of *The Confidence-Man* suggest that you might not want Melville to guide you through the dark. Since the time of the Puritans, his country has been the freest place imaginable, and yet the place where an invisible net of ideology could be flung from coast to coast, and trap everything. Its guides and prophets are canny and dislike being pinned down, even though their paradisal Romanticism is always tied to place:

> Manhattan's streets I saunter'd pondering,
> On Time, Space, Reality – on such as these, and abreast with them
>     Prudence.
>
> (Whitman, 500)

American literature is bound to American daily existence in an unbroken chain. To emerge abruptly, blinking in the sunlight of the open street, is to start the tour again.

# Afterword
## Meditations in an Emergency

But this book does have an Egress, after all. I wish it did not. On 11 September 2001, at 0858 Eastern Standard Time, a commercial airliner struck the north tower of the World Trade Center in Manhattan. For a period of minutes that now seems characteristic of a bygone age, this was taken to be an accident. At 0916, and with visible malevolence, a further hijacked plane smashed into the second tower. Thus one form of standard time, the post-1945 era, was ended, and another begun.

No one can as yet take the full measure of this event or put a name to the period that we are now living through. Everything is off the scale. There are sentiments and sentences in this book over which a darkness has now fallen. The idea underpinning the final chapter – that to depict place in the American arts is to ask questions about allegiance, at times of danger as well as desire – has only been confirmed, though I wish it were not so. America – invented, rather than discovered, and established in a Declaration of Independence – has always been founded on leaps of faith, made real by writing.

New York in particular is founded on risk, in a multiple sense that includes the importance of literature. If we return to a point just south of where the twin towers stood and look out to the Statue of Liberty, we have to lean on poetry for support, as lines from Whitman and from O'Hara's 'Meditations in an Emergency' are sculpted into the railings. And although New York has been the nation's literary capital since the time of Whitman, it is O'Hara's New York that incarnated the forms of its triumph, and that would eventually become a target. O'Hara's Manhattan was itself formed by war, by the devastation in

Europe and the arrival of its artists on American shores. Paradise, the Fall, exile, the promised land; there is no escape from these tropes. Perhaps, more happily, there is no escape either from the highpoints of the cycle for which they stand: 'Repeating the phrases of an old romance which is constantly renewed by the / endless originality of human loss...'

(Frank O'Hara, 'You are Gorgeous and I'm Coming')

# Notes

## Introduction

1  Mark Twain, *The Adventures of Huckleberry Finn*, 1st pub. 1884 (New York: Harper, 1912), 331. Subsequent page references are given in parentheses in the main body of the chapter.

2  Ann J. Lane (ed.), *The Charlotte Perkins Gilman Reader* (Charlottesville: University of Virginia Press, 1999), 5. Subsequent page references are given in parentheses in the main body of the chapter.

3  William Burroughs, *The Naked Lunch*, 1st pub. 1959 (London: Calder and Boyars, 1970), 22. Subsequent page references are given in parentheses in the main body of the text.

4  Philip Fisher, *Still the New World: American Literature in a Culture of Creative Destruction*, 1st pub. 1999 (Cambridge, MA: Harvard University Press, 2000), 160. Subsequent page references are given in parentheses in the main body of the text.

5  E. Annie Proulx, *Accordion Crimes*, 1st pub. 1996 (London: Fourth Estate, 1997), 239. Subsequent page references are given in parentheses in the main body of the chapter.

6  As given by Jed Rasula, *The American Poetry Wax Museum: Reality Effects, 1940–1990* (Urbana, IL: National Council of Teachers of English, 1996), 65. Subsequent page references are given in parentheses in the main body of the text.

7  Israel Zangwill, *The Melting-Pot*, 1st pub. 1909 (New York: Macmillan, 1919), 55.

8  F. Scott Fitzgerald, *The Great Gatsby*, 1st pub. 1925 (London: Penguin, 1950), 171.

## Chapter 1    Maps and Legends

1   Hugh Brogan, *The Penguin History of the United States of America* (Harmondsworth: Penguin, 1990), 114. Subsequent page references are given in parentheses in the main body of the chapter.

2   Gish Jen, 'Coming into the Country: The Making of a Newly American Mind', *New York Times*, 7 May 2000.

3   'Robert Creeley in Conversation with Alan Riach' (1995): *http://wings. buffalo.edu/epc/authors/creeley/interview.html*

4   See Thomas Gustafson, *Representative Words: Politics, Literature, and the American Language, 1776–1865* (Cambridge: Cambridge University Press, 1992), 49. Subsequent page references are given in the main body of the chapter.

5   Orlando Patterson, 'Everything Changes Money', *New York Times*, 7 May 2000.

6   *The Book of Daniel Drew* (West Newbury, MA: Frontier Press, 1969).

7   Thomas Jefferson, Letter to Henry Lee, 8 May 1825; as given in A. Koch and W. Peden (eds), *The Life and Selected Writings of Thomas Jefferson* (New York: Modern Library, 1944), 719. Subsequent page references are given in parentheses in the main body of the chapter.

8   See Carlos Fuentes, *Gabriel García Márquez and the Invention of America*, E. Allison Peers Lectures, 2 (Liverpool: Liverpool University Press, 1987).

9   Sacvan Bercovitch, *The Rites of Assent: Transformations in the Symbolic Construction of America* (New York: Routledge, 1993), 71. Subsequent page references are given in parentheses in the main body of the chapter.

10   Tony Tanner, *The American Mystery: American Literature from Emerson to DeLillo* (Cambridge: Cambridge University Press, 2000), 19. Subsequent page references are given in parentheses in the main body of the text.

11   P. Miller and T. H. Johnson (eds), *The Puritans* (New York: American Book Company, 1938), 686–7. Subsequent page references are given in parentheses in the main body of the chapter.

12   John Chester Miller, *Wolf by the Ears: Thomas Jefferson and Slavery* (Charlottesville: University of Virginia Press, 1991), 44–5.

## Chapter 2    American Literature and the Body Electric

1   F. O. Matthiessen, *American Renaissance: Art and Expression in the Age of Emerson and Whitman*, 1st pub. 1941 (Oxford: Oxford University Press, 1968), p. xii. Subsequent page references are given in parentheses in the main body of the text.

2   D. H. Lawrence, *Studies in Classic American Literature*, 1st pub. 1923 (Harmondsworth: Penguin, 1977), 68. Subsequent page references are given in parentheses in the main body of the text.

3  Ralph Waldo Emerson, *Essays and Lectures* (New York: Library of America, 1983), 262. Subsequent page references are given in parentheses in the main body of the text.

4  Walt Whitman, *Poetry and Prose* (New York: Library of America, 1982), 209. Subsequent page references are given in parentheses in the main body of the text.

5  Edgar Allan Poe, *Poetry and Tales* (New York: Library of America, 1984), 598–9. Subsequent page references are given in parentheses in the main body of the chapter.

6  Nathaniel Hawthorne, *The House of the Seven Gables*, 1st pub. 1851 (New York: New American Library, 1961), 11. Subsequent page references are given in parentheses in the main body of the chapter.

7  George Lippard, *The Quaker City: Or, The Monks of Monk Hall*, ed. David S. Reynolds, 1st pub. 1845 (Amherst: University of Massachusetts Press, 1995), 10. Subsequent page references are given in parentheses in the main body of the text.

8  Henry James, *Literary Criticism: Essays on Literature, American Writers, English Writers* (New York: Library of America, 1984), 370, 416. Subsequent page references are given in parentheses in the main body of the chapter.

9  See David S. Reynolds, *Beneath the American Renaissance: The Subversive Imagination in the Age of Emerson and Melville* (Cambridge, MA: Harvard University Press, 1988), 371. Subsequent page references are given in parentheses in the main body of the chapter.

10  Leslie Fiedler, *Love and Death in the American Novel*, 1st pub. 1960 (Cleveland: Meridian, 1962), 498. Subsequent page references are given in parentheses in the main body of the text.

11  Nathaniel Hawthorne, *The Blithedale Romance* (New York: Norton, 1958), 216–17. Subsequent page references are given in parentheses in the main body of the chapter.

12  Herman Melville, *Redburn, White-Jacket, Moby-Dick* (New York: Library of America, 1983), 1405. Subsequent page references are given in parentheses in the main body of the chapter.

13  William Carlos Williams, *In the American Grain* (New York: New Directions, 1953), 219.

14  I am indebted to an article on books about the death penalty by Thomas Laqueur: *London Review of Books*, vol. 22, no. 19 (5 Oct. 2000), p. 24.

15  Emerson's letter to Whitman of 21 July 1855 can be found in the Library of Congress. It is reproduced with some helpful notes in J. R. LeMaster and D. D. Kummings (eds), *Walt Whitman: An Encyclopedia* (New York: Garland, 1998), 204–7.

16  Ezra Pound, *Collected Shorter Poems* 1st pub. 1952 (London: Faber and Faber, 1973), 98.

17  George G. Foster, *New York Naked* (New York: De Witt and Davenport, n.d.). Subsequent page references are given in parentheses in the main body of the chapter.

18   Vivian R. Pollak, entry on Dickinson in LeMaster and Kummings (eds), *Walt Whitman*, 183.
19   Sylvia Plath, 'Fever 103', in *Ariel* (London: Faber and Faber, 1965), 59.
20   Thomas H. Johnson, *The Complete Poems of Emily Dickinson*, 1st pub. 1970 (London: Faber and Faber, 1975), 118–19. Subsequent references are given in parentheses in the main body of the chapter.
21   Donald E. Pease, 'New Americanists', in Pease (ed.), *Revisionary Interventions into the Americanist Canon* (Durham, NC: Duke University Press, 1994), 27.
22   Quentin Anderson, *The Imperial Self: An Essay in American Literary and Cultural History* (New York: Knopf, 1971), pp. ix–x.
23   Harold Bloom, *Agon: Towards a Theory of Revisionism* (New York: Oxford University Press, 1982), 145. Subsequent references are given in parentheses in the main body of the chapter.
24   Robert N. Linscott (ed.), *The Journals of Ralph Waldo Emerson* (New York: Modern Library, 1960), 107. Subsequent page references are given in parentheses in the main body of the chapter.
25   John O. Hayden (ed.), *William Wordsworth: The Poems*, vol. 1 (New Haven: Yale University Press, 1981), 525.
26   E. H. Coleridge (ed.), *Complete Poetical Works of Samuel Taylor Coleridge*, vol. 1, 1st pub. 1912 (Oxford: Oxford University Press, 1975), 39–40.
27   See Paul de Man, 'The Rhetoric of Temporality', in *Blindness and Insight: Essays in the Rhetoric of Contemporary Criticism*, rev. edn (London: Methuen, 1983), esp. 96–106.

## Chapter 3   Melville: Crises in Representation

1   John Bryant and Robert Milder (eds), *Melville's Evermoving Dawn: Centennial Essays* (Kent, OH: Kent State University Press, 1997), 3. Subsequent page references are given in parentheses in the main body of the chapter.
2   Herman Melville, *Typee, Omoo, Mardi* (New York: Library of America, 1982), 33. Subsequent page references are given in parentheses in the main body of the chapter.
3   John Carlos Rowe, 'Melville's *Typee*: US Imperialism at Home and Abroad', in Donald E. Pease (ed.), *National Identities and Post-Americanist Narratives* (Durham, NC: Duke University Press, 1994), 273. Subsequent page references are given in parentheses in the main body of the text.
4   John Wenke, *Melville's Muse: Literary Creation and the Forms of Philosophical Fiction* (Kent, OH: Kent State University Press, 1995), 64. Subsequent page references are given in parentheses in the main body of the chapter.
5   Herman Melville, *Pierre, Israel Potter, The Piazza Tales, The Confidence-Man, Uncollected Prose, Billy Budd Sailor* (New York: Library of Amer-

ica, 1984), 855. Subsequent page references are given in parentheses in the main body of the chapter.

6 Wyn Kelley, *Melville's City: Literary and Urban Form in Nineteenth-Century New York* (Cambridge: Cambridge University Press, 1996), 125.

7 Harold Bloom (ed.), *Herman Melville's* Billy Budd, *'Benito Cereno', 'Bartleby, the Scrivener', and Other Tales* (New York: Chelsea House, 1987), 1.

8 Hershel Parker, *Herman Melville: A Biography*, Volume 1: *1819–1851* (Baltimore: Johns Hopkins University Press, 1996), 760.

9 My information regarding Melville's doings on the day of the *Mosses* piece and the abduction is drawn from Parker's biography and from a panel discussion transcribed as chapter 11 of Bryant and Milder's *Evermoving Dawn* collection.

## Chapter 4 'Eden is burning': Literature of the Popular Imagination

1 See Robert Cantwell, 'Smith's Memory Theater', in his *When We Were Good: The Folk Revival* (Cambridge, MA: Harvard University Press, 1996). Subsequent page references are given in parentheses in the main body of the text.

2 I am indebted for information regarding Lippard's life, politics and sales figures to David S. Reynolds's introduction to *Quaker City*.

3 I am indebted for details of the Sickles case to an article by Sarah Mark in the *Washington Post*, 17 July 2000 ('In the Beginning – Washington's First Century'), which itself declares a debt to Nat Brandt, *The Congressman Who Got Away with Murder* (Syracuse, NY: Syracuse University Press, 1991), and Constance MacLaughlin Green, *Washington* (Princeton, NJ: Princeton University Press, 1962).

4 As given by Greil Marcus, 'Get into the Graveyard', booklet accompanying compact disc, Dock Boggs, *Country Blues: Complete Early Recordings (1927–29)* (Revenant 205), 14. Subsequent page references are given in parentheses in the main body of the text.

5 Dock Boggs, *His Folkway Years 1963–1968*, compact disc (Smithsonian Folkways 40108).

6 Harriet Beecher Stowe, *Uncle Tom's Cabin*, 1st pub. 1852 (Oxford: Oxford University Press, 1998), 261. Subsequent page references are given in parentheses in the main body of the chapter.

7 See Michael A. Bellesiles, *Arming America: The Origins of a National Gun Culture* (New York: Knopf, 2000).

8 Abraham Lincoln, Last Public Address, 11 April 1865, as given in *Abraham Lincoln: Great Speeches* (New York: Dover, 1991), 111.

9 See the Civil War entry in LeMaster and Kummings.

10 Tim Underwood and Chuck Miller (eds), *Bare Bones: Conversations on Terror with Stephen King* (New York: New English Library, 1990), 22. Subsequent page references are given in parentheses in the main body of the chapter.

11   Judging by his recently published memoirs, *On Writing*, King regards *Insomnia* and *Rose Madder* as overly deliberate in construction, and is sensitive (wrongly, at least in my view) to the charge that his best work was done twenty years ago.
12   Stephen King, *It*, 1st pub. 1986 (New York: New English Library, 1989) 558–9. Subsequent page references are given in parentheses in the main body of the chapter.
13   At the time of writing the dollars have not dried up, but 'The Plant' has.
14   Philip Fisher, 'Democratic Social Space: Whitman, Melville, and the Promise of American Transparency', in Fisher (ed.), *The New American Studies: Essays from Representations* (Berkeley: University of California Press, 1991), 72. Subsequent page references are given in parentheses in the main body of the chapter. An abbreviated version of the essay is included as part of Fisher's *Still the New World*.
15   Lawrence Sutin, *Divine Invasions: A Life of Philip K. Dick* (London: Paladin, 1991), 5. Subsequent page references are given in parentheses in the main body of the chapter.
16   Philip K. Dick, *Time Out of Joint*, 1st pub. 1959 (London: Penguin, 1988), 25. Subsequent page references are given in parentheses in the main body of the chapter.
17   Philip K. Dick, 'The Electric Ant', in *We Can Remember It For You Wholesale* (London: Voyager, 1994), 293. Subsequent page references are given in parentheses in the main body of the chapter.

Chapter 5   Going Fishing: Harry Smith, the *Anthology of American Folk Music*, and the Fan

1   Harry Smith (ed.), *Anthology of American Folk Music* (Smithsonian Folkways, 1997; SFW 40090: box, 6 compact discs, supplementary literature). Subsequent references to the music and other materials in the box are given in parentheses in the main body of the chapter.
2   Paola Igliori (ed.), *American Magus: Harry Smith* (New York: Inanout Press, 1996), esp. 230–67. Subsequent page references are given in parentheses in the main body of the chapter.
3   *Harry Smith's Anthology of American Folk Music: Volume Four* (Revenant: RVN 211, n.d.) (2 compact discs in book).
4   Greil Marcus, *Invisible Republic: Bob Dylan's Basement Tapes* (Basingstoke: Picador, 1997), ch. 4. Subsequent page references are given in parentheses in the main body of the chapter.
5   *Times Ain't Like They Used to Be: Early American Rural Music*, vols 1–4 (1997: Yazoo 2028, 2029, 2047, 2048).
6   The complete recordings of Ma Rainey, together with other female singers of the period, can be found on the Document label, which aspires to a reissue of the entire recorded corpus of pre-war blues. Comprehensive anthologies of female blues that are readily available include *Classic*

*Performances: The Great Women Blues Singers: The Gold Collection* (1998: Retro R2CD 40–75).

7  See Harold Rosenberg, *The Anxious Object*, 1st pub. 1964 (Chicago: University of Chicago Press, 1982), 61.

8  William Carlos Williams, *The Collected Poems 1909–39* (Manchester: Carcanet Press, 1987), 174. Subsequent page references are given in parentheses in the main body of the chapter.

9  Pete Gilpin and George Stephens, *Bascom Lamar Lunsford: 'Minstrel of the Appalachians'* (Asheville, NC: Stephens Press, 1966), 11, 13, 15, 20.

## Chapter 6   Modernism and the Subversive Imagination

1  T. S. Eliot, *Selected Essays* (London: Faber and Faber, 1969), 289. Subsequent page references are given in parentheses in the main body of the chapter.

2  Ezra Pound, *The Cantos* (London: Faber and Faber, 1968), 557. Subsequent page references are given in parentheses in the main body of the chapter.

3  Ed Sanders, *Investigative Poetry* (San Francisco: City Lights, 1976), 9.

4  Christopher MacGowan (ed.), *William Carlos Williams: Collected Poems*, Volume II: *1939–1962* (London: Picador, 1991), 157.

5  Rainer Maria Rilke, *New Poems: The Other Part [1908]*, trans. E. Snow (San Francisco: North Point Press, 1987), 3.

6  Robert Lowell, *History* (London: Faber and Faber, 1973), 194.

7  As given in N. Baym et al. (eds), *The Norton Anthology of American Literature*, vol. 2 (New York: Norton, 1979), 2485.

8  T. S. Eliot, *Collected Poems 1909–1962* (London: Faber and Faber, 1968), 63, 70, 77. Subsequent page references are given in parentheses in the main body of the chapter.

9  Miriam Allott (ed.), *Keats: The Complete Poems* (London: Longman, 1970), 541.

10  Amiri Baraka, liner notes to *Panthalassa: The Music of Miles Davis 1969–1974* (1998: Columbia, CK 67909), unpaginated. Subsequent quotations marked 'ibid.' in the main body of the chapter.

11  Amiri Baraka, *Transbluesency: Selected Poems 1961–1995* (New York: Marsilio, 1995), 54. Subsequent page references are given in parentheses in the main body of the chapter.

12  Donald Allen (ed.), *The Collected Poems of Frank O'Hara* (New York: Knopf, 1971), 256. Subsequent page references are given in parentheses in the main body of the text.

13  Baraka, 98. The poet's collaboration with musicians can be heard on *New York Art Quartet & Imamu Amiri Baraka* (1965, ESP 1004).

14  Langston Hughes, 'Po' Boy Blues', in H. L. Gates Jr and N. Y. McKay (eds), *The Norton Anthology of African-American Literature* (New

York: Norton, 1997), 1200. Subsequent page references are given in parentheses in the main body of the chapter.

15  See Raffael De Gruttola, 'Steve Jonas', in *First Offense*, 4 (Canterbury, 1988), 30. Jonas died from an overdose of glutethimide (Doriden).

16  Steve Jonas, 'Orgasm XXI', *Wivenhoe Park Review*, 2 (Colchester, n.d.), 46.

17  Stephen Jonas, *Exercises for Ear, CCXXIII. In Stephen Jonas: Selected Poems*, ed. Joseph Torra, (Hoboken, NJ: Talisman House, 1994). Subsequent references are given in parentheses in the main body of the chapter, by exercise rather than page number.

18  Jonathan Dollimore, reviewing *Shakespeare* by Kiernan Ryan, *Times Higher Education Supplement*, 1 Sept. 1989, p. 16.

19  Henry James, *The Portrait of a Lady*, 1st pub. 1881 (New York: Norton, 1972), 210.

20  Allen Ginsberg, *Collected Poems 1947–1980* (New York: Viking, 1984), 131. Subsequent page references are given in parentheses in the main body of the chapter.

21  As quoted by Graham Caveney, *Screaming With Joy: The Life of Allen Ginsberg* (London: Bloomsbury, 2001), 185–6.

22  Background information on Burroughs has been taken mostly from the better of the two biographies: Ted Morgan, *Literary Outlaw: The Life and Times of William S. Burroughs* (London: Bodley Head, 1991). See also Geoff Ward, 'The Mutations of William Burroughs', in R. Mengham (ed.), *An Introduction to Contemporary Fiction* (Cambridge: Polity, 1999), 110–23.

23  William Burroughs, *Queer* (London: Picador, 1986), 16.

24  William Burroughs, *Junky*, 1st pub. 1953 (as *Junkie*) (Harmondsworth: Penguin, 1977), 54

## Chapter 7   'Dedicated to America, whatever that is': Contemporary Literature and the Egress

1  John Muir, from *The Mountains of California*, as given in Lawrence Clark Powell, *California Classics: The Creative Literature of the Golden State* (Santa Barbara, CA: Capra Press, 1982), 143–4.

2  Jack Kerouac, *Visions of Cody* (New York: Penguin, 1993), dedication page. Subsequent page references are given in parentheses in the main body of the chapter.

3  Robert Creeley, preface to John Wieners, *Cultural Affairs in Boston: Poetry & Prose 1956–1985* (Santa Rosa, CA: Black Sparrow, 1988), 11.

4  John Wieners, *Selected Poems 1958–1984* (Santa Barbara, CA: Black Sparrow, 1986), 28. Subsequent page references are given in parentheses in the main body of the chapter.

5  Paul Goodman, 'Advance-Guard Writing, 1900–1950', *Kenyon Review*, 13 (1951), 357–80.

6   Robert Duncan, *The Opening of the Field*, 1st pub. 1960 (London: Jonathan Cape, 1969), 7.

7   Henry James, *The American Scene*, 1st pub. 1907 (New York: St Martin's, 1987), 89. Subsequent references are given in parentheses in the main body of the chapter.

8   'An Interview with John Ashbery', *American Writing Today*, vol. 1 (Washington: Forum Series, 1982), 270.

9   Brad Gooch, *City Poet: The Life and Times of Frank O'Hara* (New York: Knopf, 1993), 328.

10   Toni Morrison, *Beloved*, 1st pub. 1987 (London: Picador, 1988), 131. Subsequent page references are given in parentheses in the main body of the chapter.

11   Richard Ford, *The Sportswriter*, 1st pub. 1986 (London: Flamingo, 1987), 49. Subsequent page references are given in parentheses in the main body of the chapter.

12   Don DeLillo, *Libra* (New York: Viking, 1988), 456. Subsequent page references are given in parentheses in the main body of the chapter.

13   Thomas Pynchon, *Mason & Dixon*, 1st pub. 1997 (London: Vintage, 1998), 345.

14   Steve Benson, 'Shelter', in *As Is* (Berkeley: The Figures, 1978), 62.

15   Steve Benson, *Blindspots* (Cambridge: Whale Cloth Press, 1981), 5.

16   Lyn Hejinian, jacket comments for Steve Benson, *Blue Book* (New York: The Figures/Roof, 1988). Subsequent page references are given in the main body of the chapter.

# Select Bibliography

Abrams, W. H., *Natural Supernaturalism: Tradition and Revolution in Romantic Literature* (New York: Norton, 1971).

(O'Hara, Frank) Allen, D. (ed.), *The Collected Poems of Frank O'Hara*, 1st pub. 1971 (Berkeley: University of California Press, 1995).

——(ed.), *The New American Poetry 1945–1960*, 1st pub. 1960 (Berkeley: University of California Press, 1999).

Allott, Miriam (ed.), *Keats: The Complete Poems* (London: Longman, 1970).

Anderson, Quentin, *The Imperial Self: An Essay in American Literary and Cultural History* (New York: Knopf, 1971).

Ashbery, John, *Self-Portrait in a Convex Mirror* (New York: Viking, 1975).

Baraka, Amiri, *Transbluesency: Selected Poems 1961–1995* (New York: Marsilio, 1995).

Baym, Nina, et al. (eds), *The Norton Anthology of American Literature*, vol. 2 (New York: Norton, 1979).

Bellesiles, Michael A. *Violence and Brutality in American History* (New York: New York University Press, 1999).

——, *Arming America: The Origins of a National Gun Culture* (New York: Knopf, 2000).

Benson, Steve, *As Is* (Berkeley: The Figures, 1978).

——, *Blindspots* (Cambridge: Whale Cloth Press, 1981).

——, *Blue Book* (New York: The Figures/Roof, 1988).

Bercovitch, Sacvan, *The Rites of Assent: Transformations in the Symbolic Construction of America* (New York: Routledge, 1993).

Bloom, Harold, *Agon: Towards a Theory of Revisionism* (New York: Oxford University Press, 1982).

——(ed.), *Herman Melville's* Billy Budd, *'Benito Cereno', 'Bartleby, the Scrivener', and Other Tales* (New York: Chelsea House, 1987).

Boggs, Dock, *Country Blues: Complete Early Recordings 1927–29*, compact disc, (Revenant 205).

——, *His Folkway Years 1963–1968*, compact disc, (Smithsonian Folkways 40108).

*The Book of Daniel Drew* (West Newbury, MA: Frontier Press, 1969).

Brogan, Hugh, *The Penguin History of the United States of America* (Harmondsworth: Penguin, 1990).

Bryant, John and Milder, Robert (eds), *Melville's Evermoving Dawn: Centennial Essays* (Kent, OH: Kent State University Press, 1997).

Burroughs, William, *The Naked Lunch*, 1st pub. 1959 (London: Calder and Boyars, 1970).

——, *Junky*, 1st pub. 1953 (Harmondsworth: Penguin, 1977).

——, *Queer* (London: Picador, 1986).

Cantwell, Robert, *When We Were Good: The Folk Revival* (Cambridge, MA: Harvard University Press, 1996).

Caveney, Graham, *Screaming with Joy: The Life of Allen Ginsberg* (London: Bloomsbury, 2001).

De Gruttola, Raffael, 'Steve Jonas', in *First Offense*, 4 (Canterbury, 1988).

DeLillo, Don, *Libra* (New York: Viking, 1988).

De Man, Paul, 'The Rhetoric of Temporality', in *Blindness and Insight: Essays in the Rhetoric of Contemporary Criticism*, rev. edn (London: Methuen, 1983), 187–228.

Dick, Philip K., *Time Out of Joint*, 1st pub. 1959 (Harmondsworth: Penguin, 1988).

——, *The Man in the High Castle*, 1st pub. 1962 (Harmondsworth: Penguin, 1987).

——, 'The Electric Ant', in *We Can Remember It for You Wholesale* (London: Voyager, 1994), 290–309.

Dollimore, Jonathan, review of *Shakespeare* by Kiernan Ryan, *Times Higher Education Supplement*, 1 Sept. 1989.

Duncan, Robert, *The Opening of the Field*, 1st pub. 1960 (London: Jonathan Cape, 1969).

Eliot, T. S., *Collected Poems 1909–1962* (London: Faber and Faber, 1968).

——, *Selected Essays*, 1st pub. 1932 (London: Faber and Faber, 1969).

Emerson, Ralph Waldo, *Essays and Lectures* (New York: Library of America, 1983).

Erkkila, Betsy, *Whitman the Political Poet* (New York: Oxford University Press, 1989).

Fiedler, Leslie, *Love and Death in the American Novel*, 1st pub. 1960 (Cleveland: Meridian, 1962).

Fisher, Philip, 'Democratic Social Space: Whitman, Melville, and the Promise of American Transparency', in Fisher (ed.), *The New American Studies: Essays from Representations* (Berkeley: University of California Press, 1991), 70–111.

——, *Still the New World: American Literature in a Culture of Creative Destruction* (Cambridge, MA: Harvard University Press, 1999).

Fitzgerald, F. Scott, *The Great Gatsby*, 1st pub. 1925 (London: Penguin, 1950).

Ford, Richard, *The Sportswriter* (London: Flamingo, 1987).

Foster, George G., *New York Naked* (New York: De Witt and Davenport, n.d.).

Fuentes, Carlos, *Gabriel García Márquez and the Invention of America*, Allison Peers Lectures, 2 (Liverpool: Liverpool University Press, 1987).

Gates, Henry Lewis Jr. and McKay, Nellia Y. (eds), *The Norton Anthology of African-American Literature* (New York: Norton, 1997).

Gilbert, Sandra M., 'The American Sexual Poetics of Walt Whitman and Emily Dickinson', in S. Bercovitch (ed.), *Reconstructing American Literary History* (Cambridge, MA: Harvard University Press, 1986), 123–54.

Gilpin, Pete and Stephens, George, *Bascom Lamar Lunsford: 'Minstrel of the Appalachians'* (Asheville, NC: Stephens Press, 1966).

Ginsberg, Allen, *Collected Poems 1947–1980* (New York: Viking, 1984).

Gooch, Brad, *City Poet: The Life and Times of Frank O'Hara* (New York: Knopf, 1993).

Goodman, Paul, 'Advance-Guard Writing, 1900–1950', *Kenyon Review*, 13 (1951), 357–80.

Gustafson, Thomas, *Representative Words: Politics, Literature, and the American Language, 1776–1865* (Cambridge: Cambridge University Press, 1992).

Hawthorne, Nathaniel, *The Blithedale Romance*, 1st pub. 1852 (New York: Norton, 1958).

——, *The House of the Seven Gables*, 1st pub. 1851 (New York: New American Library, 1961).

——, *Collected Novels* (New York: Library of America, 1984).

Hayden, John O. (ed.), *William Wordsworth: The Poems*, vol. 1 (New Haven: Yale University Press, 1981).

Hounshell, David, *From the American System to Mass Production 1800–1932* (Baltimore: Johns Hopkins University Press, 1984).

Igliori, Paoloa (ed.), *American Magus: Harry Smith* (New York: Inanout Press, 1996).

James, Henry, *The American Scene*, 1st pub. 1907 (New York: St Martin's, 1987).

——, *The Portrait of a Lady*, 1st pub. 1881 (New York: Norton, 1972).

——, *Literary Criticism: Essays on Literature, American Writers, English Writers* (New York: Library of America, 1984).

Jefferson, Thomas, *Notes on Virginia*, 1st pub. 1784; in Koch and Peden, *The Life and Selected Writings of Thomas Jefferson*, 187–292.

Johnson, Thomas H. (ed.), *The Complete Poems of Emily Dickinson*, 1st pub. 1970 (London: Faber and Faber, 1975).

Jonas, Stephen, *Exercises for Ear: Being a Primer for the Beginner in the American Idiom* (London: Ferry Press, 1968).

——, *Selected Poems*, ed. Joseph Torra (Hoboken, NJ: Talisman House, 1994).

Kelley, Wyn, *Melville's City: Literary and Urban Form in Nineteenth-Century New York* (Cambridge: Cambridge University Press, 1996).

Kerouac, Jack, *Visions of Cody*, 1st pub. 1972 (New York: Penguin, 1993).

Kesey, Ken, *One Flew Over the Cuckoo's Nest* (New York: Viking Penguin, 1962).

King, Stephen, *It* (New York: New English Library, 1989).

——, *The Girl Who Loved Tom Gordon* (New York: Scribner, 1999).

Koch, A. and Peden W. (eds), *The Life and Selected Writings of Thomas Jefferson* (New York: Modern Library, 1944).

Lane, Ann J. (ed.), *The Charlotte Perkins Gilman Reader* (Charlottesville: University of Virginia Press, 1999).

Lawrence, D. H., *Studies in Classic American Literature*, 1st pub. 1923 (Harmondsworth: Penguin, 1977).

LeMaster, J. R. and Kummings, D. D. (eds), *Walt Whitman: An Encyclopedia* (New York: Garland, 1998).

Lincoln, Abraham, Last Public Address, 11 April 1865, as given in *Abraham Lincoln: Great Speeches* (New York: Dover, 1991), 109–13.

Lindberg, Gary, *The Confidence Man in American Literature* (New York: Oxford University Press, 1982).

Linscott, Robert N. (ed.), *The Journals of Ralph Waldo Emerson* (New York: Modern Library, 1960).

Lippard, George, David S. Reynolds (ed.), *The Quaker City: Or, The Monks of Monk Hall*, 1st pub. 1845 (Amherst: University of Massachusetts Press, 1995).

Lowell, Robert, *History* (London: Faber and Faber, 1973).

Marcus, Greil, *Invisible Republic: Bob Dylan's Basement Tapes* (Basingstoke: Picador, 1997).

——, 'Get Into the Graveyard', in booklet accompanying Boggs, *Country Blues*.

Mark, Sarah, 'In the Beginning – Washington's First Century', *Washington Post*, 17 July 2000.

Matthiessen, F. O., *American Renaissance: Art and Expression in the Age of Emerson and Whitman*, 1st pub. 1941 (Oxford: Oxford University Press, 1968).

Melville, Herman, *Typee, Omoo, Mardi* (New York: Library of America, 1982).

——, *Redburn, White-Jacket, Moby-Dick* (New York: Library of America, 1983).

——, *Pierre, Israel Potter, The Piazza Tales, The Confidence-Man, Uncollected Prose, Billy Budd Sailor* (New York: Library of America, 1984).

Miller, John Chester, *Wolf by the Ears: Thomas Jefferson and Slavery* (Charlottesville: University of Virginia Press, 1991).

Miller, P. and Johnson, T. H., *The Puritans* (New York: American Book Company, 1938).

Morgan, Ted, *Literary Outlaw: The Life and Times of William S. Burroughs* (London: Bodley Head, 1991).

Morrison, Toni, *Beloved*, 1st pub. 1987 (London: Picador, 1988).

Parker, Hershel, *Herman Melville: A Biography*, Volume 1: 1819–1851 (Baltimore: Johns Hopkins University Press, 1996).

Pease, Donald E. (ed.), *National Identities and Post-Americanist Narratives* (Durham, NC: Duke University Press, 1994).

—— (ed.), *Revisionary Interventions into the Americanist Canon* (Durham, NC: Duke University Press, 1994).

Plath, Sylvia, *Ariel* (London: Faber and Faber, 1965).

Poe, Edgar Allan, *Poetry and Tales* (New York: Library of America, 1984).

Pollak, Vivian R., *Dickinson: The Anxiety of Gender* (Ithaca, NY: Cornell University Press, 1984).

Pound, Ezra, *The Cantos* (London: Faber and Faber, 1968).

——, *Collected Shorter Poems* (London: Faber and Faber, 1973).

Powell, Lawrence Clark, *California Classics: The Creative Literature of the Golden State* (Santa Barbara, CA: Capra Press, 1982).

Proulx, E. Annie, *Accordion Crimes* (London: Fourth Estate, 1996).

Pynchon, Thomas, *Mason & Dixon* (London: Vintage, 1998).

Rasula, Jed, *The American Poetry Wax Museum: Reality Effects, 1940–1990* (Urbana, IL: National Council of Teachers of English, 1996).

Reynolds, David S., *Beneath the American Renaissance: The Subversive Imagination in the Age of Emerson and Melville* (Cambridge, MA: Harvard University Press, 1988).

Rilke, Rainer Maria, *New Poems: The Other Part [1908]*, trans. Edward Snow (San Francisco: North Point Press, 1987).

Rosenberg, Harold, *The Anxious Object* (Chicago: University of Chicago Press, 1982).

Rowe, John Carlos, 'Melville's *Typee*: US Imperialism at Home and Abroad', in Pease (ed.), *National Identities and Post-Americanist Narratives*, 255–79.

Salska, Agnieszka, *Walt Whitman and Emily Dickinson: Poetry of the Central Consciousness* (Philadelphia: University of Pennsylvania Press, 1985).

Sanders, Ed, *Investigative Poetry* (San Francisco: City Lights, 1976).

Smith, Harry, *Anthology of American Folk Music: Volume Four* (Revenant: RVN 211, n.d.) (2 compact discs in book).

—— (ed.), *Anthology of American Folk Music*, 1st released 1952 (Smithsonian Folkways, 1997; SFW 40090: box, 6 compact discs, supplementary literature).

Stowe, Harriet Beecher, *Uncle Tom's Cabin*, ed. Jean Fagan Yellis, 1st pub. 1852 (Oxford: Oxford University Press, 1998).

Sutin, Lawrence, *Divine Invasions: A Life of Philip K. Dick* (London: Paladin, 1991).

Tanner, Tony, *The American Mystery: American Literature from Emerson to DeLillo* (Cambridge: Cambridge University Press, 2000).

*Times Ain't Like They Used to Be: Early American Rural Music*, vols 1–4, compact discs (1997: Yazoo 2028, 2029, 2047, 2048).

Twain, Mark, *The Adventures of Huckleberry Finn*, 1st pub. 1885 (New York: Harper, 1972).

(Stephen King) Underwood, Tim and Miller, Chuck (eds), *Bare Bones: Conversations on Terror with Stephen King* (New York: New English Library, 1990).

Ward, Geoff, 'The Mutations of William Burroughs', in R. Mengham (ed.), *An Introduction to Contemporary Fiction* (Cambridge: Polity, 1999), 110–23.

Wenke, John, *Melville's Muse: Literary Creation and the Forms of Philosophical Fiction* (Kent, OH: Kent State University Press, 1995).

Whitman, Walt, *Poetry and Prose* (New York: Library of America, 1982).

Wieners, John, *The Hotel Wentley Poems* (San Francisco: Auerhahn Press, 1958).

——, *Behind the State Capitol or Cincinnati Pike* (Boston: Good Gay Poets, 1975).

——, *Selected Poems 1958–1984* (Santa Barbara, CA: Black Sparrow, 1986).

——, *Cultural Affairs in Boston: Poetry & Prose 1956–1985* (Santa Rosa, CA: Black Sparrow, 1988).

Williams, William Carlos, *In the American Grain*, 1st pub. 1925 (New York: New Directions, 1953).

——, *Collected Poems*, vol. 1: *1909–39*, ed. A. Walton Litz and Christopher MacGowan (Manchester: Carcanet Press, 1987).

——, *Collected Poems*, vol. 2: *1939–1962*, ed. Christopher MacGowan (London: Picador, 1991).

Zangwill, Israel, *The Melting-Pot* (New York: Macmillan, 1909).

# Index

AEE-9230